Ross Coulthart is an award-winning investigative journalist and writer. Previously an investigative reporter on news and current affairs program *60 Minutes* on Channel Nine and chief investigations reporter for the *Sunday Night* news program, Coulthart has won five prestigious Walkley journalism awards, including the most coveted top award for Australian journalism, the Gold Walkley. His broadcast television investigative journalism has also won the top broadcast award, a Logie.

Ross is the co-author of bestselling books *Dead Man Running* and *Above the Law*, both exposés of organised crime in Australian and international outlaw motorcycle gangs, as well as *Charles Bean*, *Lost Diggers* and *The Lost Tommies*.

IN
PLAIN
SIGHT

ROSS COULTHART

HarperCollins*Publishers*

HarperCollins*Publishers*
Australia • Brazil • Canada • France • Germany • Holland • Hungary
India • Italy • Japan • Mexico • New Zealand • Poland • Spain • Sweden
Switzerland • United Kingdom • United States of America

First published in Australia in 2021
by HarperCollins*Publishers* Australia Pty Limited
Level 13, 201 Elizabeth Street, Sydney NSW 2000
ABN 36 009 913 517
harpercollins.com.au

A catalogue record for this book is available from the National Library of Australia.

ISBN 978 1 4607 5906 6 (paperback)
ISBN 978 1 4607 1276 4 (ebook)
ISBN 978 1 4607 9005 2 (audiobook)

Cover design by Darren Holt, HarperCollins Design Studio
Index by Garry Cousins
Typeset in Adobe Garamond Pro by Kirby Jones

Printed and bound by CPI Group (UK) Ltd, Croydon, CR0 4YY

For all the truth-tellers out there. Thank you especially to all the anonymous whistleblowers with the courage to shine a light into dark places. And, once again, all my thanks and love to my wife Kerrie and my daughters Lucy & Millie. Thank you for making life a joyful journey.

Contents

Prologue

About 2.30 on a pitch-black morning on Australia's remote North West Cape, Annie Farinaccio walked out of a late-night party at the United States Naval Communication Station Harold E. Holt. It was late 1991, shortly before the US was due to hand over the site to Australia. The handover was happening amid mounting concern about the base's covert role as one of the cornerstones of America's submarine-launched nuclear missile defence. In the event of nuclear war, launch orders from the US would be sent out by the station's powerful transmitters to submarines across the adjacent Indian Ocean. Exmouth locals had no idea their sleepy town would likely be obliterated in a nuclear exchange; they just valued what the 'Yanks' brought to the local economy in this isolated community and were sad to be seeing them go.

The party at the base that night was to farewell some American friends who were returning home due to the handover. But Annie had stayed too late and now, she realised, she had no way of getting home – the few local taxis in this remote part of Australia had stopped for the night. So when two Australian Federal Protective Service police officers, who she knew as Kevin and Alan, kindly offered to give her a ride back into Exmouth, five kilometres south, she gratefully accepted.

Annie squeezed in between the two men on the bench seat of their four-wheel Toyota drive security vehicle and the three set off for town.

A few minutes into the journey along the barren cape's empty coast road, Kevin looked up. 'It's back. Grab the camera,' Annie recalled him saying. Then Alan began to fire off photographs through the windscreen at something overhead that Annie could not yet see.

'Eventually, Kevin pulled my head forward. "Look up!" he said. Then I saw it. A long diamond-shaped craft hovering overhead with the rear edge chopped off, rows of lights running towards the craft's tip. It was a dark grey colour but not as dark as the night sky. It was 100 feet above us at most. "What the fuck is that?"' Annie asked.

The policemen told her they had no idea, but that the same object had followed them the previous night. The next minute, the craft shot straight up from the right-hand side of the moving vehicle, before dropping down almost instantaneously on the left-hand-side of the car.

Annie screamed as they hurtled down the road, with the 'craft' in apparent hot pursuit. It followed them along the road for a kilometre. Then it shot up into the sky and appeared to land in the scrub a few hundred metres off the road, a light now shining from underneath.

Kevin wanted to stop and take pictures of it on the ground, but, Annie says, 'I was crying. "This is crazy. Take me home."'

The two police officers agreed and drove as fast as they could to the edge of Exmouth, where they dropped Annie off before rushing back to get their pictures.

'I ran to my home on the other side of town, and I ran into the house and locked the doors. I was so freaked.'

Today, Annie is in no doubt that what was hovering above them that night was a craft moving at incomprehensible speed. She does not care if people think her account sounds crazy. 'It moved so fast my eyes couldn't follow it,' she says. 'We were all freaking out.'

Two days later, two American military policemen walked into Annie's workplace in town and asked her to come with them. Legally, the US had no jurisdiction, but she went with them anyway. 'I didn't at that stage relate it to what we saw,' she says. 'I thought I was in trouble for being on the base drinking at night.'

The taciturn policemen drove Annie straight into what she knew was the top-secret section of the US base. 'I'm mouthing off at this stage, saying, "I must have done something really bad,"' she laughs.

Once inside, they led Annie into a room. Sitting in front of a group of Americans in uniform were the two police officers, Alan and Kevin. Annie knew most of the Americans on base but here she recognised only one – the American commander. The others had clearly flown in from somewhere else. There were also three or four men in civilian suits.

'I felt pissed off at this stage. One guy did the talking. He asked me, "What did you see?" I said, "I saw a UFO." They got me to draw it and asked me more questions about it. "You do realise that what you saw was a weather balloon?" I laughed at that,' Annie said. As a child, Annie had lived on a station outside Exmouth and her father frequently launched weather balloons. 'Weather balloons don't look like what I saw,' she recalled telling the man. 'Then one of the APS policemen sitting next to me – they both had their heads down – said: "Please shut up … Shut up before you get us all killed."'

The interrogation went on for a few hours. It was clear that the two Australian policemen had been there a lot longer – they appeared scared and dejected from the hours of questioning. Annie admits that she arced up at the Americans for trying to bully her into saying what they wanted her to say.

Annie is an intelligent university graduate who previously ran her own businesses. At the time of the sighting, she was working at the nearby Roebourne Regional Prison, counselling prisoners to help them find work. Fair to say, she was not easily rattled. 'I said to them, "I don't give a shit what you say. It wasn't a weather balloon. It was a UFO. I'm not saying what you want me to say. I know I saw a UFO."'

The Americans clearly had no idea what to do with an uncooperative Australian local and, eventually, they took her home. The first thing Annie did was ring her cousin, who had long been inquisitive about what was really going on at the base. He drove to Exmouth and they both visited Alan at his home.

Alan admitted the photographs of 'the craft' were printed at a printing shop inside the base and the two officers had shown them to colleagues. 'Next thing, they were in custody. They searched the photo-machine, and they took his camera, the pics and the negatives,' Annie says. Alan told her the photographs clearly showed an intelligently guided craft, not physically landed but hovering just above the ground. But, he said, every image he took was confiscated, along with his camera.

As Annie tells it, he was seriously rattled by the experience and told her and her cousin never to come back.

Annie's elderly mother in Exmouth also confirmed part of the story. She clearly remembers the two military policemen first came to the family home, so she directed them to Annie's workplace, where her colleagues watched her being escorted away.

* * *

Annie knows her story sounds implausible, but she's adamant it's true. And she's not alone. Witnesses to strange objects in our skies have told stories like this for decades. And yet, they are rarely investigated or taken seriously by the press. The default position for mainstream media has long been to dismiss such accounts, even to ridicule them. After all, they sound wacky and, without official corroboration, such tales are most often spiked before the public gets to hear about them.

However, overwhelming evidence shows that many governments, including Australia's, take such unidentified aerial phenomena (UAP) sightings very seriously indeed. Across the world, declassified government reports and well-corroborated witness sightings show that military and intelligence services are well aware of a persistent pattern of strange unidentified objects seen at and around sensitive military facilities such as Australia's North West Cape naval communication station. Declassified files held in the Australian government's National Archives reveal that anomalous sightings of unexplained objects at North West Cape have been officially reported to the Australian Air Force for decades by soldiers, tourists, a senior American officer at the base, and a local fireman. Annette's disturbing sighting report is not an isolated incident at all. At the very least, it warrants further investigation.

But, as I have discovered, there is a huge disconnect between the public ridicule automatically directed at claims of unidentified aerial phenomena and the long-concealed secrets now emerging of a new reality.

More recent reports of UAP sightings are increasingly being verified on radar and other sensor systems, as well as photographed or videoed, and these events are often corroborated by multiple witnesses. The sightings also feature something that even the US military now admits it cannot prosaically explain. In fact, US government and military insiders I have interviewed for this book admit they have knowledge of technology operating in our skies, oceans and orbit that far exceeds known human science. It often appears to be intelligently controlled, presenting to those who recorded it on video and tracked it on radar as a 'craft' of some kind.

Like most journalists, I'm generally reluctant to believe in cover-ups or conspiracies. But I believe that governments are not telling the public the full story about UAPs. What are these 'craft'? Is the extra-terrestrial hypothesis, albeit confronting, even able to explain this high strangeness? And why are they hiding in plain sight?

Chapter 1

Let's Hope They're Friendly

Recorded sightings of strange objects in Antipodean skies can be found right back to the 19th-century period of early European settlement. For thousands of years before that, Indigenous Australian Aboriginal rock art and dreamtime stories described the eerie alien faces of the Wandjina cloud and rain spirits, and also what are known today as the Min Min lights. European settlers later reported seeing fuzzy hovering white, sometimes colourful, orbs of light tracking them as they moved through outback country. It is part of folklore that the luminescent orbs and discs, first reported by Europeans near the settlement of Min Min near Boulia in Queensland, would follow people, often disappearing when approached and then reappearing in a different spot. I once reported a story in the Gulf of Carpentaria in Far North Queensland, interviewing a venerable Aboriginal elder known as Blue Bob, who knew the landscape like the back of his hand. Had he seen the Min Min lights, I asked? He chuckled and referred me to images of saucer- and orb-shaped objects that appear in Aboriginal art across the country. 'We see them all the time. They've always been in our stories,' he told me matter-of-factly. He thought it very funny that scientists recently claimed to have solved the mystery of these lights; it had recently been declared Min Mins were merely a trick of the light caused by distant bright truck headlights. 'Didn't see too many trucks around these parts a few thousand years ago,' he roared with laughter.

Early Australian newspapers carry intriguing accounts of odd lights and even craft or metallic airships in the sky. What is possibly the earliest official 'mystery aircraft' flap recorded in government files came in 1930 when a Royal Australian Air Force Squadron Leader George Jones was sent to Warrnambool in Victoria to investigate reports of mystery aircraft seen flying inland over the coast. 'They were not aircraft belonging to us and, as far as I could find out, they were not aircraft belonging to any other powers,' Jones later acknowledged.[1] Jones rose to lofty heights, becoming the Royal Australian Air Force's Chief of Air Staff during the Second World War, and was later Air Marshall Sir George Jones. The Air Marshall also openly acknowledged that he witnessed a 'UFO' during his career – 'a brilliant white light at the bottom of a shadowy shape like a transparent balloon' – and this convinced him of the need for serious research into the phenomenon. He even supported civilian research groups such as VUFORS – the Victorian UFO Research Society.

The 1930s was an extraordinary era of aviation exploration. One of the most fascinating sightings was by renowned British aviator Francis Chichester over the Tasman Ocean in 1931 as he attempted the first solo flight between New Zealand and Australia. He said that, after a series of 'bright flashes', he saw 'a dull grey-white airship coming towards me. It seemed impossible … Except for a cloud or two there was nothing else in the sky.' Next thing he knew, it had disappeared, then it reappeared with a dull gleam of light on its nose and back. His sighting remains unexplained.

Sir Francis Chichester's epic biography *The Lonely Sea and the Sky* acknowledged that what he saw 'seems to have been very much like what people have since claimed to be flying saucers'.[2]

Decades later, when I was a teenager living in New Zealand, shortly before Christmas 1978, I was initially intrigued then disappointed by a dramatic sighting in my home country. A cargo aircraft was flying along the north-east coast of New Zealand's South Island near the Kaikoura mountain ranges, when multiple people onboard made dramatic claims of witnessing glowing UAP lights following the cargo plane. Not only were the lights caught on radar and seen by multiple people onboard, they were also filmed on a later return flight by cameraman David Crockett and reported by Australian TV reporter Quentin Fogarty.

As this episode unfolded during the Christmas holiday silly season when the news business normally slows down, sensational claims of a filmed 'mass UFO sighting' took off in the international press after Quentin Fogarty's dramatic in-flight account was broadcast around the world. 'We've just heard from Wellington radar that we've got an object about a mile behind us and it's following us,' he reported in-flight on the darkened plane. 'Let's hope they're friendly. It's really getting a bit frightening up here. There's a whole formation of unidentified flying objects behind us.'

Through the viewfinder, following the lights shooting around the cargo plane, the cameraman described seeing a classic 'flying saucer' shaped object, with a brightly lit bottom and a transparent sphere on top. But when we all finally got to see the TV images, while they showed distant unexplained lights, the vision was underwhelming. It did not show an apparent craft or object of any kind behind the darting lights – certainly not a 'flying saucer'. After some initial excitement, like most people, I surmised the whole story was a flap about nothing much, that there would be some prosaic explanation.

One reason for my scepticism was because two months earlier, in October 1978, across the Tasman Ocean in Australia, a 20-year-old Melbourne-based pilot Frederick Valentich had disappeared while piloting a tiny Cessna aircraft over Bass Strait on a flight to King Island. Shortly before he and his aircraft disappeared, Valentich was recorded telling Melbourne air traffic control that he was being followed by a huge illuminated shiny metal craft hovering above him. Some of his dramatic last words, as his engine began rough idling, were: 'It's hovering and it's not an aircraft.' Then the transmission was interrupted by strange pulsing sounds and his radio cut out. The Valentich story was still lurid tabloid news fodder and, as news of the NZ Kaikoura sighting hit the Christmas holiday newspaper and TV news weeks later, Valentich's disappearance was still inflaming 'UFO fever'. There was frantic speculation in the press that the New Zealand Kaikoura or Australian Valentich cases were proof of aliens. I cynically took the view that the Kaikoura sighting was all a dramatic overreaction to the still unsolved Valentich mystery across in Australia.

Under political pressure to allay public concern, and with the intense scrutiny of the world's media, the Royal New Zealand Air Force delivered a report into the incident one month after the Kaikoura sighting and announced it had solved the puzzle, asserting that everyone on board the plane was simply confused by 'natural but unusual atmospheric phenomena'.[3] The public was assured that air force investigators had interviewed 'all the witnesses' involved in the sightings on the nights of 20 and 30 December 1978 and that atmospheric conditions during the sightings events caused the freak effects on radar and in visible light. The report suggested that the witnesses were confused by squid boats using powerful lights on the ocean below, or perhaps by an especially bright planet Venus. One issue with the Venus explanation was that the first sighting, at 2.30 am, was well before Venus should have been visible at that altitude, and the planet was at a very different angle in the sky to where the lights appeared. So, the report to the NZ Minister of Science suggested that what everyone saw was the 'planet substantially refracted by the atmosphere'.[4]

The air force also quaintly reassured the good folk of New Zealand that the Ministry 'totally discounts the possibility of visits to New Zealand ... of alien aircraft or other flying machines ... Defence does not share the view of those who believe we are visited from outer space'. It was definitely case closed, as far as the Royal New Zealand Air Force was concerned, and, like the majority of the public, I accepted that explanation and got on with life. However, the fact is that despite an official government investigation, the Kaikoura sighting remains one of the world's most well-recorded unexplained UAP sightings.

It was not until the early 1990s, when I was working in Australia as a television investigative journalist for the Australian Broadcasting Corporation's *Four Corners*, that I was encouraged by Australian Air Force insiders to reconsider my default dismissive attitude towards unidentified objects in our skies. One of my contacts in the air force was a very senior officer and, to my surprise, over a beer, he and another serving senior officer started talking expansively about 'UFO' or 'flying saucer sightings' they had experienced during their careers. The air force veterans encouraged me to take another look at UAP mysteries, suggesting that the media's excessive scepticism about the phenomenon meant that it was not being properly investigated, even inside government. I still have my shorthand notes of our conversation, where one told me: 'Pilots don't report this sort of stuff because it's career-ending to admit you see these things. But there is something weird happening that can't be dismissed. Too many of us have seen these objects.'

There is a very sound reason for why the media has long been sceptical about claims of unidentified objects in our skies. Back in the 1990s, most young reporters served time on night-shift news desks fielding calls from the public. Cub reporters were often the only person in the empty newsroom on the overnight shifts, monitoring police and ambulance scanners and the news wires while the senior journalists were at home with their families. It could be exciting because, if a big story happened during the night, the scoop was yours. More than a few journalists would guiltily admit they sat there late at night, praying for a ghoulish crime story or accident to break the tedium of the late shift.

But as the bars closed and TV schedules wound up for the evening, there was a type of caller you soon learned to avoid, who always seemed to phone in during those witching hours, especially during a full moon. Heaven help you if you dared to hang up though, because then you would become the focus of their aggressive paranoia. And yes, a disproportionate number of these calls and letters did seem to be about aliens and flying saucers. Some folk are absolutely convinced there is a deep conspiracy in the media to gag stories investigating UAPs, that some dark element of our intelligence services slaps a gag order on anomalous sightings. I do not believe for one moment that that is the case. The reluctance to cover stories about unidentified aerial phenomena is caused by professional scepticism, which has its origins in every editor's early journalistic memories of having their ears chewed off by moonstruck callers with rats in their attic.

As a young journalist working in New Zealand and later in Australia, so sure back then about everything I believed I knew, I pinned a quotation from my favourite science-fiction writer Isaac Asimov on my wall, because he encapsulated my view about people who rang journalists like me with crazy stories, the credulous who embraced woolly-headed beliefs in phenomena such as UFOs. Asimov thought these claims were wild and ridiculous; I admit I insensitively took the view that the people who made these claims were all nutters. Asimov wrote, 'I believe in evidence. I believe in observation, measurement, and reasoning, confirmed by independent observers. I'll believe anything, no matter how wild and ridiculous, if there is evidence for it. The wilder and more ridiculous something is, however, the firmer and more solid the evidence will have to be.'[5]

This idea of scientific knowledge as distinct from mere belief, with unimpeachable authority because of its basis in evidence, is perhaps the most important development from the Enlightenment. We should embrace critical thinking, be objectively collecting data, testing hypotheses and looking for disconfirming evidence, subjecting research to peer review, and trying to repeat the experiment as a way of proving what we believe we know. Good science is a bulwark against mysticism and superstition. But, as *Newton's Apple and Other Myths About Science*[6] argues, it is rhetoric to assert that there is in practice any accepted scientific method across science at all. If you put a bunch of scientists into a room, none of them will agree on what exactly they actually mean by scientific certainty, especially not in relation to the great taboo of UAPs. Millions of people report having observed unexplained aerial phenomena, but is there ever going to be any point at which the so-called scientific method accepts we should believe the observers? Renowned astronomer Carl Sagan, echoing Asimov, memorably said that 'Extraordinary claims require extraordinary evidence'.[7]

But sceptics often say witnesses to UAPs should *always* be ignored because witness evidence is notoriously unreliable.

A TED talk by palaeontologist Donald Prothero[8] typifies how leaders in scientific thought tackle the issue. 'There are certain rules, especially in science, that distinguish it from pseudo-science,' Prothero told his audience. 'Science is the last bastion of fact-checking. Right now, we have a media full of lies and misinformation. We have an internet full of lies; it's almost more garbage than it is truth.' Sadly, he's right so far. But what Prothero goes on to say is what often happens when scientists talk about UFOs – unidentified flying objects – or unidentified aerial phenomena, UAPs. (I prefer the less loaded term 'UAPs' because 'UFO' is so often taken to mean flying saucers and little green men.) He said, 'Really the only evidence that will convince most of the scientific community is actual physical UFOs or an actual carcass or even a live alien would be even better.' He automatically assumes that a witness to a 'UFO' or UAP is talking about an alien or ET spacecraft. He then asserts that *eyewitness evidence is not evidence* as far as we're concerned'.[9] That is a great way of shutting down debate but is it scientifically rigorous? For more often than not, the witnesses simply say they do not know what *it* was.

It is surely not sound science to make a sweeping generalisation that eyewitness evidence should *never* be taken seriously just because it pertains to UAPs. When a scientist gathers more prosaic data by observing wildlife or natural phenomena, for example, the scientific method does not reject their observations because of the supposedly notorious unreliability of humans being witness to what they see. Our criminal justice system often sends people to jail solely on eyewitness evidence. Witnesses testify and their evidence is rigorously cross-examined. Witness evidence can quite literally mean life or death for a defendant in some countries, including the United States. The biggest problem about the UAP phenomenon is that these strange sightings are not repeatable; they are not a replicable experiment, which is one of science's most commonly stated prerequisites to verify a hypothesis. But observer – eyewitness – evidence still has probative value.

One of the privileges of being an investigative journalist is the opportunity to use the skillset to indulge a curiosity – to go down the rabbit hole of a mystery, to work the sources, to delve through the documents, and to reach conclusions based on the evidence.

Some time back, that is what I started doing with the phenomenon of UAPs because, frankly, they are the biggest unsolved mystery of our age. Most of the sources I spoke to insisted on talking anonymously but what they told me was illuminating because it suggests that many governments are taking the UAP issue a lot more seriously in private than they are prepared to admit publicly.

Polls show more than two-thirds of Americans believe the US government knows more than it is letting on about the phenomenon[10] (although, to be sure, that does not make their belief true). An enormous number of people believe there is a vast conspiracy at the highest levels of the US military-industrial complex, concealing recovered extra-terrestrial (ET) craft and perhaps even the existence of aliens. I suspect scientists' reluctance to intellectually engage with the phenomenon, and their quick dismissal of any incidents without serious investigation, accompanied by ridicule and mockery, is actually encouraging this conspiratorial thinking.

In mainstream journalism, the dominant view has always been and generally continues to be that such notions of dark conspiracies are batshit crazy, and heaven help you if you transgress from that position. The UAP/UFO subject was and still is The Great Taboo.[11] If it gets covered at all, invariably there is a quizzical raising of the eyebrows or a subtle turn of phrase, or a flourish of *X-Files* music, to suggest that this is a lighter story to be taken with a grain of salt. There is little doubt that some or many people who contact media about flying saucers and aliens are sadly deluded, credulous or psychotic. But I had no idea, until I started digging, just how authoritative so many UAP sightings have been, and how poorly the evidence behind them has often been presented.

Chapter 2

Roswell: Implausible Denials

'The Germans have thrown something new into the night skies over Germany – the weird, mysterious "foo-fighter" balls of fire that race alongside the wings of American Beaufighters flying intruder missions over the Reich,' *The New York Times* reported in January 1945.[1] Throughout the Second World War and during the late 1940s, many Second World War aviators over Europe or in the Pacific theatre reported seeing luminous discs or spheres known as Foo Fighters. Bomber pilots over Europe regularly reported wingless and tailless glowing objects tracking their aircraft, 'that could turn on a dime'. Initially, it was believed they were a new German secret weapon. But when the Allies scoured German files and interrogated German scientists post-war, it became clear the objects were not German. No official explanation has ever been given for the Foo Fighter sightings.[2] Axis pilots were as concerned about the mystery as the Allies.

Around the world, sightings of unidentified aerial phenomena escalated in the years immediately after the Second World War. Perhaps this was in part because aliens and flying saucers were increasingly popular fodder for movies, comic strips and science-fiction stories. *Flash Gordon Conquers the Universe*, a popular sci-fi movie serial, aired in theatres in the early years of the war. However, it could be that, in turn, the increase in the number of sightings of strange objects at the time, especially in the western US, made Hollywood's storytellers more aware. This was the beginning of the new aviation age, where mass transit by aircraft was becoming more accessible. As modern science broadened human understanding of our place in the universe, thought turned also to the possibility that Earthlings might not be alone. In 1938, Orson Welles' radio adaption from New York of HG Wells' 1897 novel *The War of the Worlds* sparked alarm among some of his audience, who thought an alien invasion was actually underway. It has become a popular myth that Wells' radio show caused a mass national panic about an alien invasion, but recent research suggests this was exaggerated; it was whipped up after the broadcast by what would today be called a rival media 'beat-up'.[3]

In February 1946, Sweden had more than 2000 sightings of so-called 'ghost rockets', hundreds of them corroborated by radar returns, and purported physical fragments of these objects were even recovered. Theories they might be Soviet rocket tests were dismissed because the objects had no exhaust, were completely silent, and were seen flying horizontally and often super slowly in formation. Sweden's Air Intelligence Service told the Americans that 'these phenomena are obviously the result of a high technical skill which cannot be credited to any presently known culture on earth'[4]

Strange objects were also being seen in the Southern Hemisphere. In February 1947, there were three independent and well-verified sightings of a formation of five egg-shaped wingless and tailless craft flying over southern Australia, which defied official explanation. A farmer on South Australia's Eyre Peninsula reported seeing five strange oblong-shaped objects with narrow points coming up out of the sea with a smoky greyish colour around them. 'I saw them quite plainly,' a Mr Flavel told the *Adelaide Advertiser* newspaper. 'They seemed to be floating in the air from north-west to south-east and caused a shadow.' His account corroborated another made earlier by workmen at Port Augusta, 260 kilometres north-east, who also reported seeing five white egg-shaped objects flying in formation from north to south. 'Owing to their great speed, they were out of sight within a few seconds,' the *Advertiser* reported.[5] Potential explanations that the objects were meteors or mirages were discounted by the South Australian government astronomer of the day, Mr Dodwell. Dodwell told the paper, 'The phenomenon did not fit in with anything astronomical and was a complete mystery to him' and also, 'This seems to correspond with real objects and not with a mirage reflection.'[6]

The third sighting of a formation of five weird, high-speed, egg-shaped UAPs came two months later, a thousand kilometres east in New South Wales. A Gogeldrie farmer working on his rice harvest looked up to also see 'five metal bodies flying in V formation with the sun glistening on them'. The farmer, a Mr Nettlebeck, reportedly estimated the speed at about 1000 miles an hour (1600 km/h). A curious coincidence indeed that three separate sets of witnesses independently saw a similar formation of five high-speed egg-shaped objects in different locations over 1200 kilometres apart across southern Australia. These events also all happened just before a sighting event in New Mexico, USA, that, for many, is the origin myth of the great modern extra-terrestrial conspiracy theory – Roswell.

About the same time as the southern Australia sightings, in May 1947, on the other side of the planet in Washington DC, Rear Admiral Roscoe Hillenkoetter was settling into his new job as the Director of Central Intelligence, which later that year became the Central Intelligence Agency (CIA). A former commander of the battleship USS *Missouri*, Hillenkoetter had been wounded on another vessel during the attack on Pearl Harbor and a major priority in his new job was to fix the intelligence failures that had allowed the Japanese to attack undetected in 1941. The United States needed to detect and identify all craft in its airspace; it was a major issue of national security.

Almost as soon as Hillenkoetter took over the top intelligence job, the post-war flying saucer frenzy began in the American press. On 24 June 1947, businessman Kenneth Arnold had his seminal sighting of what became notoriously known in the press as 'flying saucers'. Arnold was a private pilot and, in the hope of winning a generous $5000 reward on offer for any sighting of a downed US military transport aircraft, he took a plane up to search in the vicinity of Mount Rainer, Washington, south-east of Seattle. In flight, in the middle of a bright afternoon, he at first saw a brilliant flashing light in the distance, which he was worried might be another plane, and then from a distance of 30 to 40 kilometres away, he noticed a series of bright flashes north of Mount Rainier. The objects flew towards the mountain and Arnold watched as they passed in front of its snow-covered slopes. He described their shape as convex with one object differently as crescent-shaped. As a pilot, Arnold was experienced in approximating the speed of distant objects and he estimated their speed as they tracked across the breadth of the distant mountain as being up to 1700 miles an hour (2700 km/h). Multiple locals wrote to local newspapers reporting that they saw similar objects. Within days, the *Chicago Sun* headlined its story 'Supersonic Flying Saucers Sighted by Idaho Pilot'.[7] And the sightings kept coming. On 1 July, a disc-shaped UAP was seen zigzagging across the sky in New Mexico and on 3 July, an astronomer in Maine reported seeing an object about 100 feet (30 metres) in diameter. The US Army's Air Materiel Command publicly explained it away as birds or insects, but the later air force investigation acknowledged the sighting was unexplained.[8] (The US Air Force was created as a separate branch of the military in September 1947.)

Ten days after Arnold's sighting, on the 4 July Independence Day national holiday, a United Airlines crew reported seeing five to nine disc-shaped objects that kept pace with their aircraft.[9] That same day, Portland police officers also reported seeing a large number of UAPs overhead, and a carload of people saw four disc-shaped craft going past Mount Jefferson in Oregon. It seemed flying discs were everywhere that summer holiday period. The US Army was forced to admit it had 'no idea what they are'.[10]

There was feverish public interest in the phenomenon of UAPs at this time, which should put what happened next in some context. On 5 July 1947, a ranch foreman named Mac Brazel found crash debris scattered across a cattle ranch 120 kilometres from Roswell in New Mexico. These days Roswell is a growing city with a population of about 50,000 but in the late 1940s it was a much smaller town of about 15,000, servicing local farmers and local military bases. Since the 1930s, the empty high plains of south-eastern New Mexico have been a test area for the United States' space and aerospace technology. So Brazel drove into Roswell to report his find. The earliest reports described what he saw, and collected, as including extremely strong and lightweight wires, foil, and metallic beams with strange writing on them. When Brazel alerted the local sheriff, the nearby Roswell Army Air Force Base was notified, and an intelligence officer named Major Jesse Marcel was sent to investigate.

Adding to the ensuing Roswell controversy was that it was Major Marcel's 509th Bomb Group Wing that had dropped the atomic bombs on the Japanese cities of Hiroshima and Nagasaki two years earlier in 1945. The New Mexico White Sands testing ground, two hours' drive west of the crash site, was where the

US Army had conducted the world's first-ever detonation of the 'Trinity' nuclear device on 16 July 1945. Atomic bombs and rockets were still being tested there in 1947. This barren part of New Mexico, of which Roswell was a part, was ground zero for the new atomic age.

Many believers in the extra-terrestrial (ET) hypothesis for UAPs speculate that alien spaceships were covertly monitoring the atomic bomb tests in New Mexico and that, when one crashed, it was secretly recovered by the US military with dead and live extra-terrestrial beings on board. The conspiracy theory demands we accept that the whole Roswell crash and alleged recovery operation have been the subject of a monumental cover-up to this day. The strangest irony of the Roswell affair is that the US military's clumsy response did much to encourage the perception, in the minds of a substantial portion of the American public, that there was indeed some kind of cover-up. This is because the US Air Force has given four different explanations for what supposedly happened at Roswell in 1947. Officials definitely lied and covered up; the big question is, why?

What we do know is that Roswell ranch foreman Mac Brazel took army intelligence officers Major Jesse Marcel and his colleague Captain Sheridan Cavitt out to the crash site and Marcel came back clearly convinced that a flying disc of extra-terrestrial origin had crashed on the ranch. Marcel described a massive field of debris 1200 metres long and 60 to 90 metres wide. There was allegedly a gouge in the field that extended up to 150 metres long, which looked as if 'something had touched down and skipped along'.[11] Marcel later showed his family some of the strange debris, saying it was wreckage from a 'flying saucer'.[12] This included foil metal sheets that were as light as a feather yet incredibly strong and impervious to tearing. He also described light metal beams on which there was strange hieroglyphic writing.

When Marcel and Cavitt brought their debris back to the Roswell base, their commanding officer Colonel William Blanchard sent Marcel on a flight to take the debris to the 8th Air Force headquarters in Fort Worth, Texas, to meet Brigadier General Roger Ramey. At midday on the same day, 8 July 1947, Blanchard ordered his base public information officer Lieutenant Walter Haut to issue a press release announcing that the US Army had recovered a flying disc. The story hit the newswires in the early afternoon and, coming as it did straight after the many UAP sightings over the previous weeks, the announcement had an incendiary effect on the already frantic public interest in 'UFOs and flying saucers'. Roswell's evening newspaper, the *Roswell Daily Record*, breathlessly reported, 'The intelligence office of the 509th Bombardment Group at Roswell Army Air Field announced at noon today that the field has come into possession of a flying saucer.'[13] (The Army actually never said that it was a 'flying saucer'; it only referred to a 'disc'.) The story also carried claims from locals Mr and Mrs Dan Wilmot, claiming that earlier that week they had seen a speeding disc overhead that 'looked oval in shape like two inverted saucers, faced mouth to mouth … The entire body glowed as though light were showing through from inside'. Not surprisingly, this incredible story asserting there was a recovered 'flying saucer', supposedly the first-ever official acknowledgement anywhere in the world of what was possibly extra-terrestrial life, went around the planet like wildfire, drawing huge media interest.

By the time Marcel arrived in Fort Worth, Texas, later that day, General Ramey's office had changed its mind. Just three hours after the noon Roswell press release, General Ramey issued a new statement through Associated Press asserting that the supposed flying disc was simply a weather balloon. It is a measure of how trusting America was in its military right after World War Two that, within days, the press accepted this assurance and the Roswell 'flying saucer' story disappeared without trace for over three decades.

Jesse Marcel did not speak up until 1978, but for eight years from 1978 until he died in 1986, he claimed he had been ordered to collude in a cover-up and dramatically alleged in multiple interviews that the real debris he brought with him that day from Roswell was substituted by General Ramey with wreckage from an old weather balloon, and that he actually believed what crashed at Roswell was extra-terrestrial. Marcel, who left the Air Force Reserves as a decorated lieutenant colonel in 1958, said he was forced to pose for photographs with pieces of a weather balloon to debunk the flying disc crash story. In retirement, Marcel told the 'real' story to nuclear physicist and self-described flying saucer researcher Stanton Friedman. Friedman then alleged a 'cosmic Watergate cover-up' of a recovered alien spacecraft and alien bodies.[14] The conspiracy theory was pushed along by a 1980 book, *The Roswell Incident*,[15] featuring interviews with purported witnesses who supported the claim that what happened at Roswell involved a crashed alien spacecraft.

What undoubtedly assisted the conspiracy theories was the 1994 decision by the US Air Force to change its story yet again, offering a third explanation; it admitted that its 1947 weather balloon story was indeed bunkum. There had been a cover-up of a kind, but the air force claimed it was not for the reasons the ufologists alleged.[16] The air force's 1994 report claimed the wreckage that was recovered was from a then top-secret balloon project designed to monitor Soviet nuclear tests, known as Project MOGUL. 'Air Force research efforts did not disclose any records of the recovery of any "alien" bodies or extra-terrestrial materials,' the report states.[17] We will return to the Air Force's highly entertaining fourth explanation for Roswell with double backflip and pike in a later chapter.

The initial press release issued by the US Army clearly referred to a recovered 'flying disc'. It began: 'The many rumors regarding the flying disc became a reality yesterday when the intelligence office of 509th Bomb Group of the Eighth Air Force, Roswell Army Air Field, was fortunate enough to gain possession of a disc.'[18] What has never been satisfactorily explained is why Roswell's commanding officer Colonel Blanchard so quickly concluded that what had crashed was a 'flying disc' when, supposedly, all he was shown at the base by Marcel and Cavitt were small pieces of debris.

One difficulty with the air force's 1994 Mogul spy balloon explanation is that declassified images of the Mogul balloon-train from that period show no disc and Mogul's radar reflector debris would have been clearly recognisable as conventional material, especially to Major Marcel. The Mogul balloon was largely composed of rubber balloons, balsa wood and tinfoil. The hexagonal radar reflectors on the Mogul balloon-train were not discs. So, why did Blanchard authorise issuing a press release saying a 'flying disc' had been recovered, unless he knew that for sure? Did two highly experienced army officers really let flying saucer fever get the better of them?

There are an enormous number of unanswered questions behind the official response to Roswell that do raise suspicion. As the US Congress's General Accounting Office discovered during its 1995 review of the incident's paperwork, not a single document from the Roswell Army Airfield in the crash period survives; every bit of paper relating to this 1947 incident was destroyed with no apparent authorisation.[19] Multiple alleged first-hand witnesses also suggest there was something very unusual about the debris recovered, including supposedly indestructible metal of an apparently highly advanced technology, clearly not just spy balloon wreckage. Colonel Blanchard even confided to his friend, the editor of the *Roswell Morning Dispatch* newspaper, that, 'The stuff I saw, I've never seen anyplace else in my life.'[20]

There is also the extraordinary deathbed affidavit of former US Army public information officer Lieutenant Walter Haut, who testified in 2002 that he was taken out to a hangar by Colonel Blanchard to view recovered child-sized bodies with abnormally large heads, lying under a tarpaulin at the base. In a statement released after his death, he alleged that Blanchard allowed him to see an apparent alien craft in a hangar 'approx. 12 to 15 feet in length, not quite as wide, about 6 feet high and more of an egg shape. Lighting was poor, but its surface did appear metallic'. Haut said, 'I am convinced that what I personally observed was some type of craft and its crew from outer space.'[21] Haut also alleged Blanchard's press release was a ruse to divert public attention from the main recovery operation of the craft from a different site.

Sceptics charged that Haut might not have been in full possession of his faculties so close to his own death and that the authors of *Witness to Roswell*, Don Schmitt and Thomas Carey, actually wrote the dramatic affidavit. 'Nobody worked on Walter Haut, spent more time with Walter Haut than we did, trying to get him to open up,' Schmitt told me.[22] He acknowledged they did draft what Walter told them into an affidavit, but Haut was very clearly of sound mind, approving every word. 'We prepared the statement based on all the information that Walter had provided us through the years. And he read through it; his daughter was present. There was a notary present, there was another witness present. And, as his daughter wrote in a statement, if Walter would have disagreed with a word of it, he would never have signed.'

There you have it. The ufologists hoped that would surely be the end of the matter: a notarised eyewitness sighting of what sounds like an alien spacecraft – and even aliens – secreted away in 1947 in a hangar in Roswell. One problem, of course, with Walter Haut's posthumous affidavit was that he was not around to answer further questions about it, and he had sworn a previous affidavit making no mention of recovered ETs or a craft. Other witnesses have come forward, especially family members of former members of the military who served at Roswell's Army Air Force base, offering second-hand hearsay evidence of what their father or family member admitted privately to them, verifying the alien spacecraft story. But, unless we one day get the chance to kick the tyres of a recovered flying saucer, the evidence is simply nowhere near convincing enough to nail Roswell down as the cover-up of a supposedly recovered craft.

As always seems to happen with Roswell stories, people have found other reasons to raise doubt with Walter Haut's direct witness evidence. His daughter, Julie Shuster, who witnessed his affidavit, was employed by Roswell's UFO Museum, a local tourism drawcard co-founded by her dad. The suggestion was made that she had a financial incentive to promote the extra-terrestrial hypothesis and that her dying father was happy to oblige. Schmitt, who from his many bruising clashes with sceptics has become a scrupulously precise and careful fellow, having trained as an investigator with the late celebrated 'UFO investigator' Dr J. Allen Hynek, laughed at that suggestion, saying that Julie (who has since passed away from breast cancer) was paid a nominal salary, not much higher than the minimum wage, to keep the museum going. 'It was hardly a financial incentive for her and her dad to concoct a UFO story,' he said. 'No one was in any doubt that Haut was sincere and truthful in what he said in his affidavit.'

Frankly, it is impossible to reach any definitive conclusion about what happened at Roswell in 1947. Something crashed, and it is tempting to accept the air force's explanation that the cover-up was to protect a sensitive Cold War spy project. I say that simply because journalists are trained to always believe that such a Cold War screw-up with a crashed spy balloon is more plausible than an elaborate (and surely incredible?) conspiracy to hide aliens and recovered spacecraft. This is the Ockham's razor principle: always assume the simplest explanation. Even inside the world of ufology, there are as many trenchant critics of the Roswell retrieved extra-terrestrials story as there are believers. But, on the evidence, especially in light of the US Air Force's bungled explanations and admitted lies, I do think what happened at Roswell should be treated as an open question for investigation.

One thing we can be sure of is that extraordinary measures were taken at the time to keep whatever it was secret. This does not sit easily with the claim that it was merely a Cold War spy balloon.

As the Roswell story unfolded, a new breed of aggressive sceptics also surfaced, questioning the excessive credulity of those all too willing to believe in elaborate alien cover-up conspiracies. But suspicions linger about who was driving the agendas of one or two of the more vociferous sceptics. It was only revealed after his death that Harvard astronomer and self-described 'UFO sceptic' Donald Menzel had a clandestine association with the US National Security Agency, CIA and Navy (holding a top-secret-ultra clearance). It was a secret relationship he never disclosed, even to his university. Researcher Stanton Friedman has accused Menzel of being a deep-cover disinformation agent tasked to shut down UAP stories.[23]

The ridicule by sceptics certainly had the effect of gagging much of the mainstream press and preventing them from taking the issue seriously, but public interest in 'flying saucers' actually intensified; sightings of UAPs soared. At a time when the Watergate scandal and the Vietnam War were eroding the trust many Americans had previously held in their government, the US public was beginning to question the institutions of the State like never before. Pressure was mounting on the US military to provide an explanation for the mystery in plain sight.

Chapter 3

The Launch of Project Blue Book

America's 1947 'UFO flap' did not die down after Roswell; it escalated. This was the beginning of the Cold War confrontation between the Soviet Union and the Western alliance; the US public, FBI and military were primed to be hypervigilant for any signs of communist spies and incursions into American territory. It meant strange objects seen in the sky were reported and investigated, and sightings of flying discs flooded into the military. So much so that by September 1947, General Nathan Twining, a former combat fighter pilot and World War Two commander, the head of the United States Air Materiel Command, penned a now famous letter about the flying discs, acknowledging that the phenomenon, whatever it was, was 'something real and not visionary or fictitious'. Twining described how the 'metallic' looking discs showed capabilities such as extreme rates of climb and manoeuvrability, including evasion when detected, which 'lend belief to the possibility that some of the objects are controlled either manually, or remotely'.[1] He recommended a detailed study of the UAPs, which became known as Project Sign and commenced in December 1947. Originally dubbed Project Saucer, the air force-controlled investigation ran for one year.

One insider privy to the Project Sign investigations was a US Air Force officer, Edward Ruppelt. He subsequently claimed to have seen a highly classified 1948 Project Sign report, entitled 'Estimate of the Situation', investigating the flying saucer sightings. 'The situation was the UFOs; the estimate was that they were interplanetary,' he succinctly admitted.[2] Ruppelt, who later headed Project Blue Book's UAP investigations, claimed this early report concluded that the best explanation for the phenomenon was that the craft were extra-terrestrial. But if such findings were in the original document, they were not in a heavily redacted version released almost 40 years later in 1987. Another tamer US air intelligence report, released in December 1948, side-stepped the extra-terrestrial hypothesis and suggested the numerous strange craft seen in American skies were possibly of Soviet origin.[3] At the same time, Project Sign was renamed Project Grudge.

So began a curious practice that continued for decades, whereby the US Air Force publicly and aggressively debunked all UAP sightings, but inside America's military and intelligence services, the issue was actually being taken very seriously. In late 1949, the Air Force Office of Special Investigations, investigating green fireballs seen over military sites, confidentially reported that 'the continued occurrence of unexplained phenomena of this nature in the vicinity of sensitive installations is cause for concern'.[4]

Sightings reports kept on flooding into the military, especially after Marine Corps veteran Donald Keyhoe published his dramatic article 'Flying Saucers Are Real' in the popular men's magazine *True* in late 1949. In his best-selling book of the same name,[5] he claimed the US Air Force knew that the mystery objects were extra-terrestrial but that it was playing down reports to avoid a public panic. In an apparent attempt to quell public interest, the air force's first Project Grudge report was published soon after, announcing that it would stop investigating unidentified flying objects and asserting that all such sightings were the result of mass hysteria, hoaxes or the misinterpretation of conventional objects. Project Grudge was ostensibly still seriously investigating UFOs. But as project insider Edward Ruppelt later asserted, there was a widespread view that Project Grudge was operating under a directive to debunk all sightings.[6]

But then a 9 January 1950 issue of the news magazine *Time* reported rumours that crashed 'flying saucers' and 'small humanoid looking bodies' had been recovered from crashes in New Mexico. That was followed by an astounding report to Federal Bureau of Investigation (FBI) boss J. Edgar Hoover in March 1950, telling him that an air force investigator had disclosed 'that three so-called flying saucers had been recovered in New Mexico. They were described as being circular in shape with raised centres, approximately fifty feet in diameter. Each one was occupied by three bodies of human shape but only three feet tall, dressed in metallic cloth of very fine texture'. The report, from Guy Hottel, the then head of the FBI's Washington DC field office, remains the most controversial, and the most popular, file in the FBI's archive. Seventy years later, on its website, the FBI, no doubt jaded by flying saucer conspiracists seizing on the memo, asserts that the Hottel report was never confirmed or investigated, and that the memo does not prove the existence of aliens.[7]

But right through this period, authoritative witnesses repeatedly recorded close-up sightings of strange craft not explainable as natural phenomena. In April 1950, 15 people at the Los Alamos nuclear weapons laboratory watched an object hovering at 2000 feet for 20 minutes. Seen through a telescope, the metallic-looking object was described as flat, roughly circular and about nine feet (2.7 metres) in diameter. The scientist watching it said it flew 'faster than any known conventional aircraft'.[8] In July 1952, multiple witnesses at Los Alamos saw a white egg-shaped object, larger than a jet, that was at one stage motionless in the sky and then moving extremely fast. It was dismissed by the air force absurdly as 'papers', because the witness had contrasted the odd motion of the object with 'fluttering papers'.[9]

Citizens were also catching these objects on camera. In May 1950, farmer Paul Trent and his wife from McMinnville, Oregon, had photographed a clear image of what looks like a classic flying saucer over their farm. A subsequent air force inquiry admitted, 'This is one of the few UFO cases in which all factors investigated, geometric, psychological, and physical, appear to be consistent with the assertion that an extraordinary flying object, silvery, metallic, disc-shaped, tens of metres in diameter, and evidently artificial flew within sight of two witnesses.'[10]

Another extraordinary piece of evidence often used to support the Roswell ET conspiracy hypothesis was a top-secret memo written by Canadian radio engineer Wilbert Smith to the Canadian Department of Transport in November 1950, later found in Smith's official papers in a Canadian university archive. Smith was highly regarded inside the Canadian government as he worked on a top-secret project intercepting Soviet communications. While at a conference in Washington DC in September that year, he read the just published *Behind the Flying Saucers*[11] book by Frank Scully, which alleged there had been multiple crashes and retrievals of ET flying saucers in New Mexico, and that it had been discovered the craft were propelled electro-magnetically. Smith used his own contacts at the Canadian Embassy in Washington to interview Dr Robert Sarbacher, an American scientist who consulted for the US government's Research and Development Board. Smith's memo[12] records astounding admissions allegedly made by Sarbacher that flying saucers were:

(a)   … the most highly classified subject in the United States government, rating higher even than the H-bomb.

(b)   Flying Saucers exist.

(c)   Their modus operandi is unknown, but a concentrated effort is being made by a small group headed by Dr Vannevar Bush.

(d)   The entire matter is considered by the United States authorities to be of tremendous significance

Wilbert Smith's handwritten notes of the meeting recorded Dr Sarbacher confirming that the facts set out in the Frank Scully flying saucers book (including recovered aliens and spacecraft) were 'substantially correct'. Wilbert Smith's son James has also admitted that his father told him much more, including that 'he was shown recovered bodies from a recovered craft' that were small and humanoid.[13] There has never been any attempt by the United States or Canadian governments to rebut Wilbert Smith's record of what he says he learned about the purported US 'recovered flying saucers' program, both governments remaining conspicuously silent on the issue.

The fact that Smith was a senior official in the Canadian government when he made this report does not mean his reported investigation findings were officially sanctioned. However, three years before his death in 1986, Dr Sarbacher wrote to researcher William Steinman, 'Relating to my own experience regarding recovered flying saucers, I had no association with any of the people involved in the recovery and have no knowledge regarding the dates of the recoveries … Certain materials reported to have come from flying saucer crashes were extremely light and very tough … I remember in talking with some of the people at the office that I got the impression these "aliens" were constructed like certain insects we have observed on earth … I still do not know why the high order of [security] classification has been given and why the denial of the existence of these devices.'

It might be argued Sarbacher's letter proves nothing because it was hearsay, not direct witness evidence. The same argument applies to his son, Robert Sarbacher, who admitted[14] his father told him he knew UAPs 'were real for the obvious reason that they would be going 600 mph and then make a direct 90 degree turn in mid-air without slowing down ... separated from all inertia and gravity'. While the Wilbert Smith and Dr Robert Sarbacher claims are intriguing because of the credibility of the people making them, as mere hearsay evidence, they remain unverified.

* * *

A 1952 CIA document offered prosaic explanations for many flying disc sightings at the time, including 'mass hysteria ... Hallucination and hoax'. But it also acknowledged unexplained sightings over the highly sensitive Los Alamos and Oak Ridge nuclear weapons laboratories 'at a time when the background radiation count had risen inexplicably'. Military investigators conceded, 'Here we run out of even "blue yonder" explanations that might be tenable, and we still are left with numbers of incredible reports from credible observers.'[15]

Concern about UAPs within the CIA heightened to the point where, in 1952, the agency's Assistant Director of Scientific Intelligence advised, "'Flying Saucers' pose two elements of danger which have national security implications. The first involves mass psychological considerations and the second concerns the vulnerability of the United States to air attack'.[16] His now declassified secret memorandum clearly acknowledged UAPs were an extremely important national security concern that he urged should be scientifically investigated.

That same year, Project Grudge became Project Blue Book. Blue Book's brief was to determine if UFOs were a threat to national security, and to scientifically analyse the data gathered. It just so happened that 1952 was a bumper year for unexplained flying discs, as eventful as 1947. Numerous military sightings sent to Project Blue Book detailed pilots sighting objects moving at incredible speeds, often tracked on radar. The air force project would eventually investigate 12,618 UAP reports from both civilians and military witnesses, dismissing the vast majority as misidentifications with prosaic explanations. But a small percentage was classified as 'unexplained' even after stringent analysis.

Civilian scientist Dr Josef Allen Hynek was a Project Blue Book consultant, who had previously worked as an advisor for Project Sign. He had initially been extremely sceptical of so-called 'UFO' reports, having said in his first year on Project Sign that the whole issue 'seems utterly ridiculous'.[17] Hynek later observed that the air force could easily discount civilian reports, 'but they could not discount outright their own trained personnel – the military witnesses'.[18] He said two schools of thought dominated the approach to UAPs in their investigations: the first acknowledged that they should be taken very seriously as probable ET craft and the second was the debunking view eventually embraced by the top brass in Washington DC. An air force scientific advisory board composed of top scientists declared that it was against all known science that a craft could behave in the manner attributed to 'UFOs': 'Science had said that it was impossible and the air force theorem which was to cause so much trouble later on was born: "It can't be, therefore it isn't",' Dr Hynek lamented.[19]

Project Blue Book also brought to light frustration that, while the air force exclusively collected all the aerial sightings evidence, the other arms of the military were being kept in the dark. This became a major issue in March 1952 when the Secretary of the Navy, Dan

Kimball, and Admiral Arthur Radford travelled from Hawaii to Guam on separate aircraft that were both reportedly tracked by mysterious disc-shaped objects. Kimball told his story to an audience of navy officers and air cadets in May 1952 and the story was reported by the *Boston Traveler Magazine*.[20] A copy of the story was discovered in Project Blue Book's declassified archives. The article quoted Kimball as saying, 'Somewhere out over the dark Pacific ... the pilot came back to the cabin visibly excited and reported that a flying saucer had appeared out of nowhere, had flown abeam the Secretary's plane for some distance, and had just raced ahead and shot up into the sky and out of sight. He and the co-pilot had both watched the phenomenon.' The pilot asked for permission to notify the US base at Pearl Harbor, Hawaii, but Kimball advised that the base probably would not believe the story. He suggested they alert the admiral's plane astern and keep a lookout. Then, 'In a matter of minutes, the second plane radioed excitedly that a flying saucer had just come down and flown alongside the wing tip, then had shot ahead and vanished into the sky,' Kimball said.

The co-founder of the National Investigations Committee on Aerial Phenomena (NICAP), Major Donald Keyhoe, wrote how Kimball later told him the discs flew at speeds up to 2000 miles an hour (3200 km/h).[21] Kimball personally filed a report of the sighting to the air force but was never given any response or follow-up information. Reportedly angry about this, Kimball decided to order his own naval intelligence reports on UAPs – independent of the air force's Project Blue Book. The air force then objected to the idea of a separate independent naval investigative body and the Office of Naval Research was forced to stop its official investigation. The following year (1953), Admiral Radford went on to become the chairman of the Joint Chiefs of Staff in the Pentagon. Two of the most powerful people in America's navy had reported the same mysterious direct experience with flying discs, but absolutely no official record of it happening, or findings into what the discs were, has ever been disclosed.

Project Blue Book logged numerous reports of similar sightings at crucial nuclear weapons sites, including the Atomic Energy Commission's Hanford nuclear bomb factory in Richlands, Washington. In July 1952, two pilots witnessed a flat and round flying saucer–shaped object hovering over the highly secure facility and the next day the local Dayton *Daily News* headlined its story, 'Flyers Report Saucers Near Atomic Plant'. Dr J. Allen Hynek, by now immersed in the Blue Book investigations, witnessed how the air force instructed its investigators 'to "stall" off press inquiries "with a no-comment answer"' to the Hanford incident and other such sightings.[22]

Then came the Washington DC UFO flap; the same month as the Hanford sighting on the west coast, on 19 July, radar operators across on the east coast at Washington DC's National Airport detected a large formation of UAPs near Andrews Air Force Base. They were shocked when one of the objects was tracked accelerating off the radar scope's range within seconds, reaching a speed of 7000 miles an hour (11,265 km/h). The great Washington July 1952 'UFO flap' became a huge media story because for six hours or more there were at least ten unidentifiable glowing objects moving above Washington DC. They were also detected on radar. Pilots flying over the capital saw the objects as orange lights, hovering right over America's seats of power – the White House and the Capitol building. Not quite a landing on the White House lawn, but not far off it.

Adding to the mystery, exactly one week after the first DC sighting, the objects returned. On 26 July, a dozen UAPs were again tracked on radar and seen by pilots flying slowly over the capital. When fighter jets were sent up to engage them, they disappeared from radar. Staff in the Washington National Tower said everyone in the radar room believed the targets were 'very probably caused by solid metallic objects' that were incapable of prosaic explanation.[23] The story was front-page news across the planet and even President Truman was demanding answers. In the Pentagon's biggest press conference since World War Two, the US Air Force's Director of Intelligence, Major General John Samford, dismissed the Washington DC sightings as having been caused by freak 'weather phenomena'.

In secret, though, the experts told a different story. In December that year, the US government enlisted physicist Dr Howard Robertson to convene a panel of distinguished scientists to investigate what these unidentified objects were. The director of the Central Intelligence Agency, Walter Bedell Smith, who commissioned the so-called Robertson Panel, was earlier privately advised that 'the reports of incidents convince us that there is something going on that must have immediate attention'. The sightings of UAPs raised serious national security concerns and were 'of such nature that they are not attributable to natural phenomenon or known types of aerial vehicles'.[24]

It became clear to Project Blue Book consultant Dr J. Allen Hynek that the Robertson Panel's primary role was to debunk all UAP sightings and to put control of investigations into the phenomenon back with the air force. The CIA also began playing down the sightings, in a clear change of policy. Hynek wrote, 'In short, in convening the panel, the CIA was fearful not of UFOs, but of UFO *reports*.'[25] In its January 1953 report, the panel asserted the UAPs were no threat to national security, which was an enormous cop-out in light of advice to the contrary given to the CIA Director. The panel actually recommended a condescending educational program aimed at 'training and debunking' UAPs to the public.[26] Why this denial approach was taken by the CIA, in the face of powerful evidence to the contrary, has never been explained.

In July 1953, Perrin Air Force Base in North Texas reported seeing seven UAPs in a Z-shaped formation, 'with one bright red light, on each object hovering at estimated altitudes from five to eight thousand feet'. The next month, Project Blue Book was called in to investigate a major sighting at South Dakota, where radar tracked a 'well-defined, solid and bright' object seen by people on the ground. A fighter pilot was scrambled to intercept the object, but it accelerated away. Then when the pilot returned towards the Ellsworth Air Force Base, the UAP actually followed him in.

Thousands of these sightings were recorded in the Project Blue Book files. Many remained unresolved.[27]

Chapter 4

A Worldwide Phenomenon

While the US Air Force's Project Blue Book investigation was still ramping up, UAPs were unhelpfully frustrating official efforts to suppress interest in them by regularly showing up over sensitive defence sites or buzzing civilian aircraft in other parts of the world.

Behind the Iron Curtain, the subject of 'UFOs' had initially been greeted with derision; the Kremlin's tactic was to publicly debunk all such sightings. However, Soviet pilots were also seeing strange things, although their reports were being suppressed.[1] In 1955, on a visit to the Soviet Union, the United States Senator Richard Russell, the head of the powerful Armed Services Committee, looked out of his train window in the Trans-Caucasus region to see a disc-shaped object slowly ascending vertically, with its outer surface revolving slowly and with two lights visible on the top. It sped off when it hit about 6000 feet. As Russell and his staffer watched, one minute later, another craft made the same manoeuvre. Panicked Soviet staff on the train reportedly shut the curtains across the train window and told the Senator and his colleagues not to look outside again.

The story of this incident, told in a once top-secret memo from a US Air Attaché in the American Embassy in Prague, was only revealed 30 years later by a *Freedom of Information Act* request.[2] The second object was described by one witness as being triangular in shape with three lights on each point of the triangle. Because both craft were seen being tracked with a searchlight, the report raised concerns that Senator Russell had stumbled across a secret Soviet military project working on flying disc craft, built perhaps with the aid of captured Nazi scientists. The sighting was never explained.

In the United Kingdom, unknown objects in its skies were being detected frequently. One event was described by the physicist who investigated it as 'one of the strangest and most disturbing radar-visual UFO episodes on record'.[3] On 13 August 1956, radar operators at the Suffolk NATO base RAF Bentwaters (known to be armed with nuclear weapons) tracked an object soaring towards them at speeds of up to 9000 miles an hour (14,500 km/h). A cluster of a dozen objects suddenly appeared on radar to the south-east of the base, with three objects leading the formation tracking north-east in a triangular configuration. The objects then all converged into one huge target, sitting stationary in the sky for quarter of an hour. RAF Bentwaters alerted the nearby RAF Lakenheath base and staff on the ground there saw a luminous object stationary in the sky, which then zoomed off at high speed.

The British Royal Air Force scrambled a fighter jet to intercept the object; the pilot later described locking his radar fire-control system onto 'the clearest target that I have ever seen on radar', only for the object to immediately disappear and reappear behind him. The encounter was classified until it was reported in the University of Colorado's UAP investigation project known as the Condon Committee in 1969. A physicist who investigated the British sightings for Condon, Gordon Thayer, declared that 'the apparently rational, intelligent behaviour of the UFO suggests a mechanical device of unknown origin as the most probable explanation of this sighting'.[4] A US Air Force investigator described the sightings as 'real and not figments of the imagination' because three radar sets picked up the targets simultaneously.

Then follows one of the most extraordinary official documents of all. A series of 1956 cables[5] from a US Air Force air attaché in Kabul, Afghanistan, revealed the Governor of Kataghan Province reported that a 'flying saucer' had landed near the town of Takala in January after numerous UAP sightings across the country. Wright Patterson Air Force Base in the USA was the recipient of these cables. The craft was described as 15 metres in circumference, of metal construction, with 'small, thick glass windows around leading edge of saucer shaped moving object'. (A 15-metre circumference is an 11-metre diameter.) The Afghans were planning to transport it to the Minister of Defence in Kabul. The US Air Attaché reported he would be flying to the location to view the craft the next day but there was no follow-up. The Soviet Union exerted heavy influence in Afghanistan from 1954 because of its substantial military assistance so perhaps the USSR beat the Americans in the race to recover the object. The provenance of this US Air Force cable is not in any doubt; it is an official US government document apparently confirming the recovery of a large flying disc. There is no record detailing what was ever discovered about the craft recovered.

In Australia, during the 1940s and 1950s, similarly strange sightings of unidentified craft were also being reported. Again, many were near military sites. Once-secret files, declassified by Australia's National Archives, have revealed that, as the British government began (selflessly) using remote parts of Australia for its Cold War long-range rocket and nuclear bomb research, there were similarly strange sightings of unidentified craft reported. Back in 1946, Britain's boffins had needed space to test and re-engineer captured Nazi rockets, which would eventually be used to develop the UK's own nuclear missile deterrence. Australia agreed to provide not only the land and personnel, but also a large part of the funding. The Anglo-Australian Long Range Weapons Establishment was 122,188 square kilometres of remote outback desert country five hours' drive north of Adelaide in South Australia. Later known as the Woomera Rocket Range, it was the largest land-based test range in the Western world, and was a highly secure top-secret location. It is known today as the RAAF Woomera Test Range.

When strange objects began appearing over the remote site, sightings reports were sent to Australia's Air Force intelligence branch. There are dozens of such anomalous sightings recorded, including one in May 1954 at Woomera. A security officer named Sydney Baker witnessed an object travelling across the path of an approaching Canberra aircraft (the RAAF's first jet-propelled bomber) at a speed he estimated to be three times the jet's 870 kilometres an hour velocity. 'I found it very hard to believe what I was seeing,' he told his superiors. Through binoculars, he then clearly saw that the object, the same relative size as the aircraft, was sitting stationary in front of the Canberra's flight path. 'It was perfectly circular all the time and a dark grey colour, and gave the appearance of being translucent,' he reported.[6] Baker's account was corroborated by Staff Sergeant George Trotter, who tracked the object on his radar screen travelling at 15,000 yards in ten seconds (4800 km/h), far beyond the capacities of any known aircraft. The *Adelaide Advertiser* newspaper also reported that two ladies had seen a similar object two days earlier at Henley Beach on the South Australian coast. This corroboration by multiple witnesses of an apparent unknown high-speed craft had Woomera officials gravely concerned that a superior technology was breaching their secure airspace.

An earlier secret report to the Director of Air Force Intelligence told how five 'reliable witnesses' had observed an illuminated cigar-shaped object flying over Woomera at 9 pm during an open-air movie screening. Warrant Officer EJV Hanley witnessed 'an illuminated object shaped like a cigar with a spurting light at the rear, travelling from west to east in a horizontal way'.[7] Another warrant officer named Walker described it as 'cigar shaped, tapering off towards the back. It was lit up like a neon light with a haze around it. The colouring was whitish and the exhausts or flames at the back were yellowish or cream'.[8] A young baker at the Woomera base, Joseph Ager, described one object as 'travelling at such speed, faster than any of the jets up here. It was of a dark greyish colour and of airship shape'. A Sergeant Phillips said he saw two portholes with internal lighting on the cylindrical object, which was a light grey colour. A similar object was again seen by Adelaide locals and reported in the *Adelaide Advertiser* over three days.

The majority of these early strange sightings at Woomera and other sensitive Australian military sites went unexplained. A lot of the 'UFO believers' see a conspiracy in the fact that there was often no official follow-up to these sightings of strange objects. However, knowing how military bureaucracies work, it seems more likely commanders took the view that to admit they had absolutely no idea what these objects were, was not particularly helpful to their careers. Better to politely ignore the elephant in the room.

Nonetheless, under mounting political and media pressure, Australia's Directorate of Air Force Intelligence (DAFI) began investigating the UAP reports. In 1954, Harry Turner, a Melbourne University nuclear physics professor, approached the air force asking to read its UAP files. Because the air force was being hammered to provide an explanation, Turner (who already had a security clearance) was hired by DAFI to do a classified review of recent sightings. Turner's report to DAFI subsequently concluded that 'The evidence presented by RAAF tends to support the conclusion ... that certain strange aircraft have been observed to behave in a manner suggestive of extra-terrestrial origin.'[9] However, because Harry Turner quoted US best-selling flying saucer author and National Investigations Committee on Aerial Phenomena director Major Donald Keyhoe in his research, Australia's Director of Air Force Intelligence dismissed Professor Turner's findings, after consulting with the US Air Force. He said Professor Turner had 'erred' in quoting Keyhoe because the former marine major supposedly gave the misleading impression his books had some official US government sanction. Why DAFI's director took such a harshly critical stance against his scientific advisor is unexplained, but it was quite unfair to Turner (and to Keyhoe), because the Australian intelligence UAP sightings reports he cited to support his conclusions were based on solid data and witness evidence. Keyhoe's outspokenness was clearly embarrassing at the time to Australia's friends in the American military so maybe the director thought he was doing his US intelligence chums a favour.

For example, Turner's report detailed that air force files documented that, on 5 May 1954, radar at the Woomera Rocket Range detected what was seen to be a 'misty grey disc' at 60,000 feet. It sped off at 3600 miles an hour (5800 km/h). An English scientist had simultaneously viewed the object seen on radar through his binoculars; this was a well-verified sighting. But the Royal Australian Air Force elected to heed its American ally and play down Turner's 'flying saucer' ET hypothesis. Bill Chalker, an Australian scientist and UAP researcher trained in mathematics and chemistry, was the first civilian researcher to gain access to the Royal Australian Air Force's UAP files in the early 1980s. He befriended Harry Turner late in his life and says of Turner's efforts, 'Political myopia from both the US and Australian military effectively scuttled Australia's first serious flirtation with scientific investigation of UFOs'.[10]

Fifty-four kilometres north-west of Ooldea in the Great Victoria Desert in South Australia sits the Maralinga nuclear test range where the British detonated many nuclear bombs as they developed their nuclear missile deterrence. An area of 52,000 square kilometres, during the tests it sat within the remote Woomera Prohibited Area until the land was returned to free access in 2014. One still largely untold story is the harm these reckless tests also caused to lands traditional to the Maralinga Tjarutja people, whose name for the site in their Pitjantjatjara language, *Mamu Pulka*, translates as 'Big Evil'. Incredibly, for reasons best known to themselves, the British actually set fire to and blew up lumps of highly toxic plutonium, spewing dangerous levels of radioactive waste across the outback landscape. One site known as 'Kuli' is still off-limits today because it is far too dangerous to even try to clean it up. Nearly a third of the servicemen exposed died of cancer, although proving that the cancers they suffered decades on were caused by their exposure was nearly impossible for the victims.

One of the scientists whom now-declassified files show took part in the British tests from 1956 to 1963 was a health physics officer named Oliver Harry Turner, the same Professor Harry Turner hired in 1954 to do the classified review of UAP sightings for Australia's Defence Department. Previously secret files in Australia's National Archives reveal Turner investigated[11] strange sightings of anomalous objects in the skies over Maralinga throughout the British atmospheric nuclear bomb testing. In July 1960, at 7.15 pm, above a site known as Wewak where a number of static instrumentation balloons hovered, a police constable saw a light in the sky and initially thought one of the balloons had caught fire. He and four other military and government witnesses saw the hovering light, which looked like a balloon. 'As it appeared to come nearer, or grow larger, it turned to a red colour,' the report details. However, all balloons being used at the remote site were accounted for. Turner thoroughly investigated the sighting. 'He is of the opinion that the light was not the result of a natural phenomenon but caused by an unidentified flying object, either a cone from a satellite or a "flying saucer",' the Range's security officer wrote in his report. He ignored Harry Turner's conclusion and went instead with the safer option, speculating that it was either a meteor or static electricity.

* * *

Four years earlier, in 1956, the US National Investigations Committee on Aerial Phenomena (NICAP) had begun soliciting UAP witness reports, in a direct challenge to the hold the air force's Project Blue Book had over UAP investigations. NICAP was founded by inventor Thomas Townsend Brown that year and it soon attracted the support of many high-powered former military and intelligence officials. This reflected considerable frustration from some in the top brass with the air force's dismissiveness of the UAP issue. Former CIA Director Vice Admiral Roscoe Hillenkoetter, barely a year out of the job, was one of the three former navy admirals on the NICAP board; another was Rear Admiral Delmer Fahrney, the former head of the navy's guided missile program, who would become NICAP's chairman. The very notion of a highly respected former top intelligence community insider such as Hillenkoetter taking an activist role at the helm of a UAP disclosure organisation would be laughable today, but he clearly believed something was being hidden by his government. 'It is time for the truth to be brought out in open congressional hearings,' he said in 1960. He would tell Congress, 'Behind the scenes, high-ranking air force officers are soberly concerned about UFOs. But through official secrecy and ridicule, many citizens are led to believe the unknown flying objects are nonsense.'[12]

In January 1957, Admiral Fahrney announced NICAP's belief that 'No agency in this country or Russia is able to duplicate at this time the speeds and accelerations which radars and observers indicate these flying objects are able to achieve.' He then earnestly ventured an extra-terrestrial explanation, saying, 'There are signs that an intelligence directs these objects because of the way they fly. The way they change position in formations would indicate that their motion is directed.' Admiral Fahrney also noted that many witnesses had stopped reporting their sightings to the air force because 'of the seeming frustration – that is, all information going in, and none coming out'.[13] The admiral's statement was a calculated slap in the face for the credibility of the air force's investigations into the phenomenon. The Pentagon immediately went on a public offensive to discredit NICAP.[14]

But Admiral Fahrney was getting secret sightings reports directly from the navy, including an account of an incident that happened in 1953, where an enormous rocket-shaped craft swooped down over a squadron of carrier-based fighter aircraft on a training exercise. The huge craft levelled off a thousand feet above the squadron and, as the pilots climbed towards it, the 'giant spaceship' shot away at speed.[15] This incident was verified to NICAP both by pilots and navy officers. When the air force was alerted, air force officers soon arrived on the carrier and an air force colonel grilled the navy men. Without consulting the carrier's captain, he warned them to 'Forget what you saw today. You're not to discuss it with anyone.'

While the US Air Force aggressively debunked most UAP sightings in public, privately it was taking the phenomenon very seriously. Former CIA Director Roscoe Hillenkoetter was pushing for Congressional hearings. To the air force's embarrassment, he released[16] a memo sent out in December 1959 by the Inspector General of the US Air Force. It told all bases confidentially that 'Unidentified flying objects – sometimes treated lightly by the press and referred to as "flying saucers" – must be rapidly and accurately identified as serious USAF business.'[17] It required investigators to have Geiger counters (to monitor radiation) and containers 'in which to store samples'. The air force edict begged the question, what were these mysterious flying objects, if physical 'samples' from them needed to be tested for radiation?

The frustration of Admiral Hillenkoetter and other senior military with his government's lack of transparency on UAPs was coming to a head. What he and his colleagues knew (and this is now revealed by declassified military archives) was that numerous sightings were being recorded over some of the country's most sensitive military bases, yet the US government seemed determined to ignore that potential threat.

Chapter 5

Hard Evidence

While publicly dismissing UAPs as no threat to national security and hastily rejecting as many sightings as possible with prosaic explanations, in private, the US government was taking an extraordinary interest in the phenomenon and deploying substantial resources to investigate it. This went way beyond Project Blue Book, which appears to have been largely for public show. As journalist Leslie Kean has revealed,[1] in 1953, the US Air Command had created the 4602d Air Intelligence Service Squadron (AISS) that confidentially vetted all UAP reports before they were sent to Blue Book, culling sightings that raised national security concerns. It was even tasked to collect unidentified flying objects from the field.

The 4602d AISS ran a secret project in which the US Air Force deployed covert quick reaction intelligence teams around the world to recover unidentified objects and debris from space. In 1961, an AISS operation named Project Moon Dust was tasked in a letter known as the 'Betz Memo' to 'locate, recover and deliver descended foreign space vehicles'.[2] Another project, Operation Blue Fly, was proposed to deliver the recovered objects to the Foreign Technology Division at Wright Patterson Air Force Base in Ohio. In his 1990 book, *Out There*, the *New York Times* journalist Howard Blum asserted that the 'foreign space vehicles' the US Air Force sought included craft of extra-terrestrial origin and that Moon Dust was a kind of 'UFO SWAT team'.[3] The book described the secret team's role as 'field exploitation of unidentified flying objects, or known Soviet/Bloc aerospace vehicles, weapons systems, and/or residual components of such equipment'.

Surprisingly, declassified Project Blue Book and US Defence Intelligence Agency files do show the US was involved in a covert worldwide 'UFO' investigation and recovery program. Operation Moon Dust definitely involved retrieval of 'foreign technology' from other countries, but it also specifically sought 'Unidentified Flying Objects' and 'flying saucers'.

A declassified US Air Force sighting report from 1961 of an 'unidentified object' in Pakistan acknowledged the message as a 'Project Moon Dust' message.[4] There is also a reference to 'Moon Dust' in a report about an object found near Santa Cruz in Bolivia in 1979.[5] Perhaps the most intriguing smoking gun, however, is a heavily redacted declassified Central Intelligence Agency document[6] from March 1968 that describes how a 'huge metallic disc-shaped object with a six-foot base and four feet in height was found in a crater' eight kilometres north-east of Pokhara in Nepal. Portions of a similar object were found near other villages. There is nothing in the censored files to show if any object was ever recovered or what it was. Author and researcher Kevin Randle said US Embassy staff were allowed to view three photographs of the recovered objects, but not a fourth. Intriguingly, the subject of the message was again 'Moon Dust'.[7] The codename probably became too overt for the air force because in 1987 the US Air Force said Project Moon Dust 'no longer officially exists'. It announced the name was 'replaced by another name that was still classified'.[8] That of course suggests Operation Moon Dust's successor continues –

that somewhere out there, someone is still quietly collecting UAP debris. Several sources have claimed to me and other researchers that a secret collection unit using ex-military and intelligence experts still exists but that it is run through the cover of a group of US aerospace corporations.

* * *

In 1964, Dr Robert Jacobs was a 1st Lieutenant in the US Air Force in charge of a photographic squadron based at Vandenberg Air Force Base in California. In September that year, on a hilltop near a town called Big Sur about 160 kilometres from Vandenberg, Jacobs was filming a dummy nuclear warhead that had been launched from the base aboard an Atlas intercontinental ballistic missile. The images were shot through a huge motorised telescope and captured on a 35-millimetre camera but, on the day, because the telescopic image was being filmed under a shroud, Bob Jacobs had absolutely no idea he had captured extraordinary film of an object flying around the warhead, firing beams of light.

A day or so after the filming, Jacobs was summoned by his commanding officer Major Florenze Mansmann to a screening of the footage in his office. Fifty-seven years on, Bob Jacobs obviously still has a vivid recollection of what he saw that day, as we talk on multiple Skype video calls. 'When I walked in, the major told me, "Watch this, lieutenant." He had the projector with a 16mm copy of my film set up. What it showed was amazing. Shortly after the warhead separated from the upper stage of the ICBM, the UFO suddenly appeared, chasing the warhead as it travelled downrange at thousands of miles an hour. At huge speed, it circled the warhead and, at four different points, it shot a beam of light. Then I clearly saw the warhead tumble, falling away. The UFO had knocked it out. I was just astonished.'[9]

In front of two taciturn strangers who were also present, Major Mansmann sternly challenged Jacobs, asking him if he and his men were playing around during the filming. 'He then asked me to explain what we had just witnessed. I told him that it looked to me like we got a UFO on film. The major warned me straight away never to repeat those words. He told me the incident never happened and that was the end of the matter,' he recalled.

Years later, in 1982, Jacobs wrote about his encounter for a popular magazine; a researcher following up the story tracked down Major Mansmann. Jacobs had not seen the major since he left the air force nearly 20 years earlier but Mansmann confirmed the incident happened exactly as he told it. Jacobs recalled, 'He even said that on the higher resolution imagery, they could see it was a domed disc and the strangers who were there that day were CIA agents. He also confirmed the whole event was classified top-secret.' Mansmann openly asserted his belief that the object was an extra-terrestrial craft that had released four beams of 'directed energy' of some sort to disable the dummy warhead.

Mansmann, who by 1982 held a doctorate in biomedical engineering and worked at Stanford University, backed Jacobs' account because he read how sceptics James Oberg and journalist Philip Klass were attacking Bob Jacobs with claims that his sighting was fanciful and uncorroborated. Jacobs tells me, 'To this day, I am absolutely convinced, like he was, that what we saw was some kind of craft from outer space because it was technology far beyond anything we have on this planet. I also think the UFO shot down the dummy nuclear warhead to send a message, that it disapproved of us using this technology for warfare.'

Jacobs sent me the signed letters from Mansmann confirming his account. What struck me most about Jacobs' direct witness account, corroborated and added to by his former commanding officer, was how viciously the debunkers attacked him to shut down his story. Philip Klass even tried to get him sacked from his university job because Jacobs was supposedly behaving in a manner inappropriate for an academician by even talking about 'flying saucers'. Perhaps Klass was simply an over-zealous critic, but Jacobs' corroborated account suggests strongly that there was a coordinated effort inside the US government to suppress public awareness of UAP interactions with the military.

Another extremely important sighting happened on the outskirts of Socorro, New Mexico, on 24 April 1964. Police officer Lonnie Zamora witnessed a flaming object in the sky and went to investigate. He came across a shiny whitish aluminium-coloured craft landed in a dry creek bed with two small 'people' standing in white coveralls alongside. As he began approaching, the oval-shaped object rose off the ground; he noticed it had red lettering on its side. Indentations and charred bushes were later found on the ground where the craft had landed, and independent witnesses confirmed seeing an egg-shaped craft or bluish flame about the same time as Zamora. Even the US Air Force's Project Blue Book investigators made no conclusion about the object's origins, declaring the case 'still open'. Declassified CIA files reveal the Project Blue Book officer in charge of the Zamora investigation, Hector Quintanilla, was convinced Zamora was telling the truth, describing the case as 'the best-documented case on record'.[10]

Something also crashed near the town of Kecksburg, Pennsylvania, in December 1965, which drew a huge military response. Officially, Project Blue Book wrote it off as a meteorite, but witnesses described an acorn-shaped object, 9 to 12 feet in diameter (2.74 to 3.66 metres). Two witnesses, Jim Romansky and Bill Bulebush, said the object had a gold band around the bottom with writing on it that looked like Egyptian hieroglyphics.[11] It has been ventured that the object was a Russian or US satellite but exactly what it was that crashed at Kecksburg is an open question.

Multiple witnesses say the retrieval of the object was a major military operation conducted under extremely tight secrecy. Could it have been an operation by the mysterious 4602d Air Intelligence Service Squadron?

The Americans were also reportedly monitoring objects seen over Australia. In 1967, a US Air Force sergeant was shown a film by the Central Intelligence Agency that allegedly featured clear images of a 'UFO' close up in flight. The vision was reportedly shot from a Royal Australian Air Force aircraft during a photo-mapping flight over Central Australia in about 1965. (My efforts to pry any extant film from Defence archives proved fruitless.) United States researcher Budd Hopkins related the story he was told by the air force sergeant. He claimed that the CIA's film showed a 'huge, hovering, windowed craft' filling the entire movie screen, with three smaller UAPs attached to it as a 'kind of tail'. When a door on the largest object opened, the three smaller craft flew inside. Then the large object 'canted at an angle, then disappeared in seconds'.[12]

Another Australian sighting that may have been monitored by the USA occurred in Westall in Melbourne on 6 April 1966. Twelve-year-old schoolgirl Joy Clarke was sitting in science class just before the 10.30 am recess at Westall High School in Melbourne, Australia, when a girl pushed the classroom door open. 'Mr Greenwood, Mr Greenwood, there's things in the sky. There's flying saucers in the sky,' Joy recalled the girl saying.[13] What the school children and teachers saw became known as the Westall school incident, and it remains Australia's, and one of the world's, most witnessed unexplained UAP sighting.

After rushing out onto the school's sports field, more than 100 children and adult teachers saw several hovering UAPs. 'I saw objects that looked like flying saucers, like two metallic silvery saucers with their rims against each other, and I can remember just standing there in shock,' Joy said. 'I was oblivious to whatever was going on around me because I was just looking to try and absorb what I was looking at. I was excited. I was trying to absorb the shape and the size.' Three classic 'silvery disc-shaped flying saucer craft' were hovering right above the children and teachers. The craft slowly moved to a flat hover over electrical power lines and pylons running along the edge of the school grounds.

Thirteen-year-old Colin Kelly saw the objects arrive. 'I just heard a slight whoosh, whirring sound just momentarily. I looked over my shoulder and saw the craft. I saw three of them. I definitely saw three,' Colin told me. 'One larger and two slightly smaller. They were about 18 feet across, a silvery colour. If you placed two saucers inverted on top of each other with a slight dome on top of it.' Teacher Andrew Greenwood later confirmed he too saw a silvery-green disc.

At least one of the craft moved in a slow hover to a bushland area known as The Grange, across the road to the south-east. Schoolgirl Terry Peck was one of the first children to jump across the school fence in pursuit. She told me she actually saw the craft close up in The Grange bushland, describing it as a classic silvery saucer-shaped object – she was near enough to feel its heat through her hand.[14] 'Two girls were there before me. One was terribly upset, and they were pale, really white, ghostly white,' Terry recalls. I interviewed Terry close to the 55th anniversary of the event and it was striking just how sharp her recollection was of that day's strange events. She does not suffer fools; when I asked her if the object could possibly have been the high-altitude military balloon suggested by many sceptics, she scoffed. 'I know this sounds corny, but I know what I saw,' she said. 'It was not a balloon. It was a machine, a craft.' She remembers watching as the craft lifted slowly off the ground, tilted on its side, and then shot off at an incredible speed. She is adamant there was a cover-up that day, and recalls being warned at the later school assembly not to talk about what she saw.

Light planes also appeared to be chasing the remaining objects, which were still hovering in the sky just above the power lines, but anytime the aircraft came anywhere near, the saucers jumped almost instantaneously. 'The way they moved was incredible. It was so fluid and so fast. If they wanted to go over there, they were over there. Like seconds. The movement was just incredible,' Joy Clarke said. 'It was like the saucers were playing cat and mouse with them. When the plane came close it would zoom off and the plane would slowly follow them all the way around.' The way the objects moved suggested they were under intelligent control. After a few minutes on the ground behind the trees in The Grange, one object rose again and then all three turned on their axis at 45 degrees. In an instant they whizzed out of sight, disappearing into the horizon, silently leaving the planes in their wake.

'So much happened that day,' Colin Kelly said, 'I could not forget it. I feel privileged to have seen something not a lot of people get to witness.' He too saw all three craft turn on a 45-degree angle and zoom off at great speed.

Later, Joy Clarke and a friend crept through the bush to The Grange location where the craft had apparently landed. The area was swarming with activity, police and military. 'We could see there were military people. Green army uniforms and blue, which I assume was air force. They were digging and doing stuff. We snuck in and we clearly saw this great big circle that had been flattened in the grass,' she says.

As much as I am loath to believe in cover-up conspiracies, the evidence suggests an official cover-up did take place at Westall. Soon after the incident, military jeeps and trucks full of soldiers arrived at the school. All the students were called to an assembly and warned not to talk about what they saw. Teacher Andrew Greenwood says two government agents even knocked on his door that night and warned him not to speak about what he saw.[15] Joy Clarke remembered some of the military wore the then plain green uniform of the Australian Army, but she believed some were American. There were also unknown men in black suits, who sat quietly at the end of the assembly hall as students were warned not to speak.

When, at my request, a flier was sent out to Westall witnesses, inviting them to attend the 55th anniversary of the 1966 event in April 2021 and be interviewed by this author, within days I took a call from a long-time friend who had served in a very senior position in government for many years. He was a well-respected former Federal public servant. He had heard about my interest in the mystery and revealed his own very private Westall connection – that his father was a Defence scientist who had worked for the then Federal Department of Supply in Melbourne. He told me that in the wake of the Westall incident his father had investigated the event and written a secret report about it for the Department, and that in the days after the mass sighting 'a black Humber car arrived at our family home from the Department early every morning to take him back out each day to the school'. He heard whispered discussions in the family home and knew it related to Westall but he knew nothing of what his father's report revealed, only that what his dad uncovered had 'shocked and rattled him'. Not one document on the Westall incident has ever surfaced from any government archives, despite strenuous efforts by several researchers. Knowing the credibility and integrity of my source, I am in absolutely no doubt a report was written.

All the Westall witnesses I spoke to were contemptuous of attempts to explain away the craft as crashed high-altitude balloons. 'There is just no way these were balloons,' Colin Kelly rejoindered. 'They were moving under intelligent control. Someone was driving them to dodge the planes.'

It is difficult to accept that on that crystal-clear morning half a century ago so many witnesses at Westall school somehow confused a balloon or some other mundane object for a metallic silver saucer-shaped craft. The most curious aspect of the case was that no official government explanation has ever been ventured for what the huge number of witnesses saw that day.

Researcher Shane Ryan told me he has interviewed an extraordinary tally of 122 witnesses who clearly saw a 'flying saucer' at Westall. Ryan is a dogged investigator who works in his day job at Australia's Parliament House in Canberra. He has dedicated years of his life to probing the Westall mystery. He tells me proudly that he interviewed 171 witnesses who say they saw the circle of crushed grass in The Grange bushland where an intense military operation was later watched by locals. Researcher Bill Chalker also interviewed former student Victor Zakry, who claimed to have seen the object at ground level, close enough to touch it. Zakry's drawings of what he saw portray a metallic saucer-shaped craft.[16]

'Westall stands out as an extraordinary case,' Shane Ryan said. 'It was broad daylight in a suburb of a major city and seen by such a huge number of people. I simply don't know what it was, but it should be being investigated and that's what I'm doing, collecting the data.'[17] Ryan confirmed government efforts to cover up the incident; he interviewed multiple witnesses who were warned not to speak about it, including residents who saw a layer of dirt being dug up at the landing site and taken away in trucks. 'Whatever happened, something got broken about how it was supposed to be handled. Things were swung into action to cover over that,' he said.

One sighting in Queensland that did draw the close attention of the Royal Australian Air Force occurred in January 1966. The Tully sighting by farmer George Pedley baffled investigators and remains unexplained. Pedley was driving his tractor on a cane farm when he heard a hissing noise and noticed a rising light grey saucer-shaped object eight metres long and nearly three metres wide. It rose to about 20 metres and then shot off at 45 degrees. What turned the case into a sensation were the photographs taken around where the object had landed. The so-called 'Tully Nests' showed huge round circles of flattened grass; the reeds in the swamp had actually been uprooted and swirled into a floating mat on the surface of the water. The *Tully Times* banner headlined George Pedley's story, 'I've Seen A Flying Saucer – As Told by George Pedley'.[18] The subsequent air force investigation weakly speculated the 'Nests' were caused by whirling masses of tropical air known as 'Willy Willies'. They did not even bother to engage with George's detailed account of a craft.

It is impossible to assess for sure whether the official reluctance to acknowledge anything real or mysterious about UAPs was (or is still) an active attempt at cover-up. Many ufologists are convinced there is an international conspiracy by multiple governments to suppress public knowledge of an ET presence. I suspect one explanation for the official attempt to brush off most sightings was that Australia's military simply did not like admitting that it had no idea what it was that was zooming unhindered in and out of our airspace, including over nuclear bomb sites such as Maralinga.

These sightings continue to this day. One senior Australian military intelligence insider told me UAPs are still frequently observed over sensitive military facilities, including unexplained sightings recorded over the super-secret Pine Gap US/Australian base 18 kilometres south-west of Alice Springs. But once the objects are confirmed as not being craft operated by the Russian or Chinese military or any potential foe, the prevailing view was that no one gave much more thought to what they were. I considered this to be an extraordinary admission, because surely any incursion into a prohibited Defence installation is by definition a threat? This odd lack of official curiosity into the reality of (some) UAPs invites the suspicion that someone or some agency is trying to suppress a bigger story. What we can be sure of is that among those most

active in seeking to shut down public interest in the phenomenon
are several three-letter agencies within the US government.

In August 1966, an enlightening memorandum supporting
this notion of an official cover-up was written by a university
staffer and former intelligence officer to two senior officials at the
University of Colorado. Dr Robert Low had done work for the CIA
in Albania two decades earlier, and his memo perhaps betrayed
his intelligence connections. It set out a proposed strategy for the
university's role in what became known as the Condon Report,[19]
a formal study of 'UFOs'. Dr Low foolishly divulged in writing
that 'the trick would be' to give the public the impression the
investigation was a 'totally objective study',[20] a clear admission that
the study would be anything but. The irony was that Project Blue
Book's air force investigations into UAPs were by now publicly
perceived as so seriously compromised by a debunking agenda that
Dr Edward Condon and his team of scientists had been recruited
by the air force to do an objective and independent investigation. It
came as no surprise to anyone that two years later, in 1968, the final
Condon Report declared that 'nothing has come from the study
of UFOs in the past twenty-one years that has added to scientific
knowledge'. Condon rejected the extra-terrestrial hypothesis for
UAPs and concluded that further study of them could not be
justified. One sighting the report did conspicuously acknowledge
as very likely a 'genuine UFO' was the previously mentioned 1956
RAF Lakenheath-Bentwaters radar-visual incident in the United
Kingdom.[21]

The Condon Report gave the US Air Force the excuse it was
looking for to bail out of Project Blue Book. In November 1968,
it sought and received a rubber-stamp from the National Academy
of Sciences, who reviewed and endorsed the report's conclusions.
A little over a year later, it was all over; in December 1969, the
Air Force Secretary announced Project Blue Book had been

terminated. Blue Book consultant Dr J. Allen Hynek lamented, 'this was indeed the coup de grace to the UFO era. Science had spoken. UFOs didn't exist, and the thousands of people who had reported strange sightings … could all be discounted as deluded, hoaxers, or mentally unbalanced'.[22]

It is difficult to escape the impression that Project Blue Book and the Condon Report's true purpose was an attempt to shut down public interest in and the scrutiny of UAP sightings. The public was told in the air force's 1985 summary of Blue Book's conclusions that 'nothing has happened to indicate that the air force ought to resume investigating UFOs'.[23] But this was a blatant deceit. We know now that reports where UAPs did indeed affect national security were routinely withheld from Project Blue Book's scrutiny.[24] Moreover, secret official investigations into UAPs have never actually stopped.

Chapter 6

Cracking the Cover-up

At the height of the 1970s Cold War confrontation with the Soviets, sightings of strange anomalous objects continued to be secretly recorded in official files, especially at sensitive US sites around the world, including at Exmouth in Australia. But the evident cover-up continued. By 1971, Australian Defence Department scientist Harry Turner, whose curiosity had been piqued by the mysterious UAPs seen at Maralinga in the South Australian desert 11 years earlier, was now firmly convinced the phenomenon was real and required urgent investigation. He was now the head of the nuclear science section of the then Australian Joint Intelligence Bureau's Directorate of Scientific and Technical Intelligence (DSTI). Turner had been rebuffed in 1954 when he made his controversial findings about UAPs being extra-terrestrial in his original report to the Royal Australian Air Force's intelligence branch.

As numerous controversial Australian UFO sightings were being played down in the media and by the air force, Turner was privately pushing at the very highest levels of Australia's Defence Department for a scientific investigation by the military into the UAP phenomenon. His now declassified 1971 paper, *Scientific and*

Intelligence Aspects of the UFO Problem,[1] asserted not only that these unidentified objects were real, but that there was also an ongoing deliberate official US policy to ridicule sighting events in order to stifle public awareness of the phenomenon.

'By erecting a façade of ridicule, the US hoped to allay public alarm, reduce the possibility of the Soviets taking advantage of UFO mass sightings for either psychological or actual warfare purposes, and act as a cover for the real US programme of developing vehicles that emulate UFO performance,' Turner declared. He asserted that in 1953 the US Air Force Office of Special Investigations persuaded the US Air Force to use the Project Blue Book investigation into UAPs as a 'means of publicly "debunking" UFOs' while at the same time the US was secretly launching a crash program into anti-gravity power.

Turner's paper eviscerated the 1968 Condon Committee Report, the US Air Force–funded study of UFOs under the direction of physicist Edward Condon. He said, 'The conclusions of the Condon report conflict with its own contents and has been discredited by many reputable scientists … It would appear wrong for Australia to remain ignorant of the true situation.' Turner also dismissed the official Project Blue Book UFO investigation shut down by the air force two years earlier in 1969. 'Many intelligence officers associated with the UFO problem,' he said, including former CIA boss Admiral Hillenkoetter, had 'stated that the US government knew UFOs were extra-terrestrial but was withholding this fact from the public'. Turner also met the Project Blue Book expert Dr J. Allen Hynek when Hynek visited Australia. 'It is quite clear that Dr Hynek along with many other reputable scientists do not accept the USAF explanation of misidentification, hysteria or hoax,' Turner told his superiors.

Harry Turner obtained access to the Australian Air Force's UAP sightings reports. He even proposed an Australian 'rapid intervention team' to investigate 'UFO' events, for which an aircraft was to be on standby. Researcher Bill Chalker, who interviewed Turner in retirement, says Turner had the approval of Australia's Chief Defence Scientist for this idea, so this was no idle flight of fancy on Turner's part. His concern was being taken very seriously, possibly because the sightings of strange unidentified objects at the Woomera test site were still happening. But there was bad blood with DAFI – air force intelligence – because Turner had criticised DAFI's past handling of sightings reports. Eventually, the Australian Air Force withdrew his access to their sightings files. Not long after that, Turner's plan for a rapid intervention team was also spiked. Bill Chalker told me, 'Harry was actually arguing for the air force to be given more resources and more help to investigate UFOs. That way their reports would be a lot more scientific. They took that as a criticism. It was sheer bloody mindedness by DAFI to shut him out.'[2]

Two of those official Australian Air Force sightings reports detail an incident at the United States Naval Communication Station near Exmouth on Western Australia's North West Cape, the same base where local Annette Farinaccio had her strange encounter with a triangular object in the early 1990s.

It was the height of the Arab–Israeli War, also known as the Yom Kippur War, which started on 6 October 1973 when a coalition of Arab states, led by Syria and Egypt, attacked Israel. In the days that followed, the Israelis slowly pushed back in a counter-offensive deep into Syria; Israeli artillery was even shelling the outskirts of the Syrian capital Damascus. By 24 October, Israel was routing Egypt's third army and encircling the Egyptian city of Suez. On the evening of 24 October, the Soviet leader Leonid Brezhnev told the then US Secretary of State Dr Henry Kissinger that he was considering taking unilateral military action to support Syria and Egypt. History records that a panicked White House feared the Soviets were considering deploying Soviet troops on the Syrian Golan Heights border with Israel.[3]

At 11.30 pm that same evening, Kissinger made a momentous decision to raise America's military readiness level to DEFCON-3, defence condition three. This is the highest peacetime alert status, just two steps off DEFCON-1, which is nuclear war. It meant aircraft carriers were deployed for operations in the Middle East, and US amphibious landing forces, European forces and the entire 82nd Airborne combat Division were put on alert. Near Australia, 75 B52s were recalled from Guam. The world was literally a hairsbreadth from all-out nuclear war. Had the Soviet leader gone ahead with his threat, a nuclear confrontation between the superpowers was inevitable. But for a rare dose of Cold War common sense, a remote chunk of Western Australia near the town of Exmouth would have been obliterated in a Soviet thermonuclear strike.

Today, most people who venture to Exmouth are tourists hoping to swim with whale sharks at the stunningly beautiful Ningaloo Reef world heritage site or to try their hand at game-fishing. To access the marine park's crystal-clear coral reefs, you have to drive up the peninsula north of Exmouth for five kilometres before making a sharp dogleg across to the west coast facing the Indian Ocean. As visitors turn west to climb across the dividing Cape Range mountains, few even glance at the sprawling Harold E. Holt Naval Communication Station (as it is now known), which sits on the coastal plain further north of the highway.

Built at the height of the Cold War, the imposing station transmits to United States Navy and Royal Australian Navy vessels in the Pacific and Indian oceans. The highest point of its 12 powerful antenna tower arrays is a soaring 388 metres; it is the most powerful transmission station in the Southern Hemisphere, capable of broadcasting far across and under the vast Indian Ocean beside it and beyond.

Only a handful of Cape locals know the real story about why the United States' Naval Communication Station North West Cape base (as it was then known) was built in the mid-1960s. What many locals even today do not realise is that the original primary role of the station was to send launch code orders out to American Polaris nuclear submarines in the event the United States president ordered a nuclear strike. As many Australian political leaders only belatedly realised years after it began operating, the communications station was a huge strategic threat to America's enemies; it was an absolute certainty the base and nearby Exmouth would be destroyed if war began.

When Kissinger gave that late-evening escalation order in Washington DC on the other side of the planet, it was early afternoon in Exmouth, 12 hours ahead on 25 October. Inside the US station early that evening at 7.20 pm, about seven hours after Kissinger's DEFCON escalation order was issued, Bill Lynn, an Australian fire captain working for the US Navy, was one of two witnesses who noticed an unusual object hovering in the sky near the base. In his sighting report, he said, 'My attention was drawn to a large black object which at first I took to be a small cloud formation.'

Lynn drove closer in his pick-up truck, then stopped and stepped out to watch what he could now clearly see to be a large hovering black sphere sitting in the cloudless green-blue sky. The sun had set 50 minutes earlier that night at 6.31 pm, but it was still twilight at 7.20 when he saw the black sphere. 'The object was completely stationary except for a halo around the centre which appeared to be either revolving or pulsating,' he wrote. 'After watching it for approx. 4 minutes, it suddenly took off at tremendous speed and disappeared in a northerly direction in a few seconds.' He estimated the object was approximately 30 feet (9 metres) in diameter hovering at 1000 feet over the hills due west of the base. 'It was black, maybe due to looking in the direction of the setting sun. No lights appeared on it at any time.'

The Royal Australian Air Force sightings reports[4] show both Lynn and a US officer named Lieutenant Commander Moyer or Meyer (the handwriting is unclear) independently reported seeing a revolving or pulsating object hovering in the sky that evening. The lieutenant commander, whose rank meant he was probably the deputy commander of the entire base, was driving south from the station towards Exmouth, which meant he was probably closer to the object than Lynn. In an 'Unusual Aerial Sighting' report he filed with the Royal Australian Air Force, he wrote that his attention was drawn to 'a large black object in the clear sky'. He estimated its angular size as 'approx. same as Moon when high in the sky'. It was at 2000 feet but there was absolutely no sound. It was 'hovering at first, then accelerating beyond belief,' the lieutenant commander described, and he watched as it disappeared to the north and 'accelerated at unbelievable speed and just disappeared'. Asked if he could think of any conventional explanation for what he saw, he wrote, 'Not a thing.' Then he commented, 'Have never experienced anything like it.'

The former Holt Station fire chief Bill Lynn died in 1995 aged 82 and efforts to find the other witness, Lieutenant Commander Moyer/Meyer, have failed. In 2014, Bill Lynn's son, also named Bill, wrote to UAP researcher Keith Basterfield telling him that, 'Because this happened on the US Naval Base my dad was adamant that it was swept under the carpet and was tried to be hidden from too much public disclosure. I remember him always saying that they immediately tried to dismiss his sighting, including the flock of birds theory – which he was adamant it was not. He always stated to me the vision was so clear. The experience convinced him to believe in UFOs and he was so grateful that someone else could, at least to some degree, verify his story.'[5] Bill Lynn's daughter

Kate remembers her father describing how he used the bonnet of his pick-up truck to sketch the object and to make the notes about what he saw,[6] a sketch that appears in his Royal Australian Air Force sighting report.

Curiously, there are now no records of this 1973 North West Cape sighting anywhere in declassified Royal Australian Air Force (RAAF) sighting records from 1973 held by the Australian National Archives, but the provenance of the original official sightings reports is not in question. Paperwork shows they were lawfully provided to researchers by the RAAF public relations section as part of a release of sightings reports in 1974–75, years before freedom of information laws were enacted in Australia. It has never been explained why the original files recording the 1973 sighting were subsequently *lost* from Australian Defence Department files and it is to the great credit of the Defence Public Affairs staff of that era that they recognised the importance of seeing the 25 October 1973 sighting released to the public. There is also no mention of the WA sighting in declassified US government archives but Bill Chalker has speculated it may be a sighting referred to in a heavily redacted US National Security Agency (NSA) document, previously highly protected with one of the highest top-secret-umbra security classifications, which was released in court action taken in 1980 by the US group Citizens Against Unidentified Flying Objects Secrecy.[7] An NSA official was compelled under deposition to admit that 239 UFO-related documents were held in the agency's files, including one describing 'a purported UFO sighting' in 1973; however, any mention of where this 'UFO sighting' occurred was heavily redacted.

As with Annie Farinaccio's experience in 1991, the clear suspicion is that any UAP incident over a sensitive US facility, especially one connected to nuclear weapons like the Harold Holt base, is swept under the carpet and ignored.

As in the United States, there is a clear link between UAP sightings and sensitive military sites in Australia, especially those with links to the US's nuclear missile deterrence strategy. I was briefed by military insiders on other more recent sightings of anomalous hovering objects over Australian military sites, notably the Joint (US/Australian) Defence Facility Pine Gap. Several witnesses, all serving or former military, declined to be identified but privately confirmed sightings of anomalous glowing orbs and dark spheres stretching over several decades. Pine Gap is one of the United States' most important bases anywhere in the world, playing a key role in ballistic missile launch detection and US warfighting.

* * *

Three years after that UAP sighting over Australia's North West Cape, in November 1976, Jimmy Carter was elected President of the United States. It was hoped by UFO disclosure groups such as MUFON (the Mutual UFO Network) that this most liberal of recent United States presidents would open decades of still top-secret Project Blue Book files, which it was widely known were still being withheld from public release. Canadian researcher Grant Cameron, who specialises in what American presidents have said or done about the UAP mystery, told me his search of President Carter's Presidential Library archives revealed Carter had 'an extremely high interest in UFOs during his administration, but it looks like he hit a brick wall because his efforts were stymied'.[8] On the campaign trail, Carter had openly discussed how he personally witnessed an unidentified glowing object hovering over Leary, Georgia, in 1969, and he promised American voters that if he became president he would release any US government UFO files.

According to celebrated civil rights attorney Daniel Sheehan, before Carter's January inauguration he sought a meeting with the then Director of the CIA, George Herbert Walker Bush, later the 41st president, but the CIA Director flatly refused to give the president-elect a briefing on UFOs telling Carter he had no 'need to know'. (Bush's term as CIA Director ended just before the inauguration in January 1977.) Bush suggested the incoming president instead seek a briefing through the Congressional Research Service. Once in office, President Carter pressed the issue, and the Congressional Research Service's specialist on space and aerospace, Marcia Smith, was tasked to investigate.

Marcia Smith began by asking Daniel Sheehan if he could seek Vatican approval for access to its allegedly extensive archives on UAPs. Sheehan was General Counsel for the US National Jesuit Headquarters in Washington DC at the time, but had already cemented an illustrious legal career as a federal civil rights attorney, acting for *The New York Times* during the furore over its Vietnam War Pentagon Papers leak in 1971 and suing the perpetrators of Watergate in 1972. He went on to lead cases on behalf of the nuclear whistleblower Karen Silkwood and the victims of the Three Mile Island disaster, and to sue the perpetrators of the Iran-Contra scandal. I talked to Sheehan many times over the course of several months and, although now an older man, his brain is still razor sharp. A well-respected jurist and civil rights campaigner, he also has a theatrical flourish for storytelling and an Irish charm that trial juries enjoy.

The Vatican declined Sheehan's request, but Marcia Smith came back a few weeks later and asked if, as a Jesuit representative, Sheehan would accompany some of the NASA astronauts on a lobbying tour of Congress to push for the reinstatement of full funding for the SETI program – the search for extra-terrestrial intelligence. In 1971, NASA had funded a very small SETI study but the successful bid for new funding from Congress was followed in August 1977 by the discovery of the 'Wow Signal', an extremely strong signal received by Ohio University's 'Big Ear' radio telescope. This signal remains the best candidate for an ET signal ever discovered, but it has never been detected again. After the success of his efforts for SETI, Sheehan was invited to make a presentation on the religious implications of extra-terrestrial contact at the NASA Jet Propulsion Laboratory in California.

Allegations that the now-concluded Project Blue Book was a whitewash intended to suppress public interest in UAPs was a big story in the US at this time and Sheehan saw an opportunity. He was aware of allegations that the most important UAP sightings reports had been withheld from Blue Book and so he told Marcia Smith he wanted to see 'the classified portions of Blue Book'. 'She said, "Oh no, they're not going to give that stuff to us. I'm sure they won't give it to us." I said, "Well, you never get if you don't ask",' Sheehan told me, in an interview from his Romero Institute office in Santa Cruz, California. According to Sheehan, a week or so later, Smith called him with the surprising news that permission had been given for him to view the files.

So, on a Saturday morning in Washington DC in the late spring of 1977, an eager Daniel Sheehan arrived at the still-uncompleted Madison wing of the Library of Congress for a cloak-and-dagger rendezvous with the classified Project Blue Book documents.

Sheehan said[9] that on that morning in 1977 he was met at the Madison building under intense security. As he was escorted to a basement office, he took his yellow legal notepad out of his briefcase and put it under his arm.

When they arrived at their destination, he was told to leave his briefcase in the hallway. 'No taking notes. You can't record anything,' one of his escorts warned him.

Inside the room, there were foldout tables set up with a microfiche viewing machine and shoebox-sized green cardboard boxes full of microfiche canisters. Sheehan randomly picked one canister and fed it into the microfiche viewer. 'I start looking at the documents, start trying to read them and I think, shit, if I try to read through these documents I am going to be here for ever and they'll throw me out of here before I get halfway into this thing,' Sheehan told me. 'And so, I started looking for pictures, photographs and I cranked through the whole first roll. It was all documents of some kind. Then I got another one. It was all documents. Then I get to a third or fourth microfiche and I get part way into it and here's this photograph. It's a photograph of a UFO. There isn't any doubt about it.'

Sheehan has told this story for decades, unchallenged by any official, asserting that what he saw in the multiple images was a full-scale classic saucer with a dome. The craft he saw had crashed in a field and was covered with snow. He describes how the saucer had ploughed a huge trench across the field and it was stuck at a 45-degree angle in what looked like a snowbank. There were soldiers dressed in US Air Force parkas and weather gear and some had still cameras and one was lugging what looked like a 1940s-era movie camera with film canisters mounted on top.

One of the photographs showed symbols, not any language he recognised, etched into the side of the craft just below the dome. At that point Sheehan remembered the yellow legal notepad he had snuck into the room, and he traced the odd symbols onto the inside cardboard backing of his notepad. And then he got the jitters.

'I closed up my yellow pad and to this day I kick myself in the ass for doing this, but I thought holy shit, I'd better get out of here. I've got this information; I've got these symbols on this thing and they told me I couldn't take any notes. I get up with the yellow pad, turned it lengthwise under my arm, and I walk out. I walk out and it's clear they were surprised. I kick myself for leaving so soon, actually, but it's what happened,' he recalled.

As Sheehan walked off, one of the guards demanded to see the yellow legal pad. 'He ruffles through all the pages, the yellow pages, and there was nothing on it. He handed it back to me. I was like whistling past the graveyard. I was "dum-de-dum-de-dum-de-dum." Okay, I keep walking down the hall to get to the elevator before these guys tackle me.' Sheehan laughed.

Aside from the fact that Sheehan's account has gone unchallenged, the especially troubling concern arising from Sheehan's account is that it suggests a US president was denied information on the UAP issue by the Central Intelligence Agency.

Daniel Sheehan is absolutely convinced that what he saw in the Project Blue Book microfiche files was photographic evidence of an extra-terrestrial spacecraft. Years later he worked with disclosure advocate Dr Steven Greer, vetting and legally representing dozens of government and military witnesses who came forward to speak at the National Press Club in 2001 attesting to a 'UFO cover-up', an event known as The Disclosure Project. Sheehan adamantly believes that, 20 years later, the public is now being prepared for a sanitised government admission to some of what it has been concealing about UAPs.

Sheehan says his experience investigating the UAP issue since that extraordinary 1977 viewing of the secret Blue Book files has convinced him that following the alleged 1940s UAP craft retrievals, 'The US security state set up a program to reach out and destroy the credibility of anybody who even totally innocently has an encounter with such a vehicle and tries to tell anybody about it, even to the extent of destroying their entire life and their livelihood. They felt completely justified. Anything's fair in love and war. They've viewed this as a direct appendage of the war-making in the Cold War against the Soviet Union and China.

They had to have this technology. They had to keep it secret. They had to have full and complete control over it even to the point of denying its existence.' Sheehan notably defended Harvard Professor John E. Mack in 1994 when it was revealed that the Dean of Harvard Medical School had appointed a committee of peers to confidentially review Mack's controversial clinical care and investigation of alleged alien abduction experiencers. Mack's tenure as a professor was under threat but, with Sheehan's support (funded by billionaire Laurance Rockefeller), after a 14-month investigation Harvard declared Mack's freedom to study 'what he wishes and to state his opinions without impediment'.[10]

I set out all Sheehan's allegations in a detailed letter to former Congressional Research Service aerospace specialist Marcia Smith, who produced the reports for the president. Now working privately for the Space and Technology Policy Group, she never responded to my phone messages, email and letter.

In his book *The Cover-up Exposed*, UAP researcher Richard Dolan says that two classified reports were eventually produced for President Carter, purportedly one on extra-terrestrial intelligence and the other on UAPs. The reports concluded that there were many cases in which official US Air Force investigations could not rule out the possibility that some of these vehicles were in fact extra-terrestrial.[11] Sheehan acknowledged he saw both reports written for the Library of Congress' Science and Technology Division before they were sent on to the president; alarmingly, he says neither mentioned the images of a recovered craft he claims he saw in the classified Project Blue Book files.

It has never been revealed just what President Carter or any other president was told, if anything, about the UAP phenomenon. An elderly former President Carter declined to comment when I sent questions through his press adviser. It was another intriguing stonewall. And yet, President Carter and Marcia Smith could have easily killed Sheehan's claims stone dead by issuing a short statement denying all; they never have.

I have to admit I find it an astonishing notion that the US president, the Commander-in-Chief of the US military, probably the most powerful person on the planet, could not simply click his fingers and demand a briefing on UAPs from anyone under his command. But that is the inescapable conclusion from what attorney Dan Sheehan told me he witnessed in 1977 – that the CIA Director flatly refused the president a briefing and, moreover, what the president was subsequently told in briefing documents did not reveal what Sheehan discovered. I think Sheehan's account is extremely important because, as an attorney with his reputation, he boldly challenged the US government to call him a liar on his claim that he was allowed to view an image of a recovered craft. No one in government has ever called Dan Sheehan's bluff.

It turns out the rejection of a presidential request happened a second time. The same thing occurred in July 1977 when the US's National Aeronautics and Space Administration (NASA) was asked by President Carter's science adviser Dr Frank Press to consider investigating public 'inquiries concerning UFOs'.[12] In December 1977, NASA's administrator Dr Robert Frosch responded with a remarkable rejection of the White House request, proposing instead that 'NASA take no steps to establish a research activity in this area [UFOs] or to convene a symposium on the subject'. There was never any explanation for why the president did not just order NASA to do the inquiry, which he surely could have done. Perhaps NASA simply felt it had more important things to do rather than become a clearinghouse for 'UFO' inquiries. Or perhaps someone did not want a liberal president getting the briefing he sought?

It is also extraordinary that both the official records and direct witness reports suggest that both the Australian and US military were surprisingly incurious about an incursion of a strange hovering object reported over one of their most sensitive military facilities by both a senior American officer and an Australian witness. These are witness accounts that cannot be idly dismissed. As with Daniel Sheehan's shocking discovery in the classified Blue Book files, the most notable thing about both incidents is that no one in either the government or military has ever sought to respond to, explain or acknowledge either event.

Chapter 7

Confusion or Cover-up?

While the public was assured, in the wake of Project Blue Book, that official investigations into UAPs had supposedly been shut down in the United States and most other western allied nations, including Australia, declassified archives tell a different story. The US in particular was taking a very close interest in sightings and throughout the 1970s there were a plethora of perplexing unexplained sightings that became the focus of intense official investigations, including one dramatic incident in New Zealand.

In his home next to Wellington Airport, where he was working on a Christmas night 42 years ago, John Cordy chuckles scornfully at the rushed official explanation offered at the time for what happened over the South Island region of Kaikoura in late December 1978. For John was one of the Wellington airport air traffic controllers on duty the night the unidentified objects appeared on radar screens at the capital city's airport just across Cook Strait. 'They weren't refractions or atmospherics. They were solid objects giving a radar return. There is no way that we were confused by what we saw,' he assures me.[1] 'They went with the line that we air traffic controllers didn't know what we were looking at. That's absolute rubbish.' Four decades on from Kaikoura, what surprised me most about Cordy's evidence was that air force investigators claimed to have interviewed all the witnesses, yet they never bothered to interview him.

John Cordy has long since retired, but nothing in the years since has dimmed his belief that the objects he tracked on his radar that night were in no way capable of prosaic explanation. He remains bitter that the Royal New Zealand Air Force's official finding asserted that he and other air traffic controllers at Wellington Airport were confused by anomalous faulty radar returns, yet he was never even questioned about what he saw. He knew enough to know that what the Argosy aircraft's occupants saw that night was neither squid boat lights nor the planet Venus. Yet neither is he saying the objects were aliens in flying saucers. 'They were simply unidentified. There's been lots of explanations but none of them fit the facts,' he tells me. 'We saw targets on radar that we could not explain. We were in communication with the pilot as he described the objects moving around him and we could see those on the radar. They parallel-tracked the plane for 40 miles. I'd love to have seen how squid boats could possibly be dropping their lines from the 14,000-feet altitude where we tracked these objects.'[2]

I followed the Kaikoura case as a young journalist for the *New Zealand Herald* newspaper in the early 1980s and bitterly angry letters often came in from readers suggesting the government was party to an international cover-up about the 'UFO' phenomenon. Reading the now-declassified archival files from the Minister of Defence at the time, I realise the department's investigators were copping the same abuse we copped at the *Herald*. 'You lying bastard, get your facts straight,' New Zealand's Defence Minister Frank O'Flynn was told in one especially rancorous sighting letter on file. 'You see no reason to seek an inquiry into the way the air traffic control handled this matter. Get some glasses if you cannot see this. I see every reason for an inquiry to be held.'[3]

How the Royal New Zealand Air Force conducted itself in the Kaikoura investigation does reek at the very least of a peremptory once-over-lightly effort. The air force's report declared Wellington's radar was faulty that night in 1978 and also claimed that it had interviewed all the witnesses, yet investigators failed to interview John Cordy or other key witnesses. 'It is my considered professional opinion that there was nothing wrong with the radar on either night these objects were seen,' Cordy declares. There is more than a whiff of a cover-up here, or perhaps the New Zealand government just wanted the case to go away.

As journalist Quentin Fogarty recalled when I spoke to him years later about the Kaikoura objects he filmed that night, 'All of us, the flight crew, and the air traffic controllers are adamant that we saw something highly unusual that night that simply can't be explained in mundane terms. I have never accepted the official explanation that was very quickly issued by the government to allay public concern.'[4] Quentin Fogarty passed away in 2020 but his long-time friend and colleague Dennis Grant told me the ridicule directed at Fogarty after the air force's finding took a toll on his career. 'I don't know if there was a cover-up,' Grant tells me. 'Kaikoura remains unexplained. One of the many failures was universal media scepticism when more rigour was justified in this case. The media should have asked more questions. Quentin never gave up. He stuck to his guns.'[5]

Dennis Grant later moved to Australia to work in journalism, and he became a well-respected political correspondent for one of the main television networks. He joined Fogarty on the Argosy plane's return trip from Christchurch to Blenheim that December 1978 night and saw the objects. 'It still remains the most intriguing and strange story I have ever worked on,' Grant tells me. 'I have no idea what we saw. We didn't see Venus, which is what the air force suggested. Venus was at an entirely wrong angle to where we were looking. And it wasn't reflected fishing boat lights, which was their other claim.' Dennis Grant was the only person on board the plane that night to keep contemporaneous notes. What struck him the most was that, frequently during the flight, the strange glowing orbs they all witnessed moving around their aircraft were simultaneously tracked on both Wellington radar and the plane's radar. 'We were listening in to the conversation with Wellington radar and when we said where we could see an object, they were tracking it across Cook Strait on their equipment,' he tells me.

Grant also says they were close enough to the orbs at times to see their light reflected on the ocean below, underlining the falsity of official findings that all on board were confused by squid boat lights somehow refracted on the clouds. He said the objects were lit internally; some were clearly circular but others were elongated. 'There must have been some sort of dimension, a solidity, to them because they were picked up by the radar sets as we were watching them,' he told me. Adding to the intrigue, he recalled that the plane was also in communication with Christchurch air traffic control in the South Island, as well as Wellington in the North Island, but he learned the audio tapes of the Christchurch radio exchanges were lost within a few days of the incident. I was not surprised to hear from Grant that he was not interviewed by the Royal New Zealand Air Force investigators.

* * *

Jimmy Carter's liberal presidential administration was followed by conservative Republican Ronald Reagan's presidency in 1981, and the official response to one dramatic UAP sighting at a US base in the United Kingdom dashed hopes of any greater transparency about the phenomenon. On a December morning in 1980, an American military patrol near the British Royal Air Force base RAF Woodbridge in Suffolk, England, saw lights descending into the adjacent Rendlesham Forest. Airman John Burroughs saw strange flashing red, green and blue lights in a clearing 'that threw off the image of like a craft' but he says he also never saw anything 'metallic or hard'. His colleague, Sergeant Jim Penniston, described seeing a small three-metre-wide craft composed of what looked like a black smoky glass-like material, with unfamiliar symbols inscribed on its upper side. Penniston made the astonishing claim much later that he touched the craft and recorded sketches of the hieroglyphic inscriptions in a notebook.[6] Penniston also raised dramatic claims that he and his colleagues suffered 'missing time' during the incident, that their memories were deliberately confused and blocked in some way. Nick Pope, who headed the British Ministry of Defence's 'UFO Desk' in the 1990s, told me the radiation levels tested the next day were many times higher than normal background, a finding challenged by sceptics.[7]

Two nights later, US Air Force Colonel Charles Halt, deputy commander of the nearby RAF Bentwaters base, Penniston and Burroughs' home base, led a patrol back into the forest following another reported landing by an unidentified craft, later writing a detailed memorandum of what he saw. The Rendlesham Forest incident remains one of the world's most disturbing and controversial military UAP sightings.

I interviewed retired Colonel Halt in 2009 for a television documentary. He told me he and his colleagues witnessed a hovering UAP in the forest at close-up range and he believed the vehicle was probably extra-terrestrial. Halt is an intelligent man with excellent recall, just the sort of stable character whom you would put in charge of a base that held top-secret nuclear weapons. As the eerie event unfolded that night, he had the presence of mind to audiotape his dramatic live commentary of what he saw, including how the object looked 'like an eye winking at you'. In a field, he and his patrol watched as the object, which had 'danced about in the forest', shed sparks that looked like molten metal; there was a heavy field of static electricity in the air. Perhaps most disturbingly, it shone beams of light into the nuclear weapons storage area on the base.

Sceptics such as Ian Ridpath have declared[8] that all the men saw was a nearby lighthouse, that it was a non-event misperception of distant lights, conflated into an alien encounter. But, decades on, Halt is adamant that the objects he saw were intelligently controlled and probably non-human in origin, and he derided the sceptics who were not there who dismissively asserted otherwise. 'I just know that there was something somewhere that was controlling what I saw,' Halt told me. 'It certainly is a bit scary.'[9] He said the US Air Force Office of Special Investigations (OSI) attacked the credibility of his sighting. 'I certainly believe there's a cover-up,' Halt said. He said the nearby lighthouse was easily visible and quite distinct, at least 30 degrees away, from what he saw. 'I know it was something under intelligent control that I can't explain. I have no idea what it was. I'd certainly like to know,' he laughed. Radar operators recently testified that an unknown object was indeed tracked in the area that night. As with the 1947 Roswell case, perhaps the most intriguing evidence from the Rendlesham incident were the accounts from multiple witnesses supporting claims there was an aggressive official cover-up – claims reportedly backed by British Prime Minister Margaret Thatcher, who was memorably quoted as privately admitting, 'You can't tell the people.'[10]

At the same time as the unfolding Rendlesham drama, on the evening of 29 December 1980, a UAP encounter took place near Dayton, Texas. While driving a quiet country road in dense forest at about 9 pm, Betty Cash, Vickie Landrum and her seven-year-old grandson Colby Landrum witnessed a huge glowing diamond-shaped object hovering above them, radiating massive amounts of heat. The two adults got out of the car to inspect the object, which was extremely bright, a dull metallic silver colour, and shaped like an upright diamond with the top and bottom flattened off. They also saw small blue lights ringing the centre of what they believed was clearly a craft of some kind. Both Cash and Landrum reported that the intense heat made the car body hot to the touch and that the dashboard vinyl was softened by the radiation through the windscreen.

One of the weirdest aspects of the Cash-Landrum encounter was their claim that they saw at least 23 helicopters, including multiple massive Boeing CH-47 Chinooks, approaching the object in tight formation. They watched as the object and pursuing helicopters flew off into the distance. In the days after this sighting, large painful blisters formed on Betty Cash's skin and she began losing hair. It was reported that all three suffered varying degrees of injury from what a radiologist asserted could only be ionising radiation. They sued the federal government for $20 million but in 1986 the case was dismissed for lack of proof that the object was associated with the federal government; the military denied the UAP was theirs. (More on this curious case later.)

Though not made public at the time, on 17 November 1986, the pilots of Japan Airlines flight 1628 reported seeing two glowing 'spaceships' and a gigantic mothercraft in flight near Anchorage, Alaska.

The Japanese crew of JAL 1628 were interviewed by the Federal Aviation Administration and were adamant they had seen a gigantic craft, clearly not of any known terrestrial technology, which tracked them on their journey, and they never wavered from that claim, despite a lot of harassment to persuade them otherwise. The craft they saw displayed speeds and manoeuvres far beyond the capabilities of any known technology. Captain Kenju Terauchi described two small ships and a gigantic hovering mothership, 'two times bigger than an aircraft carrier'. It appeared shortly before their descent to Anchorage Airport, at one point stopping in mid-air, then sitting on the jet's portside for 32 minutes.

Officially, the Federal Aviation Administration explained away reported multiple independent solid anomalous radar traces of this craft as 'clutter', declaring very quickly after that it could not confirm the event.[11] UFO debunker Philip Klass, an editor for the magazine *Aviation Week & Space Technology*, who was not actually a witness to the JAL sighting, rapidly dismissed it as nothing anomalous, saying the crew was clearly tricked by an atmospheric phenomenon.[12] (Klass went on to found the Committee for the Scientific Investigation of Claims of the Paranormal [CSICOP], now the Committee for Skeptical Inquiry [CSI]. He was the scourge of ufologists until his death in 2005, notable for leaving a 'curse' in his last will and testament that ufologists 'will never know more about UFOs than you know today'.[13])

Overwhelming evidence in support of an official cover-up in the JAL sighting was exposed when, after the sighting, a meeting was held at the Federal Aviation Administration's Washington office in which Central Intelligence Agency (CIA) agents confiscated all the radar evidence. John Callahan, who was the Division Chief of the Accidents and Investigation Branch of the Federal Aviation Administration when the sighting occurred, later said there was also an order made by the CIA to deny the 1986 meeting even happened. The CIA agent said revealing the existence of 'a UFO' would panic the American public, 'So therefore you can't talk about it.'

In defiance of the CIA's edict, Callahan kept a copy of the videotaped radar tapes, air traffic voice communications and paper reports that proved his story, and provided them to Steven Greer.[14]

The data strongly supported the Japanese pilots' claims. Callahan's assertion that there was a cover-up has never been challenged by any official.[15] 'As far as I am concerned, I saw a UFO chase a Japanese 747 across the sky for over half an hour on radar,' he said.

Later that decade, in 1987, back at Exmouth on Australia's North West Cape where Annette Farinaccio would see a strange 'triangular craft' hovering over the controversial US naval communications station a few years later, two warrant officers from the elite Special Air Service (SAS) Regiment were so alarmed by what they saw over the nearby Learmonth air force base they filed 'Unusual Aerial Sightings' reports to the Royal Australian Air Force. Their sightings reports from 9 June 1987 are recorded in declassified official Royal Australian Air Force files.[16]

The SAS soldiers, described by investigators as stable and reliable, were setting up a drop zone for a parachute drop. After sunset at about 7 pm, they noticed a five-metre-wide glowing light at about 5000 feet coming towards the airport. The object moved in a zigzag, and after arriving over the airstrip went into a hover and then remained stationary for six to seven minutes. The light was changing colour from white to amber and no shape could be discerned other than that it was a round light. As they watched the object, it rose into the clouds, heading north-east very slowly at first then shooting off at what one warrant officer said was an 'extreme speed'. The most disturbing aspect to this weird sighting was that, immediately afterwards, the soldiers lost radio contact with the Hercules transport aircraft that had taken off for the parachute drop. Even when the plane was at 10,000 feet directly over the airstrip, 'communication was non-existent'.

A statement by an investigating major, supporting the sighting reports, noted that three radios were used in unsuccessful attempts to raise the RAAF aircraft that was approaching, and this was the only time communications were lost over six days of exercises.

The mysterious object 'would not appear to have been an aircraft', the SAS major notes. 'It was also observed by the RAAF pilots of the aircraft in support, who refused to report the incident.' (Why the pilots refused is not known, but this author has spoken to many civilian and military pilots who said they would never report UAP sightings for fear of jeopardising their careers.)

As the 1980s drew to a close, the Cold War confrontation with the USSR was beginning to thaw. In 1987, Soviet leader Mikhail Gorbachev announced the economic liberalisation reform of *perestroika*, heralding a warming in relations with the West known in Russia as *Glasnost*, or openness. As the Soviet Union collapsed and old Cold War secrets began to leak out, it emerged that the communists frequently saw UAP incursions over sensitive nuclear and other military facilities identical to those observed in the West.

In 1978, concerned scientists from the Soviet Academy of Sciences had asked the Kremlin to support a UAP research program. The Soviet Ministry of Defence also began its own investigation into UAPs. This was largely prompted by an incident at the Russian city of Petrozavodsk near the Finnish border in 1977, when at least 170 military, police and scientists witnessed a large glowing object in the sky. Interestingly, whatever the object was, just as it appeared, numerous radios and telephones stopped working. The Petrozavodsk sighting coincided with the launch of a Vostok rocket from the Plesetsk Cosmodrome 350 kilometres north-east. A few hours before the launch, a 20-metre-wide spherical object was seen landing, and shortly before the Vostok rocket lift-off, two very large glowing spheres were seen. Later analysis revealed that strange objects were seen in the sky that September 1977 night across a huge swathe of Scandinavia and the Soviet Union.

Dual civilian and military Soviet UAP investigations programs went on for 13 years and collected thousands of UAP sightings reports. Las Vegas–based television investigative reporter George

Knapp interviewed Colonel Boris Sokolov, who headed the USSR's UAP investigations for over a decade. Sokolov related an incident over a Soviet nuclear missile base at Byelokoroviche in the Ukraine in October 1982, where a 274-metre-wide 'craft' hovered for several hours.[17] A base commander described how, while the object hovered, his missiles wound up for launch, something that should never have been possible without the necessary authorisation codes from Moscow. Mercifully, the launch countdown eventually stopped but Sokolov said a subsequent investigation could find no explanation for the event.

Declassified UAP investigation files from the British Ministry of Defence,[18] the so-called Project Condign study, also record Colonel Sokolov admitting that Soviet pilots were killed in engagements with UAPs. He said there were 40 reported cases where, 'Pilots encountered UFOs. Initially they were commanded to chase, then shoot. When our pilots would engage the UFO, it would speed up, our aircraft would give chase loose [sic] control and crash. That happened three times and twice the pilots died.' The British concluded the Russians took UAPs extremely seriously and saw them as a clear threat.

Meanwhile, around the world, the public was being told a completely different story; the US Air Force's stock standard response to public inquiries echoed Project Blue Book's findings – that UAP investigations should be shelved because they posed no such threat at all.

Chapter 8

The Black Triangles

In 1989, a huge number of witnesses, including police, described and even photographed huge triangular craft with distinctive lights on their underside, flying often at low altitudes across Belgium and into Germany. The story culminated with one of these objects being tracked on radar and F-16 fighter jets being scrambled to intercept on several occasions.

The so-called Belgian Wave sightings, witnessed from late November that year through to April 1990, inflamed speculation that some nation, possibly the United States, was operating stealthy black triangular craft capable of extraordinary manoeuvres and able to hover motionless and soundlessly in mid-air.

I interviewed some of the Belgian eyewitnesses for Australian television, and those eyewitnesses were adamant that what they saw was a solid, intelligently guided craft.

One of those interviewed was the chief of the Operations Division in the Belgian Air Staff at the time, Colonel Wilfried De Brouwer, later to become a Major General and Deputy Chief of Staff of the Belgian Air Force. He detailed the air force's evidence about these UAPs to a Washington DC press conference. 'Hundreds of people saw a majestic triangular craft with a span of approximately a hundred and twenty feet, powerful beaming spotlights, moving very slowly without making any significant noise, but, in several cases, accelerating to very high speeds,' he said.[1] '[In] the following days and months, many more sightings would follow ... On one occasion two F-16s registered changes in speed and altitude which were well outside the performance envelope of existing aircraft.'

Leslie Kean's book, *UFOs, Generals, Pilots & Government Officials Go on the Record,* included an account from the director of military infrastructure for the Belgian Army, Colonel André Almond, who, together with his wife, personally witnessed a giant triangular craft hovering in the sky above them.[2] Almond was adamant that what he saw was an unknown aerial vehicle, an intelligently guided craft displaying a technology far beyond the publicly known aerospace technological capacities of any nation. He was one of 143 witnesses to provide a statement, many of whom provided detailed drawings, photographs and videos of the strange craft they saw.

Although the eyewitness evidence was compelling, General de Brouwer acknowledged that while the F-16 radar showed solid objects, a prosaic explanation such as atmospheric electro-magnetic interference could not be ruled out. Critics such as Skeptoid's Brian Dunning[3] jumped on this admission as proof that the whole event was somehow a mass delusion. The possibility of US involvement was ruled out; the Belgian Defence Minister confirmed in 1992 that the Belgian Armed Forces were assured by the US that the craft was not some secret American intrusion of Belgian airspace. Officially, to this day, the Belgian Wave sightings are unexplained and, frustratingly, remain an open mystery, like so many UAP sightings.

A massive hovering silent black 'craft' was also witnessed at the remote Exmouth community (yet again) in Western Australia's

North West Cape in June 1990. An ex-Australian soldier told the US-based civilian UAP research group MUFON[4] in 2014 what he saw while on night patrol at 2.08 am during a 1990 exercise out of RAAF Base Learmonth. He claimed to have witnessed a massive hovering triangular-shaped 'craft' that was at least two football fields wide. The former soldier said, 'I've seen a lot of aircraft in my lifetime, but this scared the shit out of me and my patrol.' He described a black object with eight dull lights on two edges of the craft with a red light in the centre. 'It gave off a low humming noise, like a sub-woofer amp, and moved slowly at first almost like a Zeppelin airship, almost hanging still in the sky,' he recounted. He and his patrol were 'awestruck', and they laid low on sand dunes near the beach, watching for approximately 14 minutes as the 'craft' skittered from overhead to five kilometres out to sea and then shot up vertically 'in a blur'. He said that when he reported the incident, it was dismissed as being a United States Air Force Galaxy Transport aircraft resupplying the nearby US base. The sighting remains unexplained.

In late 1990, there were a series of sightings across Europe by civilian and military pilots, including the mysterious black triangle UAPs recorded on radar by Belgium's air force. In France in November 1990, as Timothy Good relates in *Need To Know*, a former French air force and Air France pilot, Jean Gabriel Greslé, was standing outside a gym where he worked as an instructor in Gretz-Armainvilliers, 25 kilometres east of Paris, when he and six of his pupils witnessed a craft '1000 feet long, with a thickness of about 200–250 feet'. It was trapezoidal in shape, with many lights and triangular sub-structures. 'It was absolutely incredible, like a city floating through the clouds,' Greslé said.[5]

As former British Ministry of Defence UAP investigator Nick Pope disclosed, at the same time as that French sighting, three Royal Air Force Tornado jets flying from the United Kingdom to Germany above the North Sea encountered a large object that sat on their wing tips and then overtook them at 'unimaginable speed'. An apparent craft, it was 'massive and covered with blue and white lights'.[6] The Ministry of Defence weakly speculated it might have been an unknown stealth aircraft. After he left the Ministry of Defence, Nick Pope detailed his inside knowledge of a major wave of UAP sightings across the UK in March 1993, all involving massive triangular-shaped craft. While with the Ministry of Defence, he had investigated a 31 March 1993 classified report from a patrol of Royal Air Force police officers at RAF Cosford base near Wolverhampton of a huge diamond-shaped object about 200 metres across, flying just a few hundred metres above them. Pope told me about this incident in a 2009 interview for Australian television. 'There's no such thing as a perfect witness, but when you've got air force professionals reporting something which in their view is highly unusual then that makes me pay attention.'[7] Pope says his superior in the Ministry of Defence told him, 'I don't believe in little green men but even I think this is highly unusual.'

Just one and a half hours after the RAF Cosford incident, there was another sighting at RAF Shawbury in Shropshire, reported by the base's meteorological officer. He saw a triangular-shaped craft with lights on its underside, about the size of a 747 jet, which at one point hovered in the sky and then fired beams of light at the ground. He watched the craft then accelerate away with 'phenomenal speed'. As Nick Pope told me, he and his superiors in the air force were flummoxed by these highly credible witness accounts of solid craft hovering over the two RAF bases; it was all declared a 'complete unknown'. He says, 'When I was doing that job, I had to come out with this party line that UFOs are of no defence significance but clearly I knew that was nonsense. When you have an incident like this with UFOs passing directly over military bases with impunity, it's got to be a defence issue. I've got no doubt in my mind whatsoever these witnesses saw something real and solid. You can take it to the bank.'

The man who led the inquiries that attempted to explain the mysterious mass Belgian sightings was Washington insider Christopher Mellon. A staffer to the powerful US Senate Select Committee on Intelligence in Washington DC, Mellon had previously worked as a legislative assistant for US Senator William Cohen, later to become Defence Secretary. He would go on to serve as a US Deputy Assistant Secretary of Defence for Intelligence and Security and Information Operations, the third highest intelligence position at the Pentagon. He also has a keen interest in UAPs.

Mellon recalls that he made exhaustive investigations with the Pentagon and intelligence services, finally declaring, 'There is no such [secret US triangular craft] program, we don't have anything like that. And so, whatever these people were seeing in Belgium, the Belgium military, and tracking, first of all the performance characteristics were unlike anything that we had or any technology we had. Secondly, it was definitely not, it was not something we had on the books, was not us,' Mellon says.[8]

Mellon is that rarest of birds, a Washington DC insider with the highest of national security clearances who is prepared to openly discuss his belief in UAPs. (In 1997, he followed William Cohen into the Pentagon as a member of the new Defence Secretary's transition team.) With his security and defence background, Mellon knows many of the deepest black world secrets held inside the United States' military and intelligence services. His role on the Senate Intelligence Committee staff required him to review top-secret Sensitive Compartmented Information (SCI) projects inside Special Access Programs (SAPs), most of which still remain classified.

One of the top-secret Department of Defence sites Mellon monitored for the Senate Intelligence Committee was Area 51, a highly secure US Air Force facility within the massive Nevada test range. First acquired by the air force in 1955 for developing aerospace company Lockheed's U-2 spy plane, Area 51's existence was not even acknowledged until 2013 and it enjoys a mythical status among UAP researchers as a location where there have been frequent sightings of strange glowing and hovering objects, as well as secret tests of more mundane but nonetheless super-secret test aircraft. During his time in service, Mellon says he was ordered by the then chairman of the Senate Appropriations Committee, Senator Robert Byrd, to investigate claims that the US was secretly working on a black high-technology aerospace project called Aurora. Another codename for the mythical craft is rumoured to be the TR3B. The Aurora has long been supposed to be a secret new hypersonic American reconnaissance aircraft and authoritative aviation writers like Bill Sweetman have claimed there is an ongoing undisclosed Aurora project.[9] Under pressure to explain the sightings of strange aircraft, in 1988 the US Air Force revealed the existence of the F-117A Night Hawk stealth attack aircraft and the B2 stealth bomber, but those aircraft did not explain what people were seeing. The speculation was rife by 1989 that America had developed a new super-stealthy craft inside Area 51, perhaps even a breakthrough in anti-gravitics, hence the mythical 'Aurora'.

Mellon visited Area 51, and had full access to review every classified project onsite. But he says he never saw anything there that equated to the kind of technology demonstrated by the UAPs that were sighted – and certainly no captured alien spacecraft. Mellon says, 'I never saw anything that involved something that was so orthogonal to our conventional understanding of science that you would think it must have come from somewhere else.' He conceded the possibility that there might be a project operating entirely outside the US government. 'I can't say that that's impossible.'

There is a moral conviction to Mellon that makes me doubt he would ever lie or dissemble to conceal some dark government secret; he is just the sort of guy you would hope a cranky Senator would put in charge of exposing dirty secrets in the defence and intelligence bureaucracy, which was effectively a large part of his role on the Senate Intelligence Committee staff. It is not hard to imagine Mellon going the extra yard to scour Area 51 for that elusive flying saucer. He was a child when his mind was first seeded with the intriguing possibility that humans are not alone. When he was seven, the principal of his boarding school showed a home movie of an object shot by one of his friends. The film showed a huge, golden disc-shaped object moving across sunny, blue skies and passing through cumulous clouds 'in a manner that would be very hard to fake'. Mellon does not know what became of the movie, but it filled him with 'wonder and awe … I remain deeply intrigued,' he says.[10] He admitted he read everything he could get his hands on about the mystery and he eventually did a research project on UFOs in college for a physics professor.

So, when Mellon says he believes there is no cover-up, it is persuasive. 'Maybe there's some super-secret program somewhere. Obviously, one can't prove a negative, right. It's impossible to prove that such a thing doesn't exist,' Mellon told Martin Willis' *Podcast UFO*.

Is it conceivable that by the 1990s the US military had designed such a craft, that it had crossed the technological Rubicon of an anti-gravity, hypersonic craft with science-fiction-style propulsion? However, if America was responsible for the Belgian UAP flap, then why would it betray the existence of such a massive technological leap by buzzing the good burghers of Belgium? Aviation journalist Jim Goodall has written 20 books on a plethora of top-secret craft, such as the SR-71 Blackbird, the F-117 stealth attack aircraft and the B-2A stealth bomber. He befriended engineer Ben Rich, the former Director of US aerospace company Lockheed Martin's Skunk Works (the pseudonym for Lockheed Martin's secretive

Advanced Developments Projects division, where many of America's most advanced aircraft have been designed). Rich, who died in 1995, had been notorious for dropping mischievous hints that the United States had achieved a huge technological breakthrough that was still being kept under wraps.

'To quote Ben Rich in his last comment to me just before he died,' Goodall told me from San Francisco,[11] '"Jim, we have things out in the desert that are 50 years beyond what you can comprehend. Not what you think we can make in 50 years but what you can comprehend. And if you've seen movies like *Star Trek* and *Star Wars*, we've been there, done that or decided it wasn't worth the effort".'

I tell Goodall that Christopher Mellon says he looked for evidence of such super-secret technological breakthroughs and, despite his high security clearances, he found no evidence the United States had made such huge leaps. 'The thing is, we may not be in charge of releasing the information,' Goodall mysteriously rejoindered with a chuckle.

Goodall also recounts an address Ben Rich gave in March 1993 to a small group of alumni at the University of California Los Angeles engineering school.

Both engineer Jan Harzan[12] and aerospace engineer T.L. Keller,[13] who were among the group, attested that Rich admitted that the US had figured out how to do interstellar travel, and that, without explanation, he said, 'there was an error in the equations'. Harzan described how when Ben Rich ended his talk, he showed a slide portraying a black disc zipping off into space, and that Rich's final words to the packed auditorium were, '"We've discovered what it is, and we now have the technology to travel to the stars" – to take ET home is what he actually said. I asked him once or twice "How does it work?" and he didn't really want to go there. After it was all over … he started to walk away. And I followed him … And

I said, "Mr Rich?" And he turned around and … looked me up and down like "who are you"? And I said, "Hi, I'm Jan Harzan, I'm an alumni. I have a real fascination with what you're talking about, particularly the propulsion side of this". And I said, "Can you tell me how it works?" And he said, "Well, let me ask you. How does ESP work?" And I was like two steps back. I wasn't really expecting a question. I was looking for an answer. And I just quipped real quickly, "I don't know, all points in space and time are connected." And that's when he said, "That's how it works." And he turned and walked out of the room.'[14]

Perhaps believers in the extra-terrestrial explanation for UAPs were far too credulous in taking the former Skunk Works boss literally. America would certainly like its strategic rivals, Russia and China, to think it now has an edge with such sci-fi-like technology, so perhaps Rich was using the opportunity to sprinkle disinformation through a prominent aerospace journalist. Ben Rich certainly enjoyed a joke; he dropped a similarly mischievous comment to another friend, the late Testor Corporation stealth aircraft model-kit designer John Andrews. Goodall gave me the letters between the two men, passed on to him by Andrews. In July 1986, Andrews had written to Ben Rich asking him to clarify whether he believed in both man-made UFOs and extra-terrestrial UFOs.[15] Rich replied in his letter, 'Dear John, Yes, I'm a believer in both categories. I feel everything is possible. Many of our man-made UFOs are Un Funded Opportunities.'[16] (Ben Rich's emphasis.) As a private aerospace company boss, Rich would no doubt have relished the massive funding opportunity that such an advanced technology represented in its potential development.

Jim Goodall told me he was in absolutely no doubt that there is a technology flying in our skies that is far beyond what has been acknowledged anywhere as within the capabilities of any country, including the United States, and he believes it might also be extra-terrestrial.

He told me how 'Dave', a retired lieutenant colonel in the US Air Force who flew the high-altitude mach-3-plus Lockheed SR-71 reconnaissance aircraft, witnessed an unidentified craft while night-flying out of Kadena Air Force Base in Okinawa, Japan, in late 1972 or early 1973. 'He told me UFOs absolutely, totally do exist,' Goodall said. 'He told me he was flying at about 78,000 feet, three-quarter moon to his starboard side. He's straight and level. You can see every star in the universe pretty much from up there. And all of a sudden, he got a glint of something metallic that was flying exactly the same direction he was, about five miles off to his starboard side and about 5000 or 6000 feet above his current altitude. He advanced the throttles on the spy-plane to try to intercept the object and as he grew closer, he could see it was not round, it had shiny metallic edges. He said that when he was a couple of miles away this thing accelerated at about a 30-degree angle of attack and left him in the dust,' Goodall told me. The pilot lost track of it between 180 and 200,000 feet, estimating its speed at 8000 miles an hour (13,000 km/h). Goodall's SR-71 pilot source, Dave, eventually became the facility manager at Area 51, the secret US test site for high-tech black world aerospace technology. 'And he started asking around, "Hey, did we ever fly anything out of here that can go eight or ten thousand miles an hour?"' The reply was always no.

The fastest jet currently flying is the United States' SR-71 Blackbird, with a top speed of mach 3.3, or 3500 km/h. The fastest manned aircraft flight ever was the October 1967 flight of the US's experimental X-15 rocket plane, a speed of mach 6.7, or 7200 km/h. The latest high-tech Lockheed Martin F-22 Raptor fighter has a top speed of (only?) 2414 km/h. No nation on the planet has an aircraft that can match what Dave saw over Japan and what many pilots and other witnesses have continued to report is flying in skies around the world to this day.

Goodall told me he also believed the controversial self-proclaimed flying saucer whistleblower Bob Lazar. Lazar is a Nevada businessman who went public in the late 1980s with incredible, and much disputed, claims that he worked as a physicist at Area 51 on reverse-engineering propulsion systems of recovered alien spacecraft. Goodall met Lazar well before he ever made the allegation that he had worked at so-called Site 4 (S-4), which is a much-rumoured but never officially confirmed secret facility supposedly located near but separate from Area 51. Goodall told me that, at their first meeting in the early 1980s, Bob Lazar was actually a UFO sceptic and both of them mocked a mutual pilot friend John Lear for his outspoken belief in UFOs. 'Bob Lazar said, "I'm a nuclear physicist and ... I wouldn't admit that UFOs are real even if you put a gun to my head,"' Goodall recalled ironically. 'This is Bob Lazar before he went to work at a place called S-4.' Years later, in 1989, Lazar went public in an interview with investigative journalist George Knapp on Las Vegas TV station KLAS, asserting (anonymously, at first) his purported employment working on a recovered extra-terrestrial flying saucer at the supposed S-4 facility, adjacent to Papoose Lake south of Area 51.

If there is a dark rabbit hole that leads to madness, the frustrating speculation about Bob Lazar's credibility will soon see you banging your head against a wall. I hear Jim Goodall out on Lazar. One turning point that persuaded him to believe Lazar came when another Area 51 source of his went treasure-hunting near where Lazar said the mythical S-4 site was located, a 30-minute south-westerly drive from the main Area 51 base. Officially, that secure area around Papoose Lake is just empty desert with old mining tenements scattered across the range. 'They were just milling around just looking for, you know, for treasures, small stuff, maybe a mining bucket or something, something old or an old bottle. And he said all of a sudden out of nowhere, there were a handful of black clad security guys with weapons wanting to know, "What are you doing here? Let's see some ID,"' Goodall said. He said what struck his source the most was that the security men did not arrive by vehicle, yet there was no evidence of any building or tunnel they came from. 'Where the hell did these guys come from?' Jim Goodall asks.

Two decades later, a former SR-71 pilot, David Fruehauf (whom I surmise was Jim Goodall's confidential 'Dave' source), went public in a television interview, partially backing Lazar's claims.[17] 'I think he's very credible,' Fruehauf asserted. Fruehauf worked at Area 51 for six years from 1979 through to 1985, commuting each day from Las Vegas to the desert site on a private charter flight named Janet Airlines. Fruehauf says he noticed a regular group of scientists and military officials who would board a bus to a facility he knew to be even more secretive than Area 51. He knew its codename was Site Four, S-4. 'We knew about S-4 but we didn't know what they did,' he says. 'All we knew was there was certain people that got on the 737 in the morning and when we got to Area 51, they were taken off in a different direction in a bus and we went on to the north going up towards the hangars.' Lazar was never at Area 51 at the same time as Fruehauf, but Fruehauf said Lazar's account was very accurate. 'He sounded totally believable to me,' Fruehauf said. He also claimed he knew witnesses who saw Lazar somewhere at Area 51.

It is impossible to resolve what truth, if any, there is behind Lazar's incredible claim that he worked on attempts to back-engineer alien spacecraft held at Area 51.. Lazar has claimed that when he went public, the official cover-up began, and this included the men in black wiping his university degree records. (As the movie franchise *Men in Black* has lampooned, a common story from UAP witnesses is that they were visited soon after reporting their sighting by strange and spooky 'men in black' who often told them to keep quiet about what they saw.) Journalist George Knapp has convincingly rebutted official denials that Lazar ever worked at Los Alamos National Laboratory in New Mexico; not only is there an old news story placing him there, Lazar sneaked Knapp into the secure facility and Lazar was clearly very familiar with the site and knew workers inside. Filmmaker Jeremy Corbell also found a witness whom Lazar said vetted him for his Area 51 security clearance.[18] But it did not help Lazar's credibility that, in 1990, he was arrested for aiding and abetting a prostitution ring, a charge eventually reduced to felony pandering, for which he served community service. As Lazar believers have impressed upon me, smearing a whistleblower with dirt from his past like this criminal charge is exactly what any black world cover-up conspiracy would exploit to discredit a troublesome snitch. It is an open question yet to be resolved if Bob Lazar's story is authentic.

* * *

It was 1991, just before the United States and its coalition allies, including Australia, invaded Saddam Hussein's Iraq after his illegal occupation of Kuwait. An orbiting American surveillance satellite tracked a mystery object speeding past it towards Earth's atmosphere, apparently coming from the inky black depths of outer space. The United States and Australia were on high alert because the Iraqi despot had short-range ballistic Scud missiles. Defence Support Program (DSP) satellite sensor systems recorded the object changing its velocity and then making a 30-degree course correction before it descended – a controlled descent. Deep inside a highly secure facility in the heart of Australia, and in similar US ground station facilities around the world, the object was logged as

100

a 'Valid IR source', and its detection notified to US and Australian defence intelligence agencies.

Few people know that an outback desert plain in central Australia is the location for the most important American military base outside of the continental United States. The Joint Defence Facility at Pine Gap nestles below the 800-metre-high McDonnell Ranges just 18 kilometres south-west of Alice Springs. Its ochre-coloured rocky ridges and undulating sandy country look like a scene from Mars. Originally a ground station for US satellites tracking the telemetry of Soviet missile launches, today Pine Gap receives electronic communications and other transmissions intercepted from space. It also collects the data from the highly sensitive infra-red DSP early-warning satellites hovering 35,000 kilometres above Earth, which capture the heat blooms of missile launches. Pine Gap's operators are constrained by their national security oaths to keep a tightly held secret – that the heat, light and infrared sensors on these satellites sometimes detect objects that are clearly not missiles and have even been seen to change course under apparently intelligent control. The codename given to these strangely moving objects is 'Fast Walkers'. The term includes mere space debris because it covers 'any orbital object seen passing through the field of view of an Earth observing sensor which is suspected of being in orbit'.[19] The object tracked in 1991, however, appeared to be under apparent intelligent control, as recently leaked documents reveal.

In June 2015, Australian Julian Assange's *Wikileaks* website dumped a cache of emails online that came from the email account of Hillary Clinton presidential campaign chairman, John Podesta. (More on this leak later.) They showed Podesta was emailed about 'UFOs' by an associate named Robert Fish revealing that Fast Walkers were routinely detected entering Earth's atmosphere from outer space by the DSP satellites. Fish told Podesta confidentially about the object he was briefed on by a US-based DSP operator at a high-security US private corporate aerospace facility in California. The UAP was recorded passing a satellite during the run-up to the Iraq War in 1991. 'So, it was under some sort of control – although whether it was "manned" or just "robotic" there's no way to tell,' Bob Fish told Podesta,[20] suggesting he ask for the data. He said information 'has existed for many years and is still available today, if one knows "where to look" and "what to look for"'. He also told Podesta 'UFO hunters' were looking in the wrong places. 'Random personal observations, fuzzy photographers, and crop circles will never "prove" the existence of anything, especially since UFO appearances to humans are transitory and somewhat related to the observer's state of mind. What needs to be collected and publicly disseminated is hard scientific data collected from instruments that are known to be accurate and reliable,'[21] Bob Fish wrote.

The enigmatic Mr Fish was clearly on John Podesta's case about UAPs; in another email,[22] Fish told him about a US Air Force non-commissioned officer he knew at the same classified facility who flew on RC-135 reconnaissance aircraft from MacDill Air Force Base in Florida to monitor Cuba. 'He said there were times when they were diverted from these missions to track UFOs off the east coast of Florida. His claim was the UFOs had a landing and take-off point in the ocean east of Miami, north of Bermuda. There was a specific electronic signature (frequency) emanating from them when they were going into or coming out of the water, so they were easy to track. On several occasions they filmed the UFO as it transitioned from water to air or vice versa,' Bob Fish told Podesta. 'High quality film of UFOs is "out there".' What caught my attention was Fish's claim that the US was actually tracking UAPs by tracing their unique electromagnetic signature.

I wrote to Bob Fish and after a few weeks he kindly responded, confirming everything he told Podesta, and more. He had never spoken publicly about UAPs before. A previously very highly security cleared defence communications intelligence insider, Fish has extensive experience working on classified programs, including President Reagan's 'Trust but Verify' nuclear missile disarmament treaty with the Soviets, and he assured me he was happy to be quoted about his strong interest and belief in UAPs. He clearly knew a lot more than he was prepared to reveal. When I asked him what he knew about the purported US ability to track such mystery craft, he told me, 'At some point, the information about "alien" stuff and true US national defence information crosses paths. Patriots with clearances do not want to be traitors to their country or their way of life. For instance, if I told you the exact electromagnetic signature of a high-mach UFO that US sensors search for, but don't attack, and you put it in a book, the Soviets/ Chinese would manufacture a bomber with sigint/elint [signals and electronic intelligence] counter measure equipment that generated that exact signature. We must find a path forward that brings about greater knowledge of the truth without endangering the civilizations we have evolved into.'[23] The intriguing thing about Fish's comment was the implication there was indeed a 'truth' still being concealed.

Fish told me he contacted Podesta because it frustrated him that no one was seeking the evidence that, because of his high security clearances, he knew was held inside government files. In the early 1990s, while working in a high security aerospace company facility, he was shown digital radar tracks showing a hypersonic UFO tracking alongside the US Air Force's SR-71 Blackbird spy plane. He said, 'There were two images streaking through the sky at Mach 3+ – one in a side-chase position to the other. The lead plane was our venerable SR-71 Blackbird; the other one was unidentified. At one point in the trace, the unidentified object made a 90-degree right turn and headed off in a different direction, rapidly gaining altitude while maintaining its speed. At that date (and it almost certainly remains true) humans simply did not have the technology to sustain that high-speed turn – g-forces would have ripped the craft's wings right off. When my friend mentioned this radar trace to the Edwards [Air Force Base] guys they sort of shrugged and asked that he erase that radar file as an unexplained anomaly. The US government, and other countries too, have captured empirical evidence – videos, imagery, electronic signatures, heat/spectral signatures, radar signatures, etc. – at various points in time that would shed light on the UFO topic. So, the question is, why hasn't it been released?' The most telling aspect of Bob Fish's story was what it revealed about the US military's reaction to such UAP incidents – whatever the government said publicly, those in the know were clearly not surprised by the mysterious phenomenon they saw on their screens; they obviously already knew all about it.

For a decade from 1988 to 1998, Charles Richard 'Dick' D'Amato served first as the chief counsel then as minority counsel for the powerful Senate Appropriations Committee in Washington DC under Senator Robert Byrd. It is well reported that D'Amato uncovered the existence of a massive $75 billion hitherto undisclosed US national security 'black budget', less so that he was also investigating UAPs, including claims of crashed craft in New Mexico. The well-respected UAP researcher Jacques Vallée described a 1990 meeting with D'Amato in his *Forbidden Science IV* edited diaries, where D'Amato frustratedly described a purported cover-up by the US intelligence community. 'These guys have been hiding their UFO data from the legislative branch for years; they behave as if they ran the country,' D'Amato said. 'They only come before us to get the appropriations for their secret projects, like their latest discoid platforms, although they're not authorized to fool the American public, or to create hoaxes or UFO simulations using taxpayers' money, as they do. I intend to find out what's been going on.'[24]

At a later meeting with Vallée, Dick D'Amato reportedly confessed he believed, 'What that stealthy group is doing is a felony ... The government can't spend appropriated money on projects that Congress doesn't know about ... That raises the question, would the president be told the truth? ... Worse, it raises the question of who is running the country. If the men who sit in this chamber cannot find out about such a project, we are no longer in a democracy ... Whatever that secret project, it must be controlled by an incredible level of fear, because nobody dares talk about it. I find no leaks anywhere.'[25] Thirty years ago D'Amato had reportedly tried to expose what he believed was a UAP cover-up. I wrote to the now elderly Richard D'Amato, but I never heard back. Mr D'Amato has obviously had a lot of folk chasing him for further comment because on his website a statement says that, after his investigation for Senator Byrd, he recommended to the Senator that the allegations about UAP crashes 'did not appear to merit any further Senate investigation',[26] whatever that assertion implies. It did not exclude the possibility that D'Amato's suspicions were validated. Perhaps someone told him to pull his head in.

My conversations with both former top-secret insider Bob Fish and aerospace journalist Jim Goodall left me thinking for the first time that, just maybe, America has cracked it; that perhaps the United States, or perhaps some other nation, is working with experimental craft using propulsion systems that must surely be based on anti-gravitics and electro-magnetic drives. However, as quickly as I weighed that possibility, my cynical journalist brain dismissed it. Surely a secret as big as that would leak? An insider with the security classification access to find out a secret like that, such as Christopher Mellon, must know because, as he says, he was legally entitled to know. As a journalist, I also know how hard it is for politicians and top public servants to keep secrets. They cannot stop themselves from blabbing.

As I dug deeper into the clandestine world of America's black projects, an alternative explanation emerged. One other possibility was that, if some aerospace corporation had secretly developed this awesome technology, then perhaps successive presidents, Congress and the American public have been lied to – that a cabal of corporate cronies have conspired, perhaps with a few headstrong generals, to keep this discovery off the books and away from all that pesky government accountability. And we all know that could never happen in the land of the free ... or could it?

Chapter 9

The Disclosure Project

When Bill Clinton became president in 1993, he asked questions about UAPs, just as Jimmy Carter had done in 1977. Clinton's Associate Attorney General Webster Hubbell claimed he was asked by the president to find out all he could about two things. "'One, who killed JFK? And, two, are there UFOs?' He was dead serious,' Hubbell claimed. As Hubbell told it in his biography *Friends in High Places*, he subsequently reported back to President Clinton that after being stonewalled by multiple agencies he could not get an answer on either the JFK or UFO mysteries. Hubbell wrote, 'I had looked into both, but wasn't satisfied with the answers I was getting.'[1] A more sensational claim has since been attributed to Hubbell – that he allegedly discovered a secret government program that was sitting on UFO secrets to which even the president did not have access,[2] but such a claim does not appear in Hubbell's book or in any media interviews quoting Hubbell. I could find no proof that Hubbell made any such statement. The claims continue to be repeated on fringe UFO websites, but Hubbell has conspicuously avoided further explanation of just what inquiries he made. He is a controversial figure, as he left office after being indicted and convicted for tax fraud and he served time in prison.

What is known is that, on entering the White House in 1993, both Bill and Hillary Clinton took a strong interest in UAPs, and after lobbying from billionaire businessman and UAP believer Laurance Rockefeller, the president ordered his new CIA Director James Woolsey to release more of the files on the subject. Two years later, a photograph of Hillary Clinton and Rockefeller shows her conspicuously carrying the book *Are We Alone?*[3] by Australian Professor Paul Davies. Rockefeller, a long-time advocate for 'UFO disclosure', gave Hillary the book as a gift; it looks at the philosophical implications of the discovery of extra-terrestrial life.

President Clinton has also admitted that he had his aides research Area 51, 'to make sure there was no alien down there'. He also pushed for the General Accounting Office's 1995 review of all the Roswell papers, which reported that the Roswell records were destroyed without authority. It is telling how overt both Clintons have been on the UAP issue. In 2014, Clinton was asked on *Jimmy Kimmel Live*, 'If you saw that there were aliens there, would you tell us?' Clinton said that he would have done so. He also admitted he believed human beings were not alone in the universe. 'If we were visited someday, I wouldn't be surprised,' he said.[4]

President Clinton wasn't the only one pushing for more information from the US authorities. An emergency physician and 'ufologist' named Dr Steven Greer was also advocating for 'disclosure'. In 1990, Greer had founded the Center for the Study of Extra-terrestrial Intelligence (CSETI), a lobby group separate from the non-profit SETI (Search for Extra-terrestrial Intelligence) Institute formerly funded by NASA. Two years later, Greer created the Disclosure Project, which advocates for the release of UAP secrets he believes are hidden within the US government and in aerospace corporations.

Dr Greer says he has personally briefed presidents and a CIA Director about the 'UFO reality'. On his website, he dramatically casts a meeting he had with the then Director of America's Central Intelligence Agency, James Woolsey, in 1993 as 'a covert briefing on the topic of UFOs under the guise of a dinner party'.[5] Woolsey denied the gathering was a briefing,[6] which a former CIA Director probably would feel obliged to do if he was embarrassed about having been exposed for conversing with Greer about a supposed UAP government cover-up. However, the most interesting part of Greer's story suggests that Woolsey, the newly appointed CIA Director under President Clinton, was prepared to investigate claims of a UAP cover-up.

Futurist John Petersen, the founder and president of The Arlington Institute, was the man who invited Woolsey and Greer to dinner that night in 1993. Petersen is a well-connected former navy flight officer, a decorated veteran of both the Vietnam and Gulf Wars. His Arlington Institute think-tank invites commentators on global futures and national security issues. Petersen, who has worked on several presidential campaigns, was twice runner-up for the job of Secretary of the US Navy. Intriguingly, Petersen told me that Jim Woolsey, a friend, 'had a passing interest in the subject of UFOs – limited to having seen a non-moving light above a lake at some point and wondering if it had been some sort of non-human vehicle'.[7] He also said that when Woolsey became Director of the CIA, Petersen visited him at his office and raised with him 'that there were a lot of highly redacted documents that the UFO community thought might relate to government knowledge of "alien stuff"'. He said Woolsey told him to get the details of the 20 most significant redacted documents, offering to check if the redacted parts had anything to do with UFOs. 'He was not offering to tell me any secrets, rather to just confirm or deny generally that the subject documents had anything to do with the UFO subject,'

Petersen told me. Petersen organised for Greer and researcher Stan Friedman to create the list of documents; Woolsey read them and came back to them saying they didn't have anything to do with UFOs. Petersen flatly denied claims that the CIA boss reached out to Greer for a briefing or that Woolsey requested the meeting. 'There was no "cover story" and no "briefing" had been requested. It was simply a social function where it was presumed that the subject of UFOs would be discussed,' Petersen says.

Greer has sometimes been the butt of ridicule for his melodramatic claims about the alleged 'UFO cover-up', asserting that dark forces were trying to kill him or his colleagues. Greer has claimed that when he sent a briefing document to President Clinton a response came back that the president 'couldn't get anywhere with [UFOs] and didn't want to push on the issue because a very good friend of his came to his home and said he would end up assassinated like Jack Kennedy. [Greer] said, "Well okay, then I'll do it". And we all almost all died subsequently.'[8]

Greer bizarrely claims that the gatekeepers of what some call 'The Big Secret' then tried to kill him with a secret remote death ray. In his book, *Hidden Truth: Forbidden Knowledge,* Greer dramatically tells how he and his fellow UAP disclosure activist colleague Shari Adamiak were diagnosed with metastatic cancers that he claimed were caused by an electro-magnetic (EM) weapons system targeting them 'from a laboratory in Utah'.[9] There is no evidence for such a claim. Nor is there any evidence to support another claim made by Greer, that former CIA Director William Colby (who died in a boating accident) was actually assassinated because he planned to help Greer's organisation. Shari Adamiak did die from cancer in 1998. Greer has claimed the reason he survived was because his golden retriever dog Yami 'bonded to me and astrally took some of the "hit" from the EM weapon system targeting us'. Poor Yami. Suffice to say, Greer does not seem to be concerned if people think he is perhaps a tad paranoid. Assuming that Greer's account of his meeting with Woolsey was correct, it suggests the CIA Director was genuinely motivated to hear and investigate Greer's claims of a UAP cover-up, which begs the question why Greer publicly exposed his potential source. His aggressive public outing of Woolsey for soliciting such a briefing (if that was true) damaged chances of persuading public officials to speak out on the issue.

When Greer went into the Pentagon in April 1997 as part of an unusual group of UFO disclosure activists and former military servicemen and was escorted to the innermost ring of America's military headquarters, the offices of the Deputy Director of the US Defence Intelligence Agency, what helped get him the invitation was that one of his companions was a legendary astronaut. Apollo 14 astronaut Edgar Mitchell knew well how his 'Right Stuff' credentials could open doors. He had earned it. It was Ed Mitchell who piloted the lunar module on 5 February 1971, becoming the sixth man to walk on the Moon, one of the legends of space exploration. Which was why in April 1997, Mitchell's renown opened the way for an extraordinary briefing with the Deputy Director of Intelligence for the US military's Joint Chiefs of Staff, Admiral Thomas Wilson.

A day earlier, Greer had held a briefing on the UAP phenomenon at a Georgetown Washington DC hotel with senior congressmen and dozens of their staffers. Around 12 witnesses, comprising defence contractors and military and intelligence insiders, gave startling first-hand testimony in the closed-door session about their claimed UAP experiences including sightings of purported extra-terrestrial space debris, claims that NASA was airbrushing photographs of flying discs, and a military pilot's account of a direct encounter with a massive craft.[10]

The next day, at 10 am on 10 April 1997, Greer, Mitchell and company were deep inside the Pentagon for their top-level meeting.

Another attendee was recently retired US Naval Reserve Lieutenant Commander Willard Miller, who served on the operations staff of the US Atlantic Command and at NORAD Space Command with Top Secret security clearances. He had also previously served as a navy reservist on Admiral Wilson's staff. The story goes that Admiral Thomas Wilson agreed to be briefed 'about UFOs' by Greer and Miller because he was one of those senior military officers whom Miller said was denied knowledge of The Big Secret. In advance of their visit, Greer had sent Admiral Wilson's staff a leaked US National Reconnaissance Office document that detailed a series of what turned out to be authentic codenames for highly top-secret so-called Special Access Programs (SAPs). It was a July 1991 security advisory, listing a series of codenames and command locations in and around the massive Nellis Air Force Base in the Nevada desert, which includes within its boundaries the notorious super-secret Area 51 sites known as Groom Lake and Dreamland.

To understand the importance of Greer's leaked classified document requires a knowledge of how Special Access Program (SAP) security classification protocols work in the US. Some black-world budget projects are hidden so deep, it is a crime for anyone read into a project to even reveal its existence.[11] SAPs are where the US Defence Department hides most of its super-secret black-budget classified projects. A further cloak of secrecy in addition to the highest top-secret security classification, an SAP designation is not actually a higher security classification than top secret. It simply means the project is compartmented, deemed Sensitive Compartmented Information (SCI), and designated a codename. Even the most senior military officials with the highest top-secret security clearance are forbidden from knowing the details behind an SAP/SCI codename unless they are *read* into it.

There are also USAPs, Unacknowledged Special Access Programs, which means the project's very existence can and must be denied by those who know about it, the true funding hidden. And there is an even higher protocol for the darkest black-world secrets of all, Waived Unacknowledged Special Access Programs, or WUSAPs. A WUSAP means the Secretary of Defence has waived all the normal oversight laws and reporting procedures; not only is its very existence concealed, it is only overseen by the so-called Gang of Eight in Congress. This includes the chair and vice-chair of the House Intelligence Armed Services Committee, the Senate Majority and Minority leaders, and a bipartisan elected group allowed to review WUSAPs.

When Admiral Tom Wilson saw the leaked document Greer sent him,[12] he was, Greer claims, very upset that there were SAP project codenames on the list that were unknown to him, the second-most powerful man in Defence Intelligence. The purpose of the document was of little consequence; it related to a security lockdown at Nellis Air Force Base in July 1991. But its reference to codenames including 'ROYAL Ops, COSMIC Ops, MAJ Ops, MAJI Ops' thrilled the world of UAP research because COSMIC and MAJ have long been rumoured to be the holy grail of UFO-related codenames.

In the 1997 Pentagon meeting, Steven Greer alleges Admiral Tom Wilson made a dramatic admission. 'He actually recognised one of these entities and made an inquiry, and it was being run by a contractor,' Greer says. 'When he called them, he said, "I'm Admiral Tom Wilson ... I want to be read into this project". Guess what happened? They said, "Sir, you don't have a need to know". This is the guy who is supposed to give the intelligence briefings for the Joint Chiefs of Staff of the United States. He was told, "You don't have a need to know"... And Admiral Wilson said, "Goddamn it, if I don't have a need to know, who does?" They said, "Sir, we cannot discuss this with you further" and they hung up and blocked his line.'[13] Whatever this program was (or is), the alleged UAP-UFO cover-up laid out by Greer, Ed Mitchell and Commander Miller is supposedly so secret that even the second-highest official in the Defence Intelligence Agency was not permitted to know about it.

The precise details of what was said at the April 1997 Pentagon briefing are unclear after nearly a quarter of a century and three of the attendees (Ed Mitchell; attorney, army reservist and disclosure activist Steven Lovekin; and Greer's CSETI colleague Shari Adamiak) are now dead. But we know Steven Greer, Willard Miller and Edgar Mitchell presented Admiral Wilson with what they were convinced was strong witness evidence to support their belief that the US government was covering up alien visitations to Earth, recovered spacecraft and alien bodies, and incredible technological breakthroughs purportedly derived from those discoveries. Greer's account suggests that Wilson actually took these incredible claims seriously. 'As the briefing progressed,' Greer says, 'he began cancelling other appointments – he was so interested in the information.'[14] Edgar Mitchell later confirmed to many friends that this meeting happened as Greer described. One of these friends was John Audette, the co-founder of Mitchell's Quantrek research organisation, who responded in detail to my inquiry about this meeting. 'Yes, Ed shared with me details about the Admiral Wilson meeting,' Audette tells me. 'Ed believed there was a cover-up by a cabal or shadow government on the ET issue and the presumed physical evidence presumed to be in government possession ... Ed believed highly secretive reverse-engineering was occurring.'[15]

Retired Navy Commander Willard Miller also supported Greer's account of Admiral Wilson's frustration. He even claimed that, just before they left the meeting, an aide to the admiral made the extraordinary admission that a long-held (and much debunked) UAP conspiracy theory called Majestic MJ-12 was actually real. Operation Majestic-12 was a supposed secret cabal of scientists, military and intelligence officials and government formed in 1947 by

President Harry Truman to facilitate the recovery and investigation of alien spacecraft. Purported secret government documents surfaced in 1984 and then later in 1996 apparently confirming the existence of MJ-12, as it is known. However, the Federal Bureau of Investigation (FBI) and even some UAP researchers have dismissed the documents as an elaborate hoax. Given the detail in them, pulling off such a hoax was a forensic achievement in itself because faking such a trove of documents citing real names, titles, offices and events was a formidably complex task.

Greer says, 'The admiral's aide turned to me and said you know the subject of Majestic MJ-12 came up and there's been a lot of debate as to, you know, whether that's real, whether it ever existed, and he said, you know we know it exists. We here at the intelligence Directorate for the Joint Staff just don't have the need to know what they do.'[16] This is why a nosey journalist like me would not survive five minutes serving in the military; fancy anyone with the remotest strand of curiosity in their DNA meekly deciding they do not have the need to know possibly the biggest secret in human history.

In another account given by Greer, Admiral Wilson (whom Greer had not named at this point) reacted with horror during their briefing. 'After he looked at all this and heard the witness, he turned to us and said: "Well I have no doubt this is true, but I am horrified that I hadn't known about it",' Greer claimed.[17] He subsequently outed Admiral Tom Wilson as that senior Defence Intelligence Agency official in his book *Hidden Truth: Forbidden Knowledge*.[18] Shari Adamiak also confirmed the Pentagon briefing took place.[19] Greer claimed Admiral Wilson was angry at the illegality of the alleged cover-up. 'During this briefing, the admiral and I discussed the risk this rogue group – that had shoved him aside – was to the United States, the rule of law and to national security ... I told the admiral that this illegal, rogue group had ARV [alien reproduction vehicle] technology that can do circles around his B2

Stealth bombers. He thought a minute and said, "Well, as far as I am concerned, if you can get people who know about this matter to talk on the record, you have my permission to go to the media with this! This group is illegal!'" Greer claimed he was told.[20]

There is something about Steven Greer's accounts of his numerous 'briefings' of military and government officials that does not ring as wholly plausible, and in some cases it seems outright implausible. I suspect it is the way he casts himself as always so much better informed than every official with whom he engages (which I concede might possibly be true, if you believe the cover-up claims). It is to Greer's credit, for example, that he was invited back in 1998 to the Defence Intelligence Agency, again with Commander Willard Miller, to brief the then Director, Wilson's immediate superior, Lieutenant General Patrick Hughes, 'on UFOs'. Greer claims that General Hughes grabbed an ET doll from the Stephen Spielberg movie, which he just happened to have on his shelf, declaring, "'Well, I have no doubt that what you are sharing is true, but I have made inquiries through channels in my agency and nobody can tell me anything! In fact, all I have gotten is this!'"[21]

It is remarkable that Greer achieved the extraordinary feat of being invited to brief top Defence Intelligence Agency officials on UAPs on at least two occasions, but the claim that both a senior admiral and a general confirmed at their first meeting with him that they both believed in a 'UFO cover-up' strains credibility for many who hear it. But, if his account is accurate, his public outing of both Defence Intelligence Agency officials, Admiral Wilson and General Hughes, sent an unhelpful message to any other official contemplating disclosure that they could not expect confidentiality from Greer.

There is another claim about Greer's meeting with Admiral Wilson that does not ring right. Sources with top-secret and compartmented security clearances say no senior military official with a Top Secret Sensitive Compartmented Information (TS-SCI) clearance should ever be surprised at such a refusal from a contractor. They said that if Admiral Wilson was not 'read onto' the Waived and Unacknowledged Special Access Program on UAPs (WUSAP) as alleged, then he would ordinarily have accepted he had no right to be angry about that. Such a refusal was normal; it was an absolute obligation. Admiral Tom Wilson would have known that even he, a Deputy Director of the Defence Intelligence Agency, had to ask to be given access, which was only then given at the discretion of his superiors.

Why would senior defence intelligence officials, entrusted with vital secrets of national security, be as candid as Greer claims they were, in a first meeting with a 'UFO disclosure' activist who, after all, believes it is corrupt senior officials inside the military and intelligence services who are conspiring to engineer this dastardly cover-up? I can understand how, since 1997, a lot of folk who heard the Greer claims about the Admiral Tom Wilson meeting dismissed the whole story as self-serving bulldust. That is certainly what former Admiral Tom Wilson has suggested.

The admiral confirmed the 1997 Pentagon meeting with Greer and Mitchell in an interview with Richard Dolan more than a decade later, but told Dolan he only agreed to it because he was 'curious why a man of Dr Mitchell's stature would be interested in such a matter'. Wilson claimed everything else about the meeting described by Greer was 'poppycock' and he then hung up on Dolan.[22] It struck me that Admiral Wilson's broad rejection of the Greer story as 'poppycock' did not address a lot of the specific questions that arise from that meeting, such as whether he, as the then Deputy Director of the US Defence Intelligence Agency, really did seek a briefing on UFOs by Greer and whether he made any specific admissions about being blocked from finding out more on the issue. I wrote to retired Admiral Tom Wilson asking about the 1997 meeting. His detailed letter in reply[23] acknowledged the meeting happened, and that it was indeed a 'briefing', saying, 'I accepted this short meeting on my schedule because Dr Edgar Mitchell was a credible and respected, retired navy captain and astronaut, and I thought it was the polite thing to do. I had had "mild" curiosity about what my guests had to say about UFOs. I recall the meeting was scheduled for 30 minutes, but possibly lasted a bit longer than that.' Wilson recalled 'my visitors' concerns about possible "special access programs" dealing with that subject. I believe, as some reports suggest, that Dr Mitchell's team's objective was to solicit my assistance in achieving access or knowledge of such programs. *I most certainly did not acknowledge or even suggest that such programs existed nor that I would attempt to gain access if they did.* In fact, I did neither then, nor since then, ever have knowledge of such programs. While they may have chosen to interpret that my polite acceptance of their briefing and understanding of their concerns left open the possibility that I would look into the issues they raised, I never had intent to do so.' (Admiral Wilson's emphasis.)

If everything Greer said about the April 1997 meeting was poppycock, as the admiral claims, and if he was in truth not blocked at all from knowing about supposed secret UAP programs, it begs the question why Wilson's Defence Intelligence Agency boss General Patrick Hughes invited Greer and Miller back to talk about UAPs months later. I suspect, in actual fact, the two Defence Intelligence Agency officials were more interested than they care to publicly admit. In light of the number of witnesses who have given their accounts of the 1997 Pentagon meeting, it is difficult to escape the conclusion that Admiral Wilson gave the impression in some way to Greer's group that he was improperly blocked from accessing UFO information (although that does not make this claim true). Multiple witnesses at this meeting – Shari Adamiak, Stephen Lovekin, astronaut Edgar Mitchell and Commander Willard Miller – have backed Greer's account.

Just a few weeks before the Pentagon meeting, one of the most widely reported UAP sightings in history happened over the city of Phoenix, Arizona. On the evening of 13 March 1997, thousands of eyewitnesses reported a massive V-shaped formation of lights as wide as several city blocks, or 'a mile wide', hovering as low as 30 metres above the city. Many perceived the object as a single black triangular or chevron-shaped craft hovering noiselessly in the night sky, with lights in each corner. The Air National Guard later implausibly claimed that all the public had seen were high-intensity flares dropped during a training exercise. Arizona's Governor Fife Symington later responded, 'As a pilot and a former air force officer, I can definitely say that this craft did not resemble any man-made object I'd ever seen. And it was certainly not high-altitude flares because flares don't fly in formation.'[24]

In my view, the historical evidence supports the suggestion there have indeed been numerous US government attempts to suppress – and on occasion, to cover up – UAP incidents, especially when the witnesses were military or civilian pilots. This does not of course prove the existence of ETs or recovered non-terrestrial spacecraft, but the evidence is overwhelming that US government agencies have gone to strenuous lengths to keep evidence of UAPs off the front page, for whatever reason. The explanations offered by the US military for the Phoenix sighting are risible in light of the clear evidence from an enormous number of witnesses; flares and a mass delusion do not cut it as an explanation. I am left in no doubt that someone senior in the US military has been trying to cover up sightings; what I struggle with is, why the cover-up? At one extreme, there are those who believe there has been an elaborate cover-up to suppress recovered extra-terrestrial technology; or alternatively, as

I am inclined to believe, maybe governments simply do not like having to admit there is a superior technology operating in their airspace displaying capabilities far beyond known human science. It is embarrassing.

One high-placed official in the US government prepared to publicly support research into UAPs at this time was John Podesta, a political consultant who served as President Clinton's Chief of Staff in the White House from 1998 to 2001, and would later serve as Counsellor to President Obama from 2014 to 2015. In 2002, shortly after leaving the Clinton White House, he supported a lawsuit fighting to get government records released on the 1965 UAP incident in Kecksburg, Pennsylvania.

He also told a Washington National Press Club press conference, 'I think it's time to open the books on questions that have remained in the dark on the question of government investigations of UFOs. It's time to find out what the truth really is that's out there. We ought to do it really because it's right. We ought to do it because the American people, quite frankly, can handle the truth. And we ought to do it because it's the law.'[25]

Chapter 10

Skinwalker Ranch

South-east of the remote US country town of Ballard in Utah sits a small farm. Once known as Sherman Ranch, it's better known in UAP legend today as Skinwalker Ranch. There have been many weird claims of supernatural happenings at the ranch since a Mormon farming family, Terry and Gwen Sherman, reported their experiences to the local *Deseret News* in the mid-1990s.[1] The Shermans claimed to have seen multiple UAPs during their 15 months on the farm. They described 'a small boxlike craft with a white light, a 40-foot-long object, and a huge ship the size of several football fields'. The family was spooked by the experiences, claiming they saw one craft emit a wavy red ray or light beam as it flew along, and orange circular doorways that seemed to appear in mid-air. Sceptics have dismissed the claims of supernatural goings-on at Skinwalker Ranch as much ado about nothing, most often suggesting witnesses misperceived prosaic objects. Everyone who interviewed the Shermans reported them to be credible and honest folk with a strong religious ethical conviction, not the sort of people who make up elaborate stories to draw attention to themselves. In fact, to the contrary, the

Shermans shunned media interest in their story after the initial reports.

There were even more alarming claims; the Shermans linked the UAP sightings to the death or disappearance of seven of their cows. Three were found dead but mutilated, with surgically precise excisions that had extracted either the poor creature's entire tongue, rectum or reproductive organs, and always with no blood. No tracks were found for possible predators; there were no tyre or footprints to suggest possible human mischief; and there was often a distinct chemical smell hanging over the scene. It was and remains a baffling mystery. The Shermans described one scene where a cow had left tracks through the snow, its hoofprints showing it had gone into a snow-covered field. But there was no sign of the cow, no tracks to show it had left the field and 'the area where the cow apparently took its last steps was surrounded by a circle of broken twigs and branches' from the trees above.[2] Their son also reported finding another dead cow, which he had seen alive just five minutes earlier, with a six-inch wide, 18-inch-deep hole cored out of its rectum well inside its body cavity, again with absolutely no blood, a chemical odour and damage to the trees above it.

It did not take long for journalists to link this sensational story to local Navajo native American legends of malevolent witches, otherwise known as the Skinwalkers. Terry Sherman also described hearing male voices speaking in an unknown language, hovering somewhere overhead; he reported his dogs were terrified. The story took off when a local retired high school teacher, Joseph Hicks, claimed to have interviewed multiple eyewitnesses who said they had seen living beings in the portholes of hovering UAPs in sightings across the Uintah Basin where the Skinwalker Ranch is located.

Sceptics speculated that the mutilated cows were all victims of predatory animals but what bolstered the credibility of at least one of the Sherman family's claims was that ranchers right across the state and into New Mexico were also reporting alarmingly similar mysterious cattle mutilations – well over 10,000. It is a matter of public record, observed by police, FBI agents and local veterinarians, that there have continued to be thousands of physical evidence reports of what witnesses say are clearly suspicious cattle mutilations across a huge swathe of the US for decades.

Cattle mutilations have also long been reported in Australia and many other countries around the world. In September 2018, Mick and Judy Cook, a farming couple near Mackay in north Queensland, Australia, reported finding a dead cow with its udder, an ear and its tongue cut out and said the cuts were so clean, they believed 'only a high-tech robot or aliens could be responsible'.[3] When I followed up with Mick Cook in March 2021, he told me the mutilations were frequent and still happening.[4] His farm, Cloverly Station, is extremely remote and inaccessible except by a road that passes right beside their farmhouse. 'No one could have got in without us knowing,' he says. Yet he estimates that, in the last couple of years, at least 15 head of his cattle had been 'surgically operated upon' on his property by unknown mutilators. Whoever or whatever it was had excised organs such as a tongue, testicles, anus and jaw from each animal's body without leaving any blood. Photographs of the wounds showed a precise hexagonal shape cut into the poor animal's carcass. He said his dogs would not go anywhere near any of these mutilated carcasses and, to add to the mystery, without any prompting, he volunteered that he and Judy had also seen strange lights doing 'weird things' over his station late at night. He said that, when he walked near one animal corpse, he felt a chemical burn on his face (echoes of similarly reported chemical smells at Skinwalker Ranch here?). Mick Cook dismissed my query if the damage could have been caused by a predatory animal. 'We're talking about surgical cuts that are so bloody neat and precise there's no blood anywhere,' he told me. 'One animal I seen, its testicle bag was cut out, but you could see the adjoining blood vessels from next to where it had been removed. No blood anywhere. What can do that?'

Repeated, verifiable, observational data from numerous reputable eyewitnesses including state police, FBI agents, scientists, veterinarians and landowners is surely the essence of what good science demands to support a hypothesis. But readers of the *Sceptical Inquirer* magazine, a journal for sceptics, were assured that it was 'obvious' the US mutilations were in fact a natural phenomenon. The whole issue of cattle mutilations was a case of 'mild mass hysteria', the report claimed.[5] An FBI investigation had conceded in 1980 that there were mutilation cases that could not be prosaically explained, concluding, without any evidence, that the mutilations were predominantly the result of natural predation. There was no explanation for what type of predator was able to excise specific organs and lumps of flesh with no apparent teeth marks, no blood and extremely surgically precise cuts. This FBI finding has been vigorously challenged over the 40 years since, including by other law enforcement officials and scientists, who continue to log anomalous apparent cattle mutilations across the US.

Author Ben Mezrich investigated cattle mutilations in *The 37th Parallel*.[6] He detailed how, across the US, for 5000 kilometres along the latitude of the 37th parallel north of the equator, there have been numerous corroborated, officially reported, often videoed and photographed, sightings of mutilated livestock – their carcasses always completely exsanguinated (in actual fact, with no visible blood spilt anywhere) and with distinct surgically precise excisions of key organs. Mezrich suggested the evidence is overwhelming that there is a link between UAP sightings and unexplained cattle mutilations. He followed research done by Chuck Zukowski, a former reserve Sheriff's deputy in Colorado, who collated more than 10,000 instances where cows and horses were found dead, consistently all missing organs, the cuts surgical and circular, every animal completely drained of blood. A massive 100 agent FBI investigation into suspected human involvement, demanded by three US State Attorneys-General, failed to solve the mystery.[7] While Chuck Zukowski was doing his investigation in the 1990s, he realised there was another well-resourced team of investigators covertly probing the same mystery. They were employees of a billionaire businessman named Robert Bigelow. 'Turns out, for the past 20 years they have been investigating UFOs,' Mezrich says.[8] It also subsequently emerged that Federal Aviation Administration manuals specifically advised civilian pilots to report UAPs to Bigelow, not to the FAA.

The enigmatic billionaire funding these investigations, Robert Bigelow, made his massive fortune through a hotel chain business named Budget Suites of America. Recognising that the UAP mystery merited ongoing investigation, in 1995, Bigelow self-funded the creation of the National Institute for Discovery Science, better known as NIDS. Bigelow was so intrigued by the Sherman family's stories that the billionaire paid $200,000 to buy Skinwalker Ranch in 1996. Bigelow funded full-time surveillance of Skinwalker Ranch as part of NIDS, ordering an investigation into the extraordinary paranormal claims.

In 1996, Dr Eric Davis was on secondment from the University of Maryland, at a US Air Force fighter wing in South Korea, when he read an intriguing ad in a physics magazine seeking to hire research scientists interested in studying the 'foundations of spacetime, the universe and the physics of consciousness'.[9] Davis started working for Bob Bigelow's National Institute for Discovery Science in July 1996. Within weeks, he had his first paranormal experience at Skinwalker Ranch.

'On the second trip there in September I saw a craft out through the kitchen window,' he said. 'And it descended, and it was still illuminated in front of the background mountain range, which was probably another 30 miles west.'[10] He watched the apparent craft's big amber light descend below tree level and glimpsed it at ground level shining through the trees, sitting there for half an hour. Later that year, in November, he was sitting with fellow scientist Colm Kelleher on the ranch-house's back porch and a similarly lit craft hurtled out from above a nearby bluff and executed a sharp high-speed 90-degree turn right above them.[11]

On another night at Skinwalker Ranch, they noticed a herd of cows was restless and the ranch manager suspected a large wildcat was lurking nearby. Eric Davis was in the corner of a field when he saw a gigantic pair of cat's eyes at the top of a tree. 'Two really large glowing yellow eyes, they looked like the eyes of a big predator cat,' he says. 'The only problem is they were too big. They were too far apart. And they were up near the top of the tree, you know, in the main bulk of the branches, but close to the top … And they're just blinking. And I'm thinking what the hell that is. I've never seen a cat that big or with eyes that wide and big. And I think, you know, that's no cat.'[12] (Anyone else thinking of *Alice in Wonderland*'s Cheshire Cat here?)

Davis alerted Colm Kelleher and Terry, the ranch manager, who were with him, and they all saw a huge creature suddenly jump down just in front of them; it was far larger than any wildcat, the size of a bear or a cow. Terry fired multiple shots into it with his rifle at point-blank range but Davis recalls, 'It didn't flinch. And it just walked off into the shrubs and disappeared.' They found no footprints in the snow, no blood; the creature, whatever it was, had disappeared. Many such anomalous paranormal experiences led Davis to the highly contentious conclusion that this was some kind of sentient non-human intelligence they were witnessing, which managed to consistently avoid detection by the Skinwalker scientists on their cameras and videos. It was a big call for any serious scientist, but his Skinwalker experiences convinced Davis that the phenomenon was real. 'We do know one thing,' Davis insists. 'They're there. They're doing something. We don't know their origin because they don't want to communicate that to us.'[13]

Sceptics have suggested[14] that what really happened at Skinwalker Ranch was that witnesses got over-excited and saw things that were not there because they went into their research credulously believing in this paranormal phenomenon, and their imagination filled in the rest. However, none of the scientists brought in by Bigelow to study this phenomenon were 'UFO believers' by background. Dr Colm Kelleher came from a cancer research centre at the University of Colorado. The team's veterinarian, Dr George Onet, was from the South Dakota State Veterinarian Office. Dr Eric Davis was with the US Air Force as a subcontractor from one of the US's preeminent public research universities. What they witnessed in their research challenged all their accepted scientific certainties. Davis has admitted he and his wife had an earlier UAP experience when he was in his late twenties,[15] but he was also at pains to debunk UAP claims when he could. National Institute for Discovery Science documents found in the newly discovered Edgar Mitchell archive files show that, while Davis was with the NIDS, he investigated a supposed alien attack and landing in Montana; he concluded it was a hoax. Amusingly, like so many before him, Davis also admits driving around the border of the secretive Area 51 government facility in the Nevada desert for a peek, provoking the security guards from Wackenhut security to rumble his car.

Las Vegas investigative journalist George Knapp is a multi-award-winning investigative journalist who has worked for Nevada's KLAS-TV for 40 years, breaking many extraordinary UAP stories. He also frequently hosts the syndicated US conspiracy and paranormal-focused radio show *Coast to Coast AM*. In 2005, Knapp co-authored a book on Skinwalker Ranch,[16] *Hunt for the Skinwalker*, with Dr Colm Kelleher, the scientist who led Bigelow's NIDS-funded scientists, engineers and analysts investigating the professed paranormal phenomena. Kelleher described a lot of 'anomalous phenomena', but none of it was captured on numerous cameras set up around the ranch. The explanation offered was that the anomalous phenomena somehow managed to mysteriously evade the cameras. Perhaps the most astounding claim in the book was that NIDS investigators witnessed a 'faceless black creature' emerging from a glowing yellow light tunnel that winked into existence from nowhere, as if from another dimension.[17] In another incident claimed by the Sherman family, a huge seemingly intelligent wolf-like animal with piercing red eyes was shot at point-blank range with a heavy calibre handgun and also a hunting rifle, yet the giant wolf reportedly wandered away unscathed.[18] 'The sound of the bullet hitting flesh and bone near the shoulder was unmistakable. The wolf recoiled but stood calmly,' the book recounts. 'Then, with a last unhurried look at the stunned family, the wolf turned slowly and began to trot away across the grass.' What caused the Sherman family to leave the ranch once and for all was when their dogs went off chasing glowing orbs of light into the trees, never to be seen again.

These were sensational (and, no doubt, many would say, implausible) claims that required independent corroboration to be believed. From what was publicly revealed about the research, the enormous amount of data known to have been collected by NIDS, such as video, electromagnetic radiation measurements, analysis of soil and cattle mutilation samples, expert reports and blood tests, did not support these extraordinary claims. If red-eyed giant wolves and sasquatches truly frequent the ranch, they were very shy when Bob Bigelow's investigators turned on their cameras.

Another intriguing character involved with the NIDS Skinwalker Ranch investigations was a now retired former US Army special forces and military intelligence Colonel John Alexander, who worked on a notorious US Defence Department remote viewing program in the 1970s and 1980s. He was one of the Pentagon 'Jedi warriors' exploring fringe ideas like purported psychic phenomena and remote viewing as potential non-lethal weapons. It was John Alexander who initiated what *New York Times* reporter Howard Blum revealed in 1990 to be a secret UFO Working Group at the Pentagon, evaluating UAP sightings and investigating alleged unexplained objects entering Earth from orbit.[19] Alexander was one of the first NIDS employees to go on watch at the ranch in the 1990s and, he claimed, 'many extraordinary events would happen with our highly skilled scientists observing'.[20] In one instance he said a ranch surveillance camera on one pole was damaged, with wires ripped out, cut and duct tape completely removed, yet a second camera oriented directly towards the damaged camera detected nothing when it undoubtedly should have recorded it happening. 'Considering the amount of physical damage that occurred, for the entire event to have happened in a little over a second (or between video frames) is simply out of the question,' he wrote.[21]

Alexander also elaborated on the extraordinary, purported sighting of a humanoid creature emerging from a three-dimensional portal on the ranch. At 2.30 am one night in August 1997, two NIDS scientists, watching from an escarpment, spotted a dim light that appeared in the vicinity of the road below them. It grew slightly in size and intensity until it was about four feet in diameter. It hovered about three feet above the ground and a third dimension was noted, giving it the appearance of a tunnel. Alexander recounted how 'the researchers were able to see the events that unfolded quite clearly. A moving dark shape appeared in the tunnel and came to the surface. Then the humanoid-like creature of considerable size –

an estimated six-foot tall and four hundred pounds – using arms pulled itself out of the tunnel of light and landed on the road. Shortly thereafter the creature walked off into the darkness …'.[22] Not surprisingly, claims of such bizarre paranormal events were met with derision from debunkers who correctly charged that little if any of the witness testimony was supported by any independent publicly released data.

But the scope of Bigelow's private NIDS investigations went beyond the Skinwalker Ranch and much of what NIDS uncovered remains confidential. The author has obtained documents previously held by the late Apollo 14 astronaut Edgar Mitchell, who died in February 2016. They shed more light on the extensive early work done in the late 1990s by Bigelow's NIDS investigators into both UFOs and cattle mutilations. Mitchell, long a proponent of research into UAPs, served on the science advisory board of NIDS and he retained some of the confidential NIDS research reports from Skinwalker and other areas visited by the Bigelow-funded investigation team.

Intriguingly, the documents show that NIDS was investigating suspected UAP-related cattle mutilations right across Utah, Nevada and New Mexico in August 1997, including a dead cow with strange haemorrhaging on its back. The NIDS report ventured this was caused by 'being dropped from a height'.[23] Another report, in September 1997, detailed interviews with UFO eyewitnesses in Dulce, New Mexico, and the investigation of a five-day-old cow mutilation in Los Brasos. NIDS investigators recorded that the poor animal's teats were missing, and its anus and tongue had been excised. They found no aberrant electromagnetic readings. Curiously, there were multiple overturned cow pats in a straight line stretching 76 metres south-west of the animal that had clearly been blown up to six metres from where they had originally been anchored to the grass. It is amusing to think of the NIDS paranormal investigation team utilising their multiple doctorates to test the adherence of cow pats but that is exactly what they did. The report reads, 'We also experimentally kicked cow pats and showed that it is difficult to move them 20 feet from their original place. We concluded that some strong wind velocity or turbulence had been responsible for overturning the cow patties [sic] near the animal. It was intriguing that no evidence of similar disturbance was in any other part of the property.'[24]

The documented Dulce UFO eyewitness reports include testimony from members of the local Jicarilla Apache tribe, including Hoyt Velarde, the then executive director of the Department of Public Safety for Dulce, with responsibilities over the police, fire and emergency services in the town.[25] Velarde told the NIDS team about an incident in 1987, when he was on a night patrol with another officer in a canyon near Dulce and they both witnessed a massive mile-long (1.6 km) UAP. The two officers first noticed a small soundless orange light about 1000 feet (300 metres) overhead. 'It was then he noticed as the light moved nearer, it was located on the edge of a huge black structure that moved slowly and silently. The object blacked out the stars and both Hoyt and his co-worker watched the object as it moved over them in the canyon … He could tell that the object was rhombus or parallelogram shaped with sides sloping upwards for a great distance. He had no way of estimating how far upwards it went, but he repeatedly affirmed that it was huge … Hoyt said that the object was about a mile from end to end. It was black and featureless except for the single light on its leading edge.'[26]

The previously undisclosed 1997 NIDS documents detail how Velarde also witnessed an egg-shaped craft while working on his father's farm many years earlier in 1964. Kelleher quoted Velarde saying, 'the craft was the same as that seen by [New Mexico Police Sergeant Lonnie] Zamora in Socorro the same year. They were sleeping on the top of the hill. The craft was about twenty feet long and it moved about a hundred feet above the trees. The craft glowed and lit up the cows, the cattle were not perturbed. It was dark but Hoyt [Velarde] saw the shape and the colour without difficulty, saying that the colour was like ivory or alabaster.'[27] The NIDS team investigated another 1997 incident where Velarde came across a small area of burning brush on his ranch. 'Upon investigating, he found three dead cows with tongues, anuses and other organs missing. One animal had its lips and the jaw skin missing.' The NIDS team went to the site and confirmed the mutilation to the three dead cows; curiously, the carcasses, shrivelled and dried out, were apparently untouched by scavengers.[28]

In the same confidential report, another local, Merl Elote, the director of the Game and Fish Department of Dulce, told the NIDS team how he witnessed a craft 75 feet (23 metres) in diameter with a single bright light; it was hovering and rotating. In a sighting two weeks earlier, Elote's brother and brother-in-law reported the same phenomenon; this time they were even closer and, although their truck engine and radios were off, the speakers began to blare loudly with static noise. One of the NIDS investigators working with Colm Kelleher during this 1997 New Mexico NIDS investigation was Gabe Valdez, a New Mexico State policeman who had strong links with the Jicarilla Apache tribe in Dulce. After his NIDS work, Valdez, who died in 2011, went public with extraordinary (and, although he did not know it at the time, almost certainly dubious) claims that a clandestine US government agency was using secret underground 'UFO bases' in the Dulce area for experiments, which explained the spate of cattle mutilations. What is intriguing is that we now know that the admitted source of these almost certainly bunkum claims was a disinformation program run from within the US Air Force itself.

In *Project Beta*,[29] researcher and author Greg Bishop told this weird story of how Valdez and a businessman named Paul

Bennewitz were fed disinformation by an officer with the US Air Force's Office of Special Investigations named Richard Doty. Doty is a notorious (but oddly likeable) villain in ufology; he has since claimed in retirement that he was under orders to lie to Valdez and Bennewitz to distract them from secret unspecified US Air Force projects that Doty was ordered to misidentify as extra-terrestrial. Intriguing then to read in the Ed Mitchell archive documents that what might have fuelled Valdez's willingness to believe Doty's disinformation was the statements of multiple local witnesses, who verified that there was indeed highly unusual UAP activity happening around Dulce. All this was detailed in the confidential document written by Colm Kelleher in 1997.[30] It suggests perhaps that the now-discredited conspiracy theory with which Bennewitz and Valdez later went public had its origins in what were in fact well-corroborated witness sightings. It was the US Air Force itself that made the implausible extrapolation of this evidence to include dubious allegations of underground alien bases at Dulce.

The debunking of the Valdez/Bennewitz conspiracy theory ensured that any claims of strange UAP activity around Dulce were treated with extreme scepticism by all mainstream media. Of course, this was exactly what any agency wanting to hide something in the mountains of New Mexico likely hoped would happen. If the government was testing some new technology in the hills around Dulce, few people would believe it after the discredited Dulce underground UFO base stories. After reading the NIDS' files, it became clear Bigelow's investigators suspected the government was up to something in the Dulce hills.

It is clear that the rumour of an underground base grew from genuine sightings by curious locals who walked the mountains. Kelleher's NIDS report contains interviews with multiple members of the Jicarilla Apache community who claimed in September 1997 to have witnessed not only hovering UAPs but even to have stumbled across a mysterious ventilation shaft dug into Mount Archuleta. Witnesses Charlie Davis and Edmund Gomez also found campsites that had been covered over with great care; the inference was that evidence of covert activity had been erased. 'Charlie described how "they" [presumably, the government] blew the side of the mountain off, all the trees were dead, presumably in order to hide something underneath. The ventilation shafts were cut into the rock with a very smooth instrument. Definitely not a natural fissure or a hole in the rock, obviously carved. A lot of draughted air was coming out strongly … Very convinced that there is a base under the mountain. Charlie agreed that he has seen plenty of craft up on Mount Archuleta,' the NIDS report reads.

The report also detailed how Dulce's Chief of Police admitted he thought there was something weird going on with UAPs and cattle mutilations. Raleigh Tafoya Sr, chief for nearly 30 years, 'was derisive about the FBI report in 1980 on cattle mutilations and even more derisive of the investigative ability of the FBI investigator … who, he said, insulted the intelligence of ranchers who had lost animals to cattle mutilations in the 1970s'. Photographs taken with two cameras by two people at one of the mutilation sites showed three round spherical airborne objects that were not visible to the photographers at the time the pictures were taken.[31]

Robert Bigelow is a shrewd and successful billionaire businessman, and most of what his NIDS team discovered across the US from 1995 to 2004 remains confidential. Bigelow is also a space industry entrepreneur who believes the UAPs are real craft. He is keen to gain an advantage in the new technology space race, so it is not unreasonable to speculate that the reason he keeps his investigations into UAPs secret is because he wants to be the first to develop the mythical anti-gravitic and electro-magnetic technology that his scientists suggest must be propelling them. In 1998, he founded Bigelow Aerospace, a space technology company based in Las Vegas, Nevada. It is prudent to surmise that he felt he got sufficient return on his NIDS research investment to justify the expense of dispatching his highly qualified investigators around the country for a solid decade of research throughout the 1990s. His archive would provide fascinating reading.

Chapter 11

Tic Tacs from Space

The morning of 14 November 2004 marks probably the most well-verified UAP event in history, although it would take 13 more years for the story to become widely known. On a clear day in the north-eastern Pacific Ocean, about 100 kilometres off the coast at a mid-point between the US city of San Diego and the coastal town of Ensenada in Mexico, the behemoth aircraft supercarrier USS *Nimitz* was undergoing preparatory training with other vessels in its carrier strike group before deploying to the Middle East. A huge swathe of ocean and sky was closed for the exercise.

The *Nimitz* is an awesome symbol of American naval might, but it was actually the accompanying Ticonderoga-class guided missile cruiser USS *Princeton* that was providing air defence protection with its then brand-new SPY-1 Aegis radar system. The *Princeton* has a passive electronically scanning radar system, which provided 360-degree coverage for the entire carrier group – still the pinnacle of current sensor technology. Unlike conventional radar, which sees a target every time the antenna rotates, the SPY-1 Aegis system is a phased array that can track hundreds of targets in all directions simultaneously.

Over the previous four days, the *Princeton*'s Operations Specialist Senior Chief Kevin Day, who was in charge of coordinating the systems that protect the entire carrier group, was increasingly concerned by anomalous radar tracks he and his team detected on their screens. Since 10 November he had tracked numerous unidentified aerial objects with no transponder return, closely clustering in groups of five to ten at a time at an altitude far above normal commercial or military aviation traffic. He verified what he saw on the *Princeton*'s CEC, the Cooperative Engagement System, which took all the radars from every source and merged them into one picture. 'I am very sure these things were real; they were solid objects,' Day tells me from his home in a beautiful part of high-country Oregon in a phone interview.[1]

The UAPs were first spotted somewhere above 80,000 feet (24,383 metres) tracking south towards the carrier fleet from around San Clemente Island (off San Diego) at an unusually slow speed for that altitude of 100 knots.[2] Aside from a weather balloon, only a handful of terrestrial aviation vehicles in history can fly that high; none fit the cluster of objects that the *Princeton*'s sensors saw. USS *Princeton* Petty Officer Gary Voorhis checked the radar system for false returns. It was recalibrated and no problems were detected. Voorhis also physically confirmed the objects were where the sensors were telling them they were. After taking a relative bearing of the objects seen on screen, he also scanned the sky through a pair of powerful binoculars. He saw something there, luminescing and hovering in the distance. 'I couldn't make out any detail at all. They were hovering there, then in an instant, they'd dart off to another direction and stop again,' Voorhis tells me by phone from the US.[3] 'I also saw them at night; they'd emit a phosphorus glow and you can see them much easier than in the day.'[4] Late on that 14 November morning, in the *Princeton*'s Combat Information Centre, Senior Chief Day again saw a cluster of 14 unidentified objects on his screen; this time, he confirmed the *Nimitz*'s radar was seeing the same thing. The aircraft carrier also sent up one of its airborne early-warning aircraft – an E2 Hawkeye – and it detected the closest object on its radar. The multiple corroboration of returns from different radar systems reassured Day that it was extremely unlikely these anomalous objects on his radar screens were false readings.

The Senior Chief was stunned by what he saw next. On his screen, the cluster of UAPs was at one moment somewhere about 80,000 feet or higher, some were lower at 28,000 feet. Then, instantly (Day calculates it to be 0.78 of a second) the UAPs plummeted to hover at a range of different altitudes, spanning from 28,000 feet to one craft hanging just 50 feet above the surface of the ocean. Day gave a memorable quote to a UFO conference in March 2019: 'It's raining UFOs. It was going choo, choo, choo, choo, choo down to the surface of the water,' he recalled.[5] In our interview, Day tells me he learned from crewmen who worked in the anti-ballistic missile defence area of the *Princeton* that they actually tracked some of these objects that day from orbit. 'Some of these things came from space,' he tells me. 'I didn't see them directly on my radar, but I know some came from orbit. We aren't alone, Ross.'[6] It is quite clear this whole event has had a profound effect on Kevin Day, that what he saw that day has rocked his world view.

What makes this sighting so astounding is that such a rate of acceleration and immediate stopping is impossible with known technologies. One study has estimated that the objects were moving at 104,895 miles an hour (168,812 km/h) at the midway point with a ridiculous acceleration of 12,250 g-forces.[7] If the objects truly did disappear from a stationary position to out of sight within a second, as accounts from Day suggest, then the maths done by the Scientific Coalition for UAP Studies suggests an even faster peak velocity of 281,520 mph (453,062 km/h). Suffice to say, it was crazy fast. Nearly two decades later, there is still nothing known to be capable of flying anywhere near that fast anywhere on Earth.

Moreover, the g-forces caused by the acceleration that Day saw on his screen make human survival impossible. Most fighter pilots can pull a maximum of about 9-G before they start to black out; even the sturdiest planes will disintegrate beyond about 15 to 17-G. The estimated 12,250-G pulled by these UAPs to zoom from 80,000 feet to hovering just above the ocean would reduce any human body to a bloody soup. Within a few hours of this sighting, the USS *Nimitz* planned to launch as many as 30 aircraft and more were scheduled to be joining the carrier group exercise from San Diego. Kevin Day decided that these strange UAPs posed a serious threat to air navigation. The swarm of unknown objects was now hovering at the lower altitudes where the planes for which he was responsible would be flying. Day recommended to the *Nimitz's* Captain James Smith that they send out aircraft to take a look, and the captain concurred.

What happened next was awe-inspiring, turning basic laws of physics and perceived holy writ constraints on known flight and propulsion limitations on their head. It was so mind-blowingly outside anyone's known experience that some might even be tempted to call it magic. As science fiction writer Arthur C. Clarke famously said, 'Any sufficiently advanced technology is indistinguishable from magic.' The most powerful navy on the planet was about to be humbled by a UAP in an aerial dogfight.

About 2 pm that afternoon the pilot of an FA-18 Hornet, Lieutenant Colonel Douglas Kurth, was directed by the *Princeton* to the closest UAP on their radar screen. Somewhere about 100 kilometres south-west of the *Nimitz*, Kurth arrived at the intercept point, but all he saw was a circular disturbance on the surface of the ocean, 50–100 metres in size. He later told an old fighter jet buddy turned journalist, Paco Chierici (who was the first to tell this now-legendary story), that the white water reminded him of a sinking ship.[8] As luck would have it, one of the carrier group's most senior pilots was already in the air. Strikefighter Squadron 41 ('The Black Aces') commanding officer David Fravor was in one FA-18F Super Hornet and his wingman, a serving female pilot who wishes to stay anonymous, was in another. Both pilots also had a weapons systems officer in their jets' backseats. All four witnesses later told much the same story of what has become one of the most compelling UAP encounters in history.

Thirty minutes into what they expected to be a routine exercise, both fighters were told they were being redirected to a 'real world situation'; they were given a heading and told to intercept an object at 20,000 feet. The pilots were asked if they were carrying any ordnance (live weapons or munitions such as missiles). They had none. But the inquiry was an indication that those watching the screens back on the *Princeton* feared things might get serious. When he reached the target point – the 'merge plot', where his radar signature matched the same position that the UAP was detected – and stared down from his FA-18 cockpit at 20,000 feet, Commander Fravor saw white water on the ocean surface below. Because the disturbance was roughly the size of a 737, he was worried that a commercial airliner might have crashed into the sea. He descended to get a better look. Remaining above, weapons systems officer Lieutenant Commander Slaight and his pilot thought it might be a submarine that was part of the exercise, but this was later ruled out by the *Nimitz's* intelligence officer in a post-flight debriefing. Subsequent evidence suggested something was under the water; USS *Princeton* Petty Officer Gary Voorhis says his sensors showed an underwater object, moving at an incredible 500 knots.[9] Whatever this strange underwater object was, it was most definitely not a craft officially acknowledged as within any country's known technological capabilities.

Descending, Commander Fravor was then shocked to discern what he can only describe as a featureless giant white 'Tic Tac'-candy shaped object with what looked like two appendages below its belly; it was hovering just above the surface of the ocean over the disturbance in the water. The Tic Tac, roughly the length of his FA-18 jet, had no windows, no visible engines, no wings, no exhaust or smoke, and no discernible markings. It was moving erratically, flitting around just above the sea. 'White, 40-foot long, just hovering over the water. Forward, back, left, right. There's no rotor wash, there's no wings. Nothing,' Fravor told *Fox News'* Tucker Carlson.[10] As Fravor descended to take a closer look, the UAP then began mirroring his movement. The Tic Tac ascended, tracking Fravor's FA-18 as if it was on the opposite hand on a clockface. This was a chilling moment for Fravor because the mirroring told him that, whatever this object was, it was intelligently responding to his fighter jet's descent. Back on board the USS *Princeton* in the Combat Information Centre everyone in the room was tense, listening to both fighter pilots' increasingly stressed communications over the speaker system. Five radar operators were each tracking the event in real time, imagery from the *Princeton*'s multiple sensor systems displayed on their screens in front of them.

As Fravor realised the object was actually ascending to close with his fighter jet, he yelled: 'Oh God. I'm engaged. I'm engaged. Oh shit!'[11] Right at that very moment the 14 other unidentified targets on the *Princeton*'s radar screen were also tracked plummeting from above 80,000 feet towards the ocean.[12] 'Pilots are screaming and everyone on the radio is screaming,' Kevin Day recalls.[13] From above, Fravor's colleague, Lieutenant Commander Jim Slaight, the weapons systems officer in the second jet, also saw the giant Tic Tac. Slaight described it as having defined edges but with a fuzzy looking border around it. 'It looked like what the heat waves would look like coming off a hot paved road or what the carrier deck looked like if you looked across it when in the Gulf in the Middle East,' he recalls.[14] He also watched as the object completed a tight circle around Fravor's plane. It stopped and, after hovering for a couple of seconds, it shot off.

'It was there … then it rifled out of sight in a split second,' Slaight remembers. 'It was as if the object was shot out of a rifle. There was no gradual acceleration or spooling up period, it just shot out of sight immediately. I have never seen anything like it before or since. No human could have withstood that kind of acceleration.' Twice, Fravor tried to lock his jet's radar onto the Tic Tac target but his system would not lock. It crossed his mind later that his system had been jammed by whatever or whoever was in the object. 'It's in a climb. We're in a descent. We're getting a great look at it. This whole thing takes probably about five minutes from the time we show up. I get over to the 8 o'clock position and it's over at the 2 o'clock position. I decide I'm going to go and see what it is and it's about 2000 feet below me. And I cut across the circle and as I get within about a half mile of it, it rapidly accelerates to the south in about two seconds and disappears … well above supersonic. Like a bullet out of a gun, it took off,' Fravor said.

So many weird things happened that November day that it is easy to overlook the significance of what happened next. Fravor and his wingman were told by the *Princeton* to fly to a prearranged rendezvous point 100 kilometres distant, which was known as the 'cap point'. This was an assigned latitude and longitude reference that Fravor had used earlier as an rendezvous position, but it was not a specific grid reference that the USS *Princeton* at any stage had transmitted to the jets on an open channel. The pilots were simply told to return to their prearranged cap point. It would have been unsettling when, as they were en route, the USS *Princeton* radioed, 'You're not going to believe this. It's at your cap.'[15] One of the UAPs was clearly tracked on the AEGIS radar hovering at 24,000 feet, right at the very spot where Fravor and his wingman were headed. Surely, no coincidence; it was as if the UAP was letting them know it was way ahead of them. No one knows how the UAP knew where the cap point was, but it suggests the UAP knew a lot more about the US Navy than the navy knew about it.

In Tucker Carlson's *Fox News* interview with Dave Fravor, the host asked if the performance characteristic of the Tic Tac was even possible with known human technology. This was the most revealing moment of the interview. Dave Fravor had clearly made a momentous decision to speak out. He knew that, for decades, military pilots rarely spoke about sightings like this. Fravor visibly gulped; he stared intently down the barrel of the camera, pressed his lips together as if he had resolved to keep on going, took a deep breath, and then the former Black Aces Squadron commander showed his hand. 'I believe,' David Fravor says, 'as do the other folks that were on the flight that, we – when we visually saw it, that it was something not from this world.'[16]

The significance of this 2004 Tic Tac encounter event is immense. For years, one of the standard military lines used to defuse public concern about UAPs has been that, after official investigation the object, whatever it was, 'is no threat to national security'. But surely, there could be no bigger threat to national security than the realisation that was hammered home to the US Navy that November afternoon in 2004 – that there was an unknown technology operating in our skies, oceans and possibly even outer space, which was far beyond the best human technology. It was almost as if the objects were teasing the American battle fleet that day. Inside the USS *Princeton*'s Combat Information Centre astonished operators watched as, once Fravor and his wingman returned to the USS *Nimitz*, in a fraction of a second, the swarm of other objects that had descended towards the ocean shot back above 80,000 feet. They resumed tracking south at a gentle 100 knots as if nothing had happened, as if a dogfight with the US Navy was a minor distraction to their high-altitude afternoon cruise. Kevin Day believes some of the objects were underwater just before they zoomed back up to 80,000 feet, the upper atmosphere, 'maybe even higher because it was above the scan volume of our radar at the time'.[17] As Commander Fravor later pointed out, any craft flying above 80,000 feet (24,380 metres) is on its way to space: 'Just think of the physics – 80,000 feet is where you can start to see the curvature of the Earth. It's considered space; they're coming from above that.'[18]

What clinched the evidence for the 2004 Tic Tac UAP sighting was that it was captured on multiple independent sensor systems, including video. As Commander Fravor and his wingman returned to the USS *Nimitz* from their Tic Tac encounter that 14 November afternoon, a third pair of aircraft headed out. One of the pilots, Lieutenant Chad Underwood, had what is called an ATFLIR pod on his jet. This is an electro-optical targeting pod that fighter jets use to navigate and direct bombs. Its combined thermographic (heat-detecting) camera, low-light television camera and laser rangefinder make it a perfect piece of kit for chasing and videoing an evasive UAP. En route, Underwood's weapons systems officer checked the cap point where the previous pilots Dave Fravor and his female pilot wingman last saw the UAP and, sure enough, there it was waiting for them. Disturbingly, as the US Navy jet tried to lock on to the object with its radar, there were clear indications of deliberate jamming, which Commander Fravor says could be perceived as a hostile act, as technically an act of war'.[19]

The weapons systems officer sitting behind Underwood was eventually able to lock on to the object using the pod's infra-red mode, meaning it showed up on his screen as a white object in a black background. What was most revealing about the infra-red mode, however, was what could not be seen. There was no sign of any jet exhaust or of any gases at all blasting from the UAP, as you would expect to see from any conventional propulsion system. 'It was simply hanging in mid-air,' Chierici wrote. The video showed the object eventually shooting off screen with a sudden dart to the left. The pilot who shot the video on his ATFLIR, Lieutenant Chad Underwood, took 15 years to finally go public with what he saw, only speaking in December 2019 to *New York Magazine*:

'The thing that stood out to me the most was how erratic it was behaving. And what I mean by "erratic" is that its changes in altitude, air speed, and aspect were just unlike things that I've ever encountered before flying against other air targets. It was just behaving in ways that aren't physically normal. That's what caught my eye. Because, aircraft, whether they're manned or unmanned, still have to obey the laws of physics. They have to have some source of lift, some source of propulsion. The Tic Tac was not doing that. It was going from like 50,000 feet to, you know, a hundred feet in like seconds, which is not possible.' The awesome implication from what Underwood conclusively filmed was that someone, somewhere, had indeed achieved a technological breakthrough that showed such manoeuvres were actually possible.[20]

The ATFLIR video of the encounter was downloaded when Lieutenant Underwood returned to the USS *Nimitz*; conspiracy theories abound among crewmen who saw the video while the ship was still at sea. Some say that the public has still not seen the full video obtained by the US Navy that day, that it was either a higher resolution or much longer in duration. A former Petty Officer Jason Turner, on board the USS *Princeton* in 2004, claimed to have seen a fuller version of the video on a console monitor in what is called the ship's Signal Exploitation Space. He described the Tic Tac making a series of manoeuvres not seen on the very brief 76-second clip later released by the Pentagon. 'This thing was going berserk, like making turns. It's incredible the amount of G-forces that it would put on a human. It made a manoeuvre like they were chasing it straight on, it was going with them, then this thing stopped turning, just gone. In an instant. The video you see now, that's just a small snippet in the beginning of the whole video,' Turner said.[21] System technician Petty Officer Gary Voorhis testified that he saw a much clearer video that was eight to ten minutes long. Kevin Day explains to me that it is standard in such an intercept for him to order 'tapes on' onboard the aircraft before the intercept begins; he estimates the full Tic Tac video would have to be at least ten minutes long.

There is a lot about the Tic Tac story that is mystifying. It was exceedingly strange that one of the most powerful carrier battle fleets in the world engaged with an apparently intelligent technology that was clearly vastly superior, but that the navy appeared incurious. Fleet commanders made no effort to follow the dozens of UAPs that were tracked on radar continuing to drift slowly southwards at 100 knots after the dogfight encounter. Kevin Day recalls asking his captain on the *Princeton* afterwards what he thought the object was. 'He told me, "I think the objects were spontaneously forming ice falling from space".' Day laughs at the absurdity of such a conclusion. His captain left him with the clear impression he knew a lot more than he was letting on about the phenomenon.[22] No further jets from the USS *Nimitz* were sent up to engage the craft. The pilot who videoed the encounter, Chad Underwood, says that soon after landing, he answered a few questions in a phone call with someone from NORAD, the North American Aerospace Defence Command,[23] but no pilots were formally debriefed at the time about what occurred. What the returning pilots did get was a good-natured ribbing about their 'flying saucer' sighting from the USS *Nimitz*'s deck crew, some of whom were wearing tin-foil hats in jest.

Curiously, it was only after the Tic Tac video mysteriously surfaced in 2007 on a German website that someone began investigating. Commander Fravor did not disclose who the government investigator was, or where they were from, but he said he was first questioned about the Tic Tac incident in 2009.[24] It was very clear that, behind the scenes, the US Navy took the Tic Tac encounter extremely seriously indeed. When former fighter pilot Paco Chierici researched his 2015 story about the Tic Tac incident, he learned that all of the personnel involved, including from the E2-Hawkeye, had now been interviewed. Someone was doing an investigation, very discreetly.

To add to the intrigue surrounding the Tic Tac encounter, there was also the whiff of a cover-up. The morning after the dogfight, Senior Chief Kevin Day went to the USS *Princeton's* communications room to get a copy of the radio communications from the previous day so that he could get the data he needed to write up an after-action report. It was routine for all communications to be permanently stored on optical disk. But he was shocked to learn that the data for the Tic Tac encounter had been wiped. 'As it turns out, all of our comms had been erased. Now, every time you key a mic on the ship, it stamps the optical disk with a date and time stamp. All the date and time stamps were there but the actual comms were all missing. And that was another anomalous thing because as far as I know I don't even think that's possible. But it happened,' Day recalls.[25]

Immediately after the incident, two unknown individuals, presumably serving military, arrived by navy helicopter on board the *Nimitz*. Petty Officer Patrick Hughes, whose job included securing the hard drives from the airborne early-warning E2 Hawkeye aircraft, was ordered to hand the 'data bricks', as they are called, to two air force guys'.[26] On board the *Princeton*, Gary Voorhis was also ordered to turn over the data tapes from the ship's Combat Engagement Centre and, in defiance of normal procedure, he was also ordered to erase everything including blank tapes.

In April 2019, aviation journalist Tyler Rogoway, who writes for *The War Zone* blog on Time Inc's *The Drive*, underlined just how uncomfortable the questions were that the 2004 Tic Tac sighting posed for the most powerful nation on Earth. He wrote that 'The main revelation is that technology exists that is capable of performing flying manoeuvres that shatter our perceptions of propulsion, flight controls, material science, and even physics. Let me underline this again for you, the *Nimitz* encounter with the Tic Tac *proved* that exotic technology that is widely thought of as the domain of science fiction actually exists. *It is real.* It isn't the result of altered perception, someone's lucid dream, a stray weather balloon, or swamp gas. Someone or something has crossed the technological Rubicon and has obtained what some would call the Holy Grail of aerospace engineering.'[27]

Chapter 12

The Hunt for 'The Big Secret'

In about 2008, one of the most powerful politicians in Washington DC, Democrat Senator Harry Reid, received an intriguing letter written by a senior US Defence Intelligence Agency (DIA) scientist (likely a physicist named James Lacatski, although he was never named), whose world view had been transformed by extraordinary events he witnessed at Skinwalker Ranch. As Reid somewhat implausibly tells it, that letter alone prompted a new secret multi-million-dollar investigation by the US military into Unidentified Aerial Phenomena. I suspect the Nevada Senator was holding his cards tight and that, in 2008, he knew much more than he was prepared to publicly reveal to justify his push for the UAPs to be investigated.

Now retired, Harry Reid is a political veteran, born the dirt-poor son of a rock miner in the desert town of Searchlight, Nevada, serving first as a Congressman in the Lower House from 1983 and then as a Senator from 1987 to 2017. Over his 30 years of Senate service, he rose to become one of the most influential senators in the Democratic Party, reaching Senate Majority Leader. He also served for two years on one of the Senate's most powerful committees, the Select Committee on Intelligence. Having served as both a Senate Minority and Majority leader, Reid was for years one of the so-called 'Gang of Eight', entitled to be briefed into highly classified intelligence matters including Waived Unacknowledged Special Access Programs. So, if anyone knows for sure if the US has ETs or a spacecraft tucked away in a cave somewhere in the desert, the now 80-year-old former Senator Harry Reid is likely one of those who was briefed into The Big Secret. Reid has long admitted a strong interest in UAPs. One of the secret sites he visited during his term was the Area 51 air force base in his Nevada home state, the scene of so much conspiratorial speculation about strange glowing craft and science-fiction-style future aerospace technology.

It was billionaire aerospace entrepreneur Robert Bigelow who sent Reid the letter from the senior Defence Intelligence Agency physicist. Reid did not name the scientist, but he said he visited Bigelow's Skinwalker Ranch, presumably about 2007–08, and what the DIA scientist saw there convinced him it was a real phenomenon that needed to be investigated. Bob Bigelow has also revealed that the DIA scientist told him that what shocked him at the ranch was an incident where a three-dimensional object suddenly materialised in front of him, which looked like the triangular metallic 'bent bell' cover art on the front of the Mike Oldfield album *Tubular Bells*. 'That's the closest thing I can come to as to what the structure of this looked like,' Bigelow says he was told.[1]

Senator Reid also says the scientist was clearly very rattled by his purported paranormal Skinwalker experience and that he told the Senator he felt it was time such phenomena be properly investigated. Reid claims that this one incident prompted him to seek Congressional funding for a study.[2] I suspect Harry Reid was being deliberately vague and that he knew a lot more from the classified intelligence world to prompt his interest in the phenomenon than just that one DIA scientist's letter. But the letter gave him the excuse he needed. The Senator approached his colleagues, Democrat Senator Daniel Inouye and Republican Senator Ted Stevens, to get $22 million funding for a study into the UAP mystery. 'We found that there were a lot of things unknown about what these things are. Now, I don't know what they are. I don't know, okay? I have no idea. But I do know we should continue studying,' he says enigmatically.[3]

Senator Daniel Inouye was a World War Two war hero who died in 2012, a recipient of the Medal of Honor for conspicuous gallantry, the highest military award in the US. A solid patriot, Inouye was well known for warning of the risks posed by covert government power. During the Iran-Contra Senate investigations into secret US military assistance given to Iran and the Nicaraguan Opposition, Inouye was very critical of those he held culpable for the scandal. He decried their apparent notion of 'a shadowy government with its own air force, its own navy, its own fundraising mechanism, and the ability to pursue its own ideas of the national interest, free from all checks and balances, and free from the law itself. It is an elitist vision of government that trusts no one.'[4] It was telling that Inouye now chose to support an investigation into UAPs. What had he and Reid learned that compelled them to spend $22 million of taxpayer money to investigate UAPs?

Reid's other backer, Senator Ted Stevens, who died in a plane crash only two years later, also needed no convincing; he admitted he saw UAPs as a pilot during World War Two. 'Whatever you want, you get it from me,' Stevens told Senator Reid. He explained he saw a UAP during one wartime flight. 'We need to take a look at this,' he told Reid.[5]

Much of the Pentagon funding went to a Robert Bigelow company, Bigelow Aerospace Advanced Space Studies (BAASS). Bigelow hired several of the same scientists who had served on his private decade-long National Institute for Discovery Science investigations. Not giving a damn what anybody thinks of his opinions, Bigelow makes no secret of his view that alien intelligences have been visiting this planet for a long time. He has described how his grandparents had a close encounter with a zooming UAP that filled up the windscreen of their car and then took off at a right angle and shot away into the distance. He is so fascinated with aliens that an alien logo is painted on the exterior of his massive Bigelow Aerospace building in Las Vegas. He even went on the top-rating US public affairs program CBS *60 Minutes* and told correspondent Lara Logan that he was 'absolutely convinced' aliens exist.[6]

Logan: 'Do you also believe that UFOs have come to Earth?'

Bigelow: 'There has been and is an existing presence, an ET presence. And I spent millions and millions and millions – I probably spent more as an individual than anybody else in the United States has ever spent on this subject.'

Logan: 'Is it risky for you to say in public that you believe in UFOs and aliens?'

Bigelow: 'I don't give a damn. I don't care.'

Lara: 'You don't worry that some people will say, "Did you hear that guy. He sounds like he's crazy?"'

Bigelow: 'I don't care.'

Logan: 'Why not?'

Bigelow: 'It's not gonna' make a difference. It's not gonna' change reality of what I know.'

Logan: 'Do you imagine that in our space travels we will encounter other forms of intelligent life?'

Bigelow: 'You don't have to go anywhere.'

Logan: 'You can find it here? Where exactly?'

Bigelow's final answer was the most intriguing: 'It's just like right under people's noses.'

Which of course all begs the tantalising question, what is it that Robert T. Bigelow's millions of dollars in research taught him about a supposed extra-terrestrial presence here on Earth that the rest of us do not know? Bigelow did not respond to requests for an interview. He is notoriously media shy, with the *60 Minutes* interview a notable exception. His more controversial research, into what some might dub the magical and mysterious, has always been done in the shadows. One of Bigelow's first hires in 2007 was former USS *Nimitz* FA-18 jet pilot Marine Lieutenant Colonel Douglas Kurth, the first witness to the Tic Tac UAP in November 2004. Just over three years after his involvement in that sighting, Kurth, now a civilian, began work in December 2007 as a program manager for the investigation team. Their UAP investigations began even before the Defence Intelligence Agency money came through in July 2008, when Senator Reid guaranteed the black budget funding for what was to become known by its clunky acronym, AAWSAP. The full title was a mouthful, no doubt intended to be as opaque as possible since this was a secret 'black' UAP investigation program hidden in plain sight on the Pentagon books. AAWSAP stood for the 'Advanced Aerospace Weapons Systems Applications Program'. An invitation to tender for the contract was issued by the Defence Intelligence Agency in August 2008 and Bigelow was the sole bidder, securing $10 million funding for the first year, with a five-year option for the contract.

What sticks out like a sore thumb in all that has been written about the investigation is that, from the very beginning, it was intended to assess what it described as 'threats' to the United States, without ever articulating what those supposed threats were meant to be. Much of the work was done under a different project name – AATIP, the Advanced Aerospace Threat Identification Program – which was funded from the same budget. The contract made no reference at all to UAPs but it was very clear that the 'foreign threat' to be investigated was UAPs.[7] 'In past interviews, [former Senator] Reid has indicated the interested parties at the DIA felt it prudent to avoid any language that might cause someone to realise the underlying focus of the AATIP program was UFOs,' Tim McMillan, a writer specialising in defence and intelligence stories, explained.[8] His story clarified that the contract was just part of a broader investigative program inside the Defence Intelligence Agency, including AATIP, which was clearly all about UAPs even if no one wanted to admit it. Nor was any explanation given for why these strange UAPs might be seen as a 'threat' but perhaps one explanation was that the Tic Tac, which so comprehensively outperformed the best fighter attack jets in the US Air Force, was clearly a potential threat worthy of intense investigation.

In an interview with George Knapp, former National Institute for Discovery Science scientist Dr Eric Davis was one of those brought into the Bigelow investigation team working on the AATIP. In a 2018 radio interview with George Knapp on *Coast to Coast AM*, Davis said, 'The *Threat* in AATIP refers to the fact that the UFO phenomenon has interfered with operations. The phenomenon was officially branded a threat, and the threat had to be studied.'[9] What he was referring to was extensive evidence showing that, for years, UAPs have been tracked and observed interfering with nuclear weapons facilities as well as air force aircraft.

America's foremost expert on this link between UAPs and nuclear weapons is researcher Robert Hastings, the author of *UFOs and Nukes*.[10] In the almost 50 years since 1973, Hastings has personally interviewed more than 150 former US military witnesses to anomalous UAP sighting incidents at nuclear bases, storage areas and test sites. He pieced together incidents at intercontinental ballistic missile (ICBM) sites across the US, including Malmstrom, Minot, F.E. Warren, Ellsworth, Vandenberg and Walker air force bases. He also found evidence UAPs were taking an interest in nuclear weapons storage areas at the air force's Wurtsmith and Loring bases, as well as the RAF Bentwaters base in England. 'It's clear they're tampering with the weapons. Now is it because they have our best interests at heart?' Hastings tells me. 'Is that what's going on? Or do they have a need for this planet and they don't want us to screw it up with radioactivity. Do they plan to invade, and they don't want to inherit a radioactive husk of a world? I doubt that anyone in the Pentagon or in the Soviet, or the Russian [Federation] nowadays, government infrastructure even has the answers to that. I'm not optimistic that anyone on the planet really knows what's going on.'[11] But Hastings is in no doubt that whatever *it* is, it is intelligent and highly advanced.

Former Bigelow NIDS scientist Dr Eric Davis has admitted that his team was responsible for the covert investigation into the 2004 Tic Tac USS *Nimitz* incident and they too reached a dramatic conclusion as to who or what was behind it. In a radio interview, he volunteered his official Defence Intelligence Agency-funded investigation's dramatic final conclusions about the 2004 Tic Tac UAP: 'the take on it is that it's a legitimate UFO ... this is not a technology that is made on Earth by humans, anywhere. ... we came to the conclusion that these are legitimate unidentified objects. They are anomalous. They are real vehicles. They are under intelligent control and they are an advanced technology.' Importantly, Davis suggested the UAPs were also a mystery to his masters at the Defence Intelligence Agency. 'And we got to do something about them because they are interfering with military deployments in the ocean and they have interfered with air force deployments in the atmosphere wherever the air force is flying their planes,' he said.[12]

Dr Davis went on to give Knapp's listeners an astonishing amount of additional detail about supposed US government 'crash retrievals', suggesting the controversial 1947 Roswell crash was indeed a genuine crashed extra-terrestrial spacecraft. 'If you're going to throw your bets on Roswell, your bet is really good,' he said.

Incredible as such claims may sound, independent researchers and witnesses have long asserted there were several other secret craft recoveries in addition to the Roswell event, where purported extra-terrestrial spacecraft were supposedly recovered by the US military during the 1940s and 1950s. (No explanation was ever offered for why these presumably highly advanced craft kept on crashing in remote parts of the US.) So it was intriguing to hear Dr Davis citing one of those other claimed extra-terrestrial spacecraft crashes in his interview with George Knapp – the 5 December 1950 case known as Del Rio, which allegedly involved a crashed craft near the town of Del Rio, Texas, that was subsequently recovered by the US Air Force.

Another purported recovery of an intelligently controlled extra-terrestrial spacecraft is also claimed to have taken place at Aztec, New Mexico, on 25 March 1948. Authors Scott and Suzanne Ramsey and Dr Frank Thayer tracked down an extraordinary number of witnesses to corroborate what they allege was a giant '100-foot diameter (30-metres) flying saucer' found lying on a mesa above Hart Canyon east of the town of Aztec.[13] This craft was also allegedly retrieved by the US military under a cloak of secrecy. The US government's stated position is that such UAP crash recoveries are a fiction; officially, they never happened. I spent several days with the Ramseys in May 2021, walking the Aztec site, and reviewing their extremely detailed evidence, including direct witness sightings of a craft (and purported alien beings). What I come away most sure about is that in 1950 there was a determined effort by the FBI and the air force to smear businessman and scientist Silas Newton, who was pushing the story of a recovered craft at Aztec. Why was there such a determined official hatchet job on Newton if the whole Aztec story was a fiction as has long been suggested? (I would need to see the aliens and the craft for myself to ever be able to accept the Aztec story.)

Talking about his work for the Bigelow BAASS Defence Intelligence Agency contract, Dr Davis went on to tell George Knapp there were indeed recovered ET craft, the information about which had not yet been revealed or published. 'We have crash retrievals,' he went on to repeat, 'and they have been analysed and unfortunately our laboratory diagnostic technologies and our material sciences and the understanding of physics that we had were not advanced enough to be able to make heads or tails of what it is, of what they had their hands on.'

Dr Davis's claims of crash retrievals are shocking in that context because he is a trusted government scientist with a very high top secret compartmentalised security clearance. His interview intimated that he knew what he was saying from his time inside secret government projects. If his claims were untrue, it would not have been unreasonable for an angry US government, embarrassed by such a reckless assertion, to have stripped him of his security classification and to have sacked him from his job at his current employer, the federally funded Aerospace Corporation. But Dr Davis remains a much-valued and trusted government employee at time of writing. Curious.

And it was not just Davis making this claim. Former National Institute of Discovery Science investigator Dr Colm Kelleher went on to investigate UAPs with the BAASS investigation team. In 2004, Kelleher was flatly asked by *Coast to Coast AM*'s Art Bell whether he thought the US military had had contact with aliens.[14] Dr Kelleher replied, 'We have had information over the last several years that seems to indicate that, certainly, pieces of technology have been recovered.' Where is this claim coming from?

To add spice to the mystery, in June 2009, then Senator Harry Reid wrote to the US Secretary of Defence requesting the Advanced

Aerospace Threat Identification Program (AATIP) be given the status of a Special Access Program (SAP). The Senator's letter gave clues as to why such strict classification was now necessary, asserting that 'substantial progress' had been made with the identification of 'several highly sensitive, unconventional aerospace-related findings. Given the current rate of success, the continued study of these subjects will likely lead to technology advancements that in the immediate near-term will require extraordinary protection. Due to the sensitivities of the information surrounding aspects of this program, I require your assistance in establishing a Restricted Special-Access-Program (SAP) with a Bigoted Access List for specific portions of the AATIP.'[15] The Senator was clearly hinting that there might be an imminent breakthrough. The obvious question was, did it have anything to do with the Bigelow team's claims of recovered ET technology?

Reid's letter, leaked to Las Vegas KLAS-TV investigative journalist and Coast to Coast AM host George Knapp, argued for continued support of the existing AATIP program, saying, 'Associated exotic technologies likely involve extremely sophisticated concepts within the world of quantum mechanics, nuclear science, electromagnetic theory, gravitics, and thermodynamics. Given that all of these have the potential to be used with catastrophic effects by adversaries, an unusually high degree of operational security and read-on discretion is required,' the Senator wrote. 'The technological insight and capability gained will provide the US with a distinct advantage of any foreign threats and allow the US to maintain its pre-eminence as a world leader.' It was a strong sell but the Senator's request for Special Access Program status for the Advanced Aerospace Threat Identification Program investigation was rejected.

We now know that the Defence Intelligence Agency's Advanced Aerospace Weapons Systems Applications Program (AAWSAP) investigation was given an extra US$12 million in

2010 appropriations to produce a dozen more reports. But a 2009 Pentagon review determined the reports were of limited value, recommending that upon completion of the contract the project be passed to an agency better suited to oversee it.[16] The Bigelow team's investigations began in late 2008 and reportedly ended in 2012. There is some uncertainty about this because AAWSAP was only funded for two years – $10 million in its first year and $12 million in its second year, a total of $22 million. Most of the Bigelow team were terminated by mid-2010.

There has been speculation that the reason why Senator Reid tried in 2009 to get the Pentagon's UFO investigation program classified as a Special Access Program was because Bigelow's dogged investigators had already tracked down the secret project codenames that pointed to a purported secret UAP program hidden inside the US government and private aerospace, which is supposedly still attempting to re-engineer recovered alien technology. The story goes that the team needed the Special Access Program status so that it could be formally 'read into' the secret UFO program it had discovered. George Knapp was chasing this claim when he asked Senator Reid in 2019 if the reason why he wanted the program to be given Special Access Program status was because he knew of evidence, other studies and programs, 'that had not yet been made public?'. Reid's answer was revealing. He agreed with Knapp's proposition, answering that he knew of, 'Other programs that have been done and information they have, including different pieces of evidence.'[17] It begs the question, was the Senator referring to physical recovered evidence? Could such a claim really be true?

Then in May 2021, in an interview with Gideon Lewis-Kraus of The New Yorker magazine, former Senator Reid went even further with an extraordinary admission:

'I was told for decades that Lockheed had some of these retrieved materials,' he said. 'And I tried to get, as I recall, a classified approval by the Pentagon to have me go look at the stuff. They would not approve that. I don't know what all the numbers were, what kind of classification it was, but they would not give that to me.' Reid told The New Yorker the Pentagon provided him with no explanation for its refusal and he confirmed that was why he'd requested Special Access Program status for AATIP. Reid said, 'Yeah, that's why I wanted them to take a look at it. But they wouldn't give me the clearance.'[18] That same week, former senior US Defence Department official Christopher Mellon told Joe Rogan's podcast audience that he also had multiple 'inside sources' who asserted there was truth to the claims that the US has secretly retrieved alien craft.[19]

At time of writing, as the June deadline for the UAP Taskforce report loomed, Reid and Mellon appeared to be disclosing as much as possible in a bid to try to force the US government to reveal what it knows. I suspect that, as a former member of the Congress' Gang of Eight SAP oversight group, Harry Reid knew full well what the US government was concealing. While being careful never to say outright the US had such alien technology the former Senator came very close to suggesting exactly that, which is mind-blowing in its potential implications. Equally as disturbing is the claim that the Pentagon blocked the Senator's request. If such a senior congressman with oversight responsibilities was not allowed to see what the Pentagon is hiding then it begs the question, who is actually holding these military officials to account?

You could be forgiven for thinking that the US Defence Department UAP investigations were really just a short-lived indulgence to appease Senator Harry Reid and that the Pentagon was never really that interested in the UAP issue. I suspect that is what the Defence Department wanted us all to think. However, the truth was very different.

Chapter 13

Would the President Know?

In late 2011, the Obama White House made a statement on behalf of the president that I suspect it may live to profoundly regret. It responded to a Change.org petition demanding immediate disclosure 'of the US government's knowledge of and communications with extra-terrestrial beings'.[1] In a definitive statement, the first time since 1947 that the executive branch of the US government had issued a formal position in writing on the issue of extra-terrestrials and UAPs, the White House Office of Science and Technology Policy declared, 'The US government has no evidence that any life exists outside our planet, or that an extra-terrestrial presence has contacted or engaged any member of the human race. In addition, there is no credible information to suggest that any evidence is being hidden from the public's eye.'[2] If the White House denial was true, then Dr Eric Davis is a liar, and so are several of his colleagues.

In 2011, former *Los Angeles Times* reporter and author Annie Jacobsen published a history of Area 51 that also gave credence to the seemingly implausible notion that the US had recovered an alien spacecraft at Roswell in 1947, a very big call for a respected historian and mainstream journalist to make after the government's adamant denials. Jacobsen wrote that in July 1947, US Signal Corps engineers tracked two anomalous objects flying across the south-western United States, the craft sometimes hovering before continuing to fly on. One of the flying objects crashed near Roswell and 'immediately, the office of the Joint Chiefs of Staff ... took command and control and recovered the airframe and some propulsion equipment, including the crashed craft's power plant, or energy source'.[3] The craft was nothing like any conventional aircraft, with no wings or tail, a round fuselage and a dome on the top, with secret army memos declassified in 1994 referring to it as a 'flying disc'. Where her book courted most controversy was Jacobsen's extraordinary assertion that what crashed at Roswell was actually Russian, crafted by captured Nazi Germany scientists. Her even more dramatic claim – that bodies found on the craft were those of 'grotesquely deformed'[4] children with unusually large heads and abnormally-shaped oversize eyes – was savaged by sceptics. Jacobsen made the eye-popping assertion that Nazi doctor Josef Mengele made a deal with Stalin just before the end of the war in which he was allowed to continue his eugenics experiments, hence apparently the deformed kids. Joseph Stalin supposedly intended the craft to land at New Mexico and cause a *War of the Worlds*-style panic. Jacobsen's source also claimed the deformed children were 'comatose but still alive'. It is impossible to assess the veracity of Annie Jacobsen's confidential sources other than to speculate that the best way to put a well-respected journalist like Jacobsen off the scent of what happened at Roswell would be to feed her disinformation so absurd that her source's admissions of a recovered craft at Roswell would be largely ignored and ridiculed by the mainstream press. And that is what has generally happened for most of the last few decades every time claims of retrieved alien spacecraft are made.

In February 2015, on his final day as Counsellor to President Obama, John Podesta tweeted, 'Finally, my biggest failure of 2014: Once again not securing the #disclosure of the UFO files. #thetruthisstilloutthere cc: @nytimesDowd'. Podesta had enjoyed huge success securing Executive Order 12958 under President Clinton, declassifying millions of pages of national security documents, including many UAP files. But it was significant that one of Podesta's last acts for Obama was to acknowledge his failure to crack open the door on UAPs.

A month later, in March 2015, President Obama went on *Jimmy Kimmel Live* and Jimmy had the gall to ask him what he knows about aliens, as he does each president. It was one of those interviews where everyone was laughing because the question was all about 'UFOs', but the entire viewing audience was also full-laser-locked onto the president's reaction to see if he would make any admission. Jimmy launched with, 'If I was the president ... the moment I was inaugurated, my hand would still be hot from touching the Bible, and I would immediately race to wherever they hold the files about Area 51 and UFOs. And I would go through everything to find out what happened. Did you do that?'

President Obama (smiling): 'That's why you will not be president. That's the first thing you would do. [laughing] Aaah – the aliens won't let it happen. You'll reveal all their secrets. They exercise strict control over us.'

Jimmy: 'Well, you know, there are a lot of people that are going to examine your facial expressions here [Obama is laughing], every twitch, everything and say – So, did you look, did you see, did you explore?'

President Obama (slightly more serious): 'I – I can't reveal anything.'

Jimmy: 'Oh really. Because President Clinton said he did go right in and he did check and there was nothing.'

President Obama: 'Well you know, that's what we're instructed to say.'[5] (The president is laughing and obviously joking at this point.)

The show entitled its YouTube video of the exchange *President Barack Obama Denies Knowledge of Aliens*, which was misleading, because the one thing the president did not do with Jimmy Kimmel was deny any knowledge of aliens. Obama conspicuously avoided the question.

The other seminal UAP event in 2015 was that punk pop rock star Tom DeLonge quit his band Blink-182. Like a lot of folk, I scoffed when I first read about DeLonge's 'UFO obsession' but, as you will see, he has achieved more than anyone in the past five years to push the US government to admit what it knows about the issue. DeLonge does not put an exact date on an event that convinced him the phenomenon was real but sometime before quitting the band, he camped out with two friends near the secret Area 51 base in Nevada. It was late on a chilly desert night, somewhere north of a small town named Tonopah, which sits midway between Las Vegas and Reno. This is the place to be to see strange glowing craft that go *whoosh* in the middle of the night. DeLonge admits to having been obsessed with UAPs for much of his life. He is absolutely convinced that alien intelligences have been visiting Earth for millennia and equally certain the US government is hiding what it knows about non-human intelligences and their advanced technology. By 2014, DeLonge had also become increasingly fascinated with what is called CE5, Close Encounters of the Fifth Kind. The idea of CE5 is that, by meditating and focusing your mind (and often, by paying thousands of dollars to the 'experts' who teach you how to do it), it is possible to make contact with extra-terrestrial intelligence. And that was what DeLonge was determined to do that night in the desert.

Earlier, DeLonge and his friends had gone through the CE5 protocols, deeply meditating and trying to project their intent into the aether. 'We were up mad late, but nothing happened,' DeLonge recalls. 'I kept telling the guys: if anything was going to happen, it would happen at three in morning, because that's the time when things like this happen. Don't ask me why. We put about four logs on the fire, and everything is illuminated by the fire, and we fall asleep round one or two.'[6] At 3 am, the world-famous rock musician, author and filmmaker woke up hearing dozens of strange voices outside his tent. He says he was completely paralysed. 'My whole body felt like it had static electricity and I open my eyes and the [campfire] is still going and there's a conversation going on outside the tent,' DeLonge recalls. 'It sounded like there were about 20 people there, talking. And instantly my mind goes, "Okay, they're at our campsite, they're not here to hurt us, they're talking about shit, but I can't make out what they're saying. But they're working on something". Then I close my eyes and wake up, and the fire is out, and I have about three hours of lost time.'

Next morning, DeLonge roused his friends and asked if they heard anything. One had slept right through; however, the other said, 'Yes! They were all around our tent. They were talking.' This freaked DeLonge out, a lot, because in his mind it confirmed his experience was not simply sleep paralysis and a lucid dream. To try to understand what had happened to him, he read the works of Professor John Mack, the onetime head of the Psychiatry Department at Harvard Medical School. 'He almost lost his job because he started writing books about UFOs and people getting abducted,' DeLonge says. 'But when you read his books and study what he was doing, a lot of people who have these contacts talk a lot about chatter, like you're in the middle of people working. How fucking crazy is that?'[7] (No doubt, many of you are thinking, very crazy.)

DeLonge is a charismatic and highly intelligent rock star with a taste for hipster beanies, who started writing punk rock songs as a teenage skateboarder and, no doubt, a lot of folk reading this are wondering why he is at all pertinent to the serious investigation of UAPs. But there was a method in DeLonge's splendid seeming madness. By 1999, as Blink-182's lead singer, DeLonge was a megastar, packing stadiums full of fans across the US and around the world. Punk purists mocked the band as more pop than punk; the cranky Sex Pistols veteran punk John Lydon, aka Johnny Rotten, dismissed them as 'a bunch of silly boys',[8] but Blink had the last laugh. In June that year, the band released their hugely popular *Enema of the State* album, featuring buxom porn star Janine Lindemulder in a nurse's uniform donning a rubber glove. One of the new songs was *Aliens Exist*, which owes a lot to the many books and articles on the UAP mystery that DeLonge devoured on his band's endless road trips. He told the *Los Angeles Times* the track was about aliens that come to Earth and 'fly up your butt. And it's true'.[9]

'What if people knew that these were real, I'd leave my closet door open all night,' DeLonge's 'Aliens Exist' lyrics scream to the MTV generation. The more he read about the subject, the more convinced DeLonge became that UAPs were real, but what he craved was hard evidence. *'I know the CIA would say, What you hear is all hearsay, I wish someone would tell me what was right,'* his song laments.

The incredible bonkers, crazy thing about Tom DeLonge's obsession with UAPs is that I am now certain that very senior government officials, claiming to be protecting one of the United States' most closely held secrets, briefed DeLonge on what they assured him was the truth about a genuine UAP cover-up. It is an extraordinary story how this all came to light. If what these senior officials told DeLonge is actually true, then a monstrous lie has been perpetrated. What we can be very sure of is that Tom DeLonge secured astounding access, far more than anyone else studying the phenomenon, speaking secretly with very senior US generals, spies and aerospace executives, whom he claims briefed him on an American seven-decade history of contact with alien intelligences. Maybe they figured, who was ever going to believe a crazy rock star?

For years, DeLonge was publicly mocked as a nutty kook for his fascination with UAPs, his obsession given the indulgence that big-time rock stars get for being a bit eccentric. Even his bandmate Mark Hoppus mocked DeLonge in a *Rolling Stone* interview: 'He believes in aliens. Honestly, he believes anything he reads. You could say, "I read in a magazine that an alien landed in Australia. A doctor found him and did an autopsy – there's footage on the internet." And Tom wouldn't even question it. He would take it as gospel and go around telling everybody.'[10]

But what even DeLonge's own bandmembers did not realise until too late was just how serious his fascination was becoming. In early 2015, DeLonge quit Blink-182, or rather his relationship with the band went on 'indefinite hiatus', in part because he wanted to focus on researching the mystery of UAPs. There were hints in interviews he gave just before the split, revealing just how deep down the rabbit hole he had fallen, where he told of meeting people who were secretly gathering testimony at the time for Congressional hearings intended to expose US government UAP projects and a supposed secret US space program. (One of these people was probably disclosure activist Steven Greer.) DeLonge told the press he feared his phone was tapped and how one person he was dealing with (I speculate it was probably Greer telling him this) 'was being awoken in the middle of the night with clicking and buzzing noises and falling on the ground vomiting, every morning at 4 am. I know that those are artifacts from mind-control experiments, where the same technology that we use to find oil underground, we can zap somebody at the same frequency that the brain operates on, and it can cause some really horrible things to happen'.[11] Yes. Needless to say, it all sounds batshit crazy. Greer's Utah death rays again. But who knows, maybe it will turn out to be true.

DeLonge laid out the conspiracy to his millions of fans. 'The phenomenon has been around forever. All the ancient religions were written down based on witnessing this phenomenon in various forms. Governments of the world watched the phenomenon and tried to replicate the technology, but they did it in secret ... So, in order to hide what the governments are building in secret, they blame it on spaceships and aliens that eat your brains and all this weird stuff, but it's all in an effort to hide what we're really building, something that is real but is exotic and esoteric, and it's all part of a plan.' It all made it way too easy for the media to take the piss with DeLonge. The rock star who made a living writing pop-punk songs with often facile lyrics was now demanding to be taken seriously about aliens. But DeLonge stuck to his guns. 'I can't tour nine months of the year with enough time to do the enormity of what I'm setting out to do,' he said.[12]

Most people had no idea what on earth DeLonge was talking about with such earnestness. But, behind the scenes, DeLonge's critics would have been shocked to see the extraordinary connections he was making. Shortly before he left Blink-182, the rock star was invited to an open house for families of a top defence aerospace contracting company to MC at a function where his job would be to introduce someone he would only describe as a lead aerospace executive. DeLonge says that he agreed to do the families' event on one condition: that he got five minutes alone with that executive to discuss an issue of his choosing. Defence contracting giant Lockheed Martin has since confirmed to Tyler Rogoway's *The WarZone* column that its Skunk Works division did meet with DeLonge. 'Tom DeLonge reached out to Skunk Works with interest in collaborating on a documentary focused on secret machines and advanced development projects,' Lockheed Martin said in a statement. 'Multiple members of the Skunk Works team met with DeLonge to explore his vision for the documentary, as we would with any individual or organisation interested in telling the story of Skunk Works and the technologies we've developed. We ultimately decided to not move forward with our participation in the documentary. During this exploration period, DeLonge attended a Skunk Works employee event.'[13]

But the statement did not tell the full story. Skunk Works is a nickname for Lockheed's advanced development programs and it has an illustrious super-secret black-budget history for its role in developing the U2 and SR-71 Blackbird spy-planes, the F-117 Nighthawk stealth attack aircraft, the F-22 Raptor fighter and the F-35 Lightning stealth jet – all by far the most advanced known aerospace defence technology of their day on the planet. DeLonge figured that if any private aerospace corporation was likely involved in the mythical UFO research he had been reading about for years, Lockheed Martin's Skunk Works was a great start. It is also a fair bet that the executive whom DeLonge subsequently met at the families event was Rob Weiss, the Lockheed executive vice-president and GM of Skunk Works until 2019. There are very sound reasons to believe that Tom DeLonge's version of what actually happened was much closer to the truth.

'When the meeting came, I took the bull by the horns and I pitched him the idea … I had for a project that could help the youth lose their cynical view of the government and Department of Defence,' Tom writes in a foreword to his 2016 science-fiction thriller *SeKret Machines: Chasing Shadows*. He says he was invited back a second time, this time to a secure concrete bunker actually inside Area 51. He says he went through four layers of security: guns, electronic code entry systems, hallways with speakers playing 'white noise, and a series of solid doors flanking my view, each with rotary locks and not a single window in sight'.[14]

When I read DeLonge's account of this meeting, I took a cynical view that what he must have done was hide his real intentions about UAPs in his pitch to Skunk Works to get in the door, a classic naughty media ruse if one is being honest. All this talk of changing the jaundiced attitudes of young people to make them think sweet, rosy things about the military-industrial complex sounded implausible. As things turn out, it clearly did not make sense to Lockheed either; they were on to DeLonge in a flash. 'What are your intentions with the … *conspiracy stuff?*' he was asked. DeLonge admits that when the executive he called 'BossMan' (probably Skunk Work's then General Manager Rob Weiss) walked into the meeting, he was told, 'We cannot be involved in any type of project whatsoever that has this topic associated with it, specifically because there's never been any evidence whatsoever that this stuff even exists.'[15]

The way DeLonge tells it, he told BossMan/Weiss, 'If Edgar Allen Mitchell – the sixth man to walk on the Moon – is out there telling every kid in the world that this topic is real, then we have a problem. But that's okay, we don't need to talk about this subject, or include this information, we just need to address these credibility issues at some point. But give me your time, please, to hear me out.'[16] He then asked for a five-minute meeting alone with the BossMan and it was agreed that all the other executives and engineers would leave the room. 'Now, I cannot tell you what I said to this man in that meeting, and I cannot tell you about the hour-long conversation I had with the other two executives right afterward. But I can say that over the next few months things started to go lightspeed for this project,' DeLonge says.[17]

However, in an interview with George Knapp in March 2016,[18] DeLonge actually revealed a lot of what he said in that one-on-one moment with the BossMan. Deep inside this concrete bunker in the desert, with everyone else out of the room, DeLonge sat two feet from the boss in a suit and explained that he understood the national security implications about UAPs, telling BossMan, 'I am not naïve to the topic. I think if you hear me out you are going to see that there is merit in what I am about to propose.' DeLonge told him, 'Over the past thirty years there's been a program to indoctrinate people to the idea that this [UFOs/UAPs] might be real. But the problem is, all the young adults of the world, they use the internet, they have iPhones, they talk to each other much quicker than people ever have so this program that everyone's been following from the 50s is far outdated, it's antiquated, people have surpassed it and now they don't trust you guys. Now they don't like you guys.' DeLonge also claims he told BossMan he knew about 'some bad things that have happened on this subject'. He says BossMan demanded to know, 'What kind of bad things has the government done with this subject?' DeLonge says he detailed 'a couple of things that I can't say here and I said, "If you allow me to do this, what I am trying to do then I am going to ask you for some help. I need advisers. I need people to help guide me so I don't keep disinforming people".'

DeLonge says that was the breakthrough point. He says he sent the BossMan a draft prologue he had been working on for a non-fiction book he was writing about UFO/UAPs in his *SeKret Machines* series. Quite why that prologue helped open the door to the secret UAP gatekeepers is baffling because the version DeLonge eventually published is all about the aggressively debunked, hugely controversial (and potentially very frightening, if true) 'contactees and abductee aspect of the [UAP] phenomenon'. In *SeKret Machines: Gods, Man & War*,[19] DeLonge and co-author Peter Levenda suggest that it is possible to prove there are physical effects on UAP contactees and that those abducted (presumably by non-human intelligences/aliens?) show signs of post-traumatic stress disorder. To be frank, I would have thought the very idea of discussing anything to do with alien abductions would be highly toxic for BossMan and his secretive gatekeeper colleagues, but that is what Tom says helped get his pitch over the line. DeLonge claims that within two weeks of that meeting he was introduced to senior top brass from across the military, including US Air Force generals, intelligence officials, high-ranking NASA bureaucrats and senior officials in the White House. Then came a meeting straight out of a black world spy movie, where DeLonge described being told to fly to a regional American airport and found himself sitting down at its hangar restaurant with a man he calls 'The General'. The very first thing The General said to him he found terrifying: "'It was the Cold War and we found a lifeform'. And that's when I start shitting my pants.'[20]

Chapter 14

We Can Handle the Truth

Rock star Tom DeLonge has given a series of strange rambling media interviews about his secret meetings about UAPs with government and corporate officials. Perhaps the wackiest was the one he recorded with podcast host, comedian and mixed martial arts commentator Joe Rogan. DeLonge told Rogan on *The Joe Rogan Experience* that he was given the greenlight by his defence and intelligence black world mentors to spread the word about an imminent US government disclosure of amazing UFO secrets; he also claimed he was schooled by them on how not to reveal too much of what he now knew. He claimed his military sources even did a mock *Newsweek* magazine interview with him so that they could analyse his answers and rehearse him before he gave a real interview.[1]

It is instructive to get across the detail of what DeLonge said in his 100-minute-duration Joe Rogan interview and a four-hour George Knapp interview because, frankly, if any of what he says he was told is true, the implications are huge. I know a lot of you will think DeLonge sounds crazy but, as you will see, I believe there is strong evidence that certain former and serving senior officials of the US government and military definitely met with and briefed Tom DeLonge. The issue to be debated is whether what he claims they told him was in any way true. DeLonge claims he was told by these senior officials that the US government had indeed secretly retrieved alien spacecraft ... and aliens; that there is a secret struggle underway to master the technology and to protect humanity from an imminent threat. I am in no doubt whatsoever that, whether true or not, these briefings happened. I have to admit I still find it extraordinary that former and serving military officials decided to brief DeLonge but maybe they thought what he might say would sound so batshit crazy that if he went public with it, no one would believe him anyway.

'Things like this do not happen at the White House, they do not happen on The Hill,' DeLonge said he was told by an extremely self-important someone from the spook world at the Pentagon. 'They happen at places like this, at tables like this, where a few men get together and decide to push the ball down the field.'[2] (Phwooar – what a jerk, I can hear you thinking. Do people still really talk like that? It has overtones of Jack Nicholson's Colonel Jessup in the movie *A Few Good Men*, 'You can't *handle* the truth! Son, we live in a world that has walls, and those walls have to be guarded by men with guns. Who's gonna' do it? You?') From DeLonge's account, there was a lot of this bravado alpha male talk from these anonymous men in uniform and the spook world that is downright disturbing; it suggests an egregious disregard for democratic accountability and government oversight. Let us assume for a moment that what DeLonge was told is all true (which is, I admit, a massive stretch). What is worrying is that he seems to have bought the sweetness and light narrative that everything these anonymous officials are supposedly doing (presumably with little or no accountability at all to the American people) is benevolently inclined; or at least we should just have to take their word for it.

In his interview with George Knapp, DeLonge was at pains to ensure people understand 'The General' is a great, well-intentioned guy, but on reflection DeLonge's account suggests there is a glint of fanaticism in The General's embrace of secrecy that suggests he and his colleagues are zealots who are desperate to conceal what are potentially crimes on the Republic. For, if any of what DeLonge is saying is true then presidents have been lied to, Congress has been lied to, and the entire world has been deceived about the UAP phenomenon. And unpleasant things have been done to many people to protect The Big Secret. DeLonge, however, thinks we should just trust them.

'They really want people to know these things, but they don't want it to mess up their efforts. The more I started to find out the more I thought it's a pretty heroic tale, that these were really good men and women ... he must have brought up what was best for the Republic, what was best for the free Republic, he brought that up probably eight different times. It is very, very important for these men what is best for the United States as a free country, free-thinking man and the republic we built. They're not these crazies running around, they're not warmongers,' DeLonge asserted.[3] Heroic? Hmmm ... So who do you think is pulling the strings here really, Tom DeLonge or The General? George Knapp pulled DeLonge up at one stage and asked, 'People will say, this guy's a rock musician, they're not going to tell this stuff to him or they're going to tell him stuff that they're going to have plausible deniability ... if this goes wrong, they can discredit you, or deny it?'

'Well, they can do that to anybody,' DeLonge replied. 'They can do that to presidents. You're talking about levels of power that we can't comprehend as civilians. Frankly, I don't care if anyone doesn't believe me. I'm in the middle of something very important. I just gotta' do what I said I'll do.'[4]

Say again, 'levels of power that we can't comprehend as civilians'? Hopefully, DeLonge understands that the executive arm of government, including the Pentagon, CIA, Defence Intelligence Agency and every other three-letter agency, only have any power at all because authority is vested in the executive by the people, for the people, through the Congress? Does history not teach us something about unaccountable military and intelligence officials making reckless decisions in secret – the CIA Cointelpro program against domestic America, Cuba, Iran/Contra, Vietnam, Iraq? These comments are actually frightening if someone in the military actually believes such delusions of grandeur.

I am very sure that 90 per cent of readers have called bullshit on DeLonge's spiel by this stage, if not long before now. The idea that a punk-pop rock star could achieve what decades of UAP conspiracy whistleblowers have tried to do and failed – forcing the whole purported US government UAP conspiracy out into the open – is surely ridiculous. And yet, that was exactly what DeLonge set out to do. He pitched to his government black-world insiders a massive entertainment concept of novels, feature films, non-fiction books and documentaries to raise public awareness. 'I knew more than most that this phenomenon was scary, and everything that we did over the past 60 years was based on the enormity of the unbelievable task at hand. We had to rethink religion, history, national security, secrecy, physics, defence, space exploration, cosmology, *humanity*.'[5]

Think about the implications if, just maybe, what DeLonge is saying he was told is remotely *true*. Many Americans are likely to be outraged by the notion that a bunch of self-important blowhard generals, spooks and scientists are secretly colluding with private corporations to keep advanced mind-blowing technologies from the knowledge of everyone else – giving them, to quote DeLonge, 'levels of power' that are incomprehensible to us mere mortals. The way DeLonge tells it, their argument seems to be that we had to keep this secret from you because it might scare you and because the aliens are a terrible threat. Assuming this is true, is there any plan to actually consult with the planet before we start declaring war on the first non-human intelligence we meet? A citizenry should be sceptical about any claims by its military that it needs billions – perhaps trillions – of dollars to combat a secret threat that it can't tell you about for your own good. DeLonge has talked a lot about this supposed malevolent threat, which he claims the Pentagon has told him about, so let us take a closer look at the claims. For starters, DeLonge claims he learned, from these mysterious gatekeepers with the insider knowledge, that humanity was already in touch with aliens. 'I think this generation was meant to have this stuff come out. I don't believe that some of the events happened on accident. Some have been on purpose. Pushing humanity in a very specific direction. They also time travel. When you use the technology, there's a time difference between what they're doing in an artificially created bubble of gravity and your time.'[6]

Podcaster Joe Rogan has often dabbled with the subject of UAPs and the paranormal, and, in a major interview with Tom DeLonge, he did a great job teasing as much as he could out of DeLonge, despite DeLonge's Pentagon interview evasion training, which was supposed to have restrained him from revealing too much. It is amusing to think of how a bunch of stiffs in uniforms tried to teach Tom DeLonge how not to reveal secret stuff because, with no disrespect to DeLonge, he would be a hopelessly indiscrete spy. He could not restrain himself from excitedly blabbing it all out to Joe Rogan. Whether it is true or not, DeLonge obviously adamantly believes what he was told by his gatekeeper mentors. 'I believe not only that the [ET] technology exists – that we've figured out how to play with it,' DeLonge said. 'But I'm not going to get into that here ...'

'Is this in the hands of the US government?' Rogan asked.

'I don't want to get into this. I definitely have to watch what I say,' DeLonge nervously responded, leaving listeners and viewers with the impression that, because he had revealed too much, a pitiless Delta Force commando team was about to kick in Rogan's studio door and drag both of them off in chains to a dark prison cell in a secure cave at Groom Lake, where Area 51 is located.

The way DeLonge told it, his black world advisors were agonising about how to break the news about extra-terrestrials to the planet. DeLonge said he told them, 'You struggle with telling disclosure. I don't think everyone should know everything. And then you say they can't handle it, don't tell them anything. And I'm like there's a middle road there and here's the way I would do the middle road. And it resonated with them.' (Why the hell, I hear you shouting, would Tom DeLonge ever agree that the public should not be told everything? DeLonge, believe us. As the movie showed, Colonel Jessup was proven wrong. We *can* handle the truth.)

DeLonge was told that aliens had engaged with humans for millennia and that the remains of crashed or recovered extra-terrestrial craft were retrieved by the US government. 'The problem is these are extraordinarily advanced civilisations that have been coming here like, forever. That's why it's in all the ancient fucking scripts and texts and carved into rocks and all that shit. But, trying to figure it out, trying to connect the dots, and looking at debris that they probably still have, we have no fuckin' clue how to make this or back-engineer this stuff.'[7] (His insider advisers who were telling DeLonge this totally contradict themselves on this point later, as you will see.) When he told Rogan that The General had told him in the airport restaurant about a recovered crashed alien spacecraft in the 1940s, Rogan quite reasonably asked what we were all thinking, 'Ever think this guy is bullshitting you?'

'Oh, fuck no,' DeLonge replied. 'That's why you've got to hear the real story.'

If what follows is a *true* story, it was probably driving DeLonge's UAP-gatekeeper minders insane with frustration to hear how much he revealed. US National Reconnaissance Office (NRO) surveillance satellites, he claimed, were seeing these UAP objects coming in and out of the atmosphere all the time, and he had seen the evidence. 'One of my advisers was from the NRO. High up. And they call it episodic visits. That's all I know. I saw a paper where the Department of Defence figured out an algorithm on how to compute when they fly in and collect smaller ships. They tested that and it was successful,' DeLonge effused to an increasingly agog Rogan.

He said that two weeks after asking his informants for insiders who could give him the UAP information he needed, he was summonsed to meet a general and a colonel at Colorado Springs (the base for the US Air Force Space Command), who greenlighted his access and his media awareness campaign.[8] DeLonge was chosen to be a vehicle for soft disclosure by those in the US government who wanted the story out. 'You've been given permission, shut the fuck up and get to work,' the colonel told him. It is surely a very perverse notion that DeLonge or anyone needed 'permission' to talk about this stuff from a potty-mouthed, unaccountable, military officer who might well be committing serious crimes against the great American republic by concealing it from the Congress and the people. It also implies some element of military control over DeLonge's agenda. DeLonge confessed to Joe Rogan that he got into trouble with some gatekeepers of The Big Secret because of an interview he did on the hugely popular *Coast to Coast AM*, a conspiracy and paranormal radio show. 'Next thing I'm approached by somebody from a certain agency. I was interrogated for two days straight. "We need to know who you are. You know shit you shouldn't know",' he claimed. The implication behind this unnamed agency's approach, if true, is of course that some arms of the US government still disagrees that the public has any right to know this stuff. Thank heavens then that this is all nonsense and it is all a figment of DeLonge's imagination.

The offending show in question was probably one hosted by Las Vegas investigative journalist George Knapp in 2016.[9] In it, DeLonge intimated hugely significant revelations were imminent. 'We're also going to be shown scientific breakthroughs that will seem like magic to people,' he gushed. (At the time of writing, well over five years later, we are still waiting.) He told Knapp that when the public learned about the secret spending there would be an uproar but that once the truth was out the public would be grateful. (Of course, the public would be grateful; why should Americans get upset about billions of dollars of public money being secretly spent on weapons purportedly to fight aliens when the government cannot protect its citizenry from a killer virus?)

The grand conspiracy that Tom DeLonge painted was that, since the 1940s, the US government has hidden a UAP research program, including developing their own craft, inside private industry corporations. 'Yes, we have cracked gravity, and we are building machinery that has anti-gravity. And yes, I was told that it's a big deal ... They may be building things that truly have anti-gravity,' he said. (Here is where he or his advisers contradicted themselves; remember DeLonge said earlier that his mentors admitted they still had no idea how to back-engineer this alien technology?)

DeLonge also expanded, in his interview with George Knapp,[10] on that first meeting with 'The General' who made the extraordinary and apparently terrifying claims about a recovered alien 'lifeform'. 'These are the first, the very first, words that he said to me, "It was the Cold War and every single day we lived under the threat of nuclear war. Every single day, we believed and really thought in the deepest part of our souls that nuclear war could happen at any given moment." And then he stops. And then he says: "And somewhere in those years," and he looked me in the eye, "we found a lifeform. And everything that we did and every decision that we made with that lifeform was because of the consciousness at that time". And I said: "Sir, when taking into account things that this lifeform has done, for example, turning our nuclear weapons on and readying them for launch …". And then he interrupts me, puts a finger on my face and says [with reference to a Soviet-era missile commander]: "There are heroes in Russia, heroes. And under grave risk to himself and to his country, they did not fire back." And at that moment I realised, it had already started, this game I was in …' DeLonge says. (Goddamn, this really is starting to feel like Jack Nicholson's fantastic Col Jessup rant, 'I have a greater responsibility than you can possibly fathom … You have the luxury of not knowing what I know … You fucken people, you have no idea how to defend a nation …'.) DeLonge claimed he was told that the lifeform was discovered in 1989, at the end of the Cold War, and that the discovery supposedly changed the course of history.

Over his extraordinary four-hour interview with George Knapp, DeLonge claimed that his contacts said the whole 'UFO reality' was being kept secret from humanity, not because the government was maliciously hiding the truth, but because its research into the phenomenon was still going on and they did not yet fully understand it, which was why they were pouring so much money into it. So relax, good people of the world, the gatekeepers of The Big Secret are only giving themselves plausible deniability by flagrantly lying about UAPs to protect you, and they are telling this supposedly true story to DeLonge because they know you will never believe him and they do not want to scare you. This makes perfect sense, so be quiet and leave them alone to spend billions of dollars in absolute secrecy without any effective government oversight.

Then, of course, DeLonge did proceed to scare the bejabbers out of us with what he had been told. He claimed to Knapp that there were ongoing government investigations into victims of alien abductions and cattle mutilations, and that 'this [ET] intelligence is pinning different countries against each other based on religion on purpose, and it's a scary scenario. It's a multiple-front war'.[11] And, just when you thought things could not get much weirder, DeLonge also started talking about gods. 'The entire UFO phenomenon is about multiple gods that fight amongst themselves and by design factionalise mankind into different religions to step back and let us fight each other because it has other things it wants to accomplish, and we don't notice them because we're too involved fighting each other. Our government knows that. It knows that The Others are instigating wars among mankind.'[12] He even suggested that supernatural myths about demons were related to the UFO/ UAP phenomenon. 'What you have is something that doesn't like man, and either feels jealous of, or has some kind of plan for what man is to be,' he said. Oh yes, you also need to know that ancient civilisations such as Easter Island, the Maya and the Inca supposedly disappeared because they 'did not obey, thus encouraging the story to be kept … Except this time, when they come to wipe us out like the other ones, we are actually ready for them. And that readiness is another example why things have been quiet for so long and has been a strange international partnership indeed.'[13] There were also UFO crashes in Nazi Germany, China and Russia, all of which were covered up, he added.

What was going on in secret, he claimed, was an international collaboration between countries to be prepared for The Others. 'We started working like crazy with the brightest minds and huge amounts of money, with passion and with resilience and with everything at our disposal to come up with a way to protect everybody … When people find out about this, they're gonna' lose a lot of their cynicism about the government,' DeLonge said. Very reassuring. Not. Cynical. At all. The essence of what he is claiming to know is that humanity has been kept in the dark by a bunch of zealot generals, who do not want us to know that the gods worshipped by humanity for thousands of years might have a few malevolent rivals. And that they are getting ready for war with aliens.

Okay. So that is the mega-UFO/UAP conspiracy theory as set out by rock star Tom DeLonge.

Perhaps, in deference to the military's love of acronyms, it should be called TBSMT: Tom's Benevolent Spooks & Military Theory, the idea that we should believe that what is probably the biggest secret outside of what happens after death – the knowledge of the existence of other intelligent life in the universe – is supposedly being kept secret from us all because our governments just want to protect us from getting scared; and we are meant to believe this in an era when public trust in government is at rock bottom.

Let us assume for a moment that what DeLonge is saying he has been told is remotely true. The Pew Research Center has monitored public trust in the US government since the 1950s. Back in 1958, about the time (according to DeLonge's anonymous contacts) when the world's governments allegedly started colluding to hide the existence of The Others, about three-quarters of Americans trusted their government to do the right thing almost always or most of the time. But, since about 2007, public trust in government has never been lower, about 30 per cent. Politicians are way below even journalists on the trust scale. So even if our governments come out tomorrow and admit to this ostensible true story of the phenomenon, there must surely be a worry in the minds of those anonymous – and indubitably arrogant – powerbrokers, who are supposedly really pulling the strings, that nobody is ever going to believe them anyway. Is it any wonder public trust in government is so low if they truly are keeping a secret like this one?

Call me cynical, but I find it a more plausible explanation that if this is true (and that is one hell of an *if*), what the reticent gatekeepers of The Big Secret (if there is one) are truly most worried about is being hauled before Congress in chains and asked to explain why this incredible secret was withheld from public knowledge, and why billions of dollars are being spent on black budget programs re-engineering purported alien technology that is also being hidden from the taxpayers who are copping the bill. More than a few citizens would no doubt suggest that politicians, spooks and generals hiding any such secret should be tarred and feathered, tied to a Humvee bumper bar, and dragged around Washington DC for public excoriation as lying deceitful crooks who corrupted their oaths of office, but I could not possibly comment.

I know what you are thinking. The only sensible explanation for this is that what Tom DeLonge said to George Knapp and Joe Rogan about a gigantic secret conspiracy to hide the truth of UFOs/UAPs is a huge steaming pile of bull dung. He was never told this by anyone. His supposed sources in government are a fiction of his lurid imagination. He made up all this stuff about flying around North America meeting The General in an airport hangar and Skunk Works in its underground bunker. DeLonge needs help. It simply did not happen.

Well, I wish I could be so sure. This is where the story really starts to get crazy interesting ... thanks to some dastardly Russian hackers.

RECORD PHONES
Business Office 2288
News Department
2287

Leased Wire
Associated Press

Roswell Daily Record

ROSWELL, NEW MEXICO, TUESDAY, JULY 8, 1947.

Claims Army Is Stacking Courts Martial

Indiana Senator Lays Protest Before Patterson

RAAF Captures Flying Saucer On Ranch in Roswell Region

House Passes Tax Slash by Large Margin

Defeat Amendment By Demos to Remove Many from Rolls

Security Council Paves Way to Talks On Arms Reductions

No Details of Flying Disk Are Revealed

Roswell Hardware Man and Wife Report Disk Seen

Ex-King Carol Weds Mme. Lupescu

US Air Force intelligence officer Major Jesse Marcel posing with the remains of a weather balloon at the 8th Air Force headquarters in Fort Worth, Texas, July 1947. Three decades later, Marcel claimed that he was ordered to collude in a cover-up and that the real debris he recovered from near Roswell was extra-terrestrial in origin. *(University of Texas at Arlington Library)*

The mysterious so-called 'Foo Fighters' – the white shapes in this photo – became a common sight tracking military aircraft during World War Two. The Americans thought it was a German or Japanese secret weapon; the Axis thought it was the Americans. The Foo Fighters pictured here were claimed to be tracking these Tachikawa Ki-36 fighters over central Japan in 1945. *(Mary Evans Picture Library)*

'The Salem Lights', photographed on 16 July 1952 from a US Coast Guard station on Winter Island, Salem, Massachusetts. Three days later, Washington DC was buzzed by unknown objects in a massive Unidentified Aerial Phenomenon flap. Seventy years later, both incidents remain unexplained. *(Library of Congress)*

During the 1950s and early 1960s, American science magazines like this one openly touted rumours of imminent United States' breakthroughs in anti-gravitic (AG) propulsion. Then it all went quiet. The big question: did the AG program go black? *(Public Domain)*

Members of the US Air Force's Project Blue Book, the code name for the group that studied UAPs for the USAF from 1952 to 1969, often derided for its perceived over-zealousness in aggressively debunking almost all UAP sightings. *(Mary Evans Picture Library)*

ABOVE: Joy Clarke, aged 12, standing in the circle of flattened grass where she and multiple other witnesses from Westall High School in Melbourne, Australia, saw an alien craft land in 'The Grange' in April 1966.

RIGHT: Joy Clarke today, standing on the same field where she saw the craft. *(Author)*

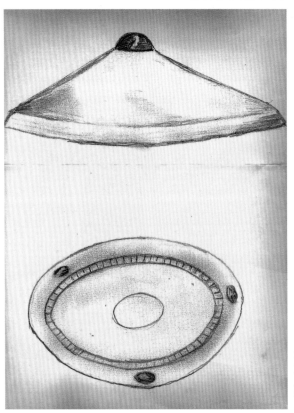

A sketch rendered by researcher Bill Chalker from an account by Victor Zakry, who witnessed a craft hovering over Westall in April 1966. *(Courtesy of Bill Chalker)*

One rare local newspaper report about the Westall sighting in 1966, which includes an image of one of the witnesses, then schoolteacher Andrew Greenwood. Greenwood says the article led to the subsequent visit to his home by government and military officials, and threats for him to keep quiet about what he saw. *(Courtesy of Shane Ryan)*

A photograph taken by a Balwyn, Melbourne, resident (who wishes to remain anonymous) shortly before the Westall school sighting in April 1966.

LEFT: The telescope Bob Jacobs used near Big Sur, California, to film a missile launch in 1964. When the US Air Force falsely claimed Jacobs never filmed from Big Sur he provided this photograph to prove it happened. *(Courtesy Dr Bob Jacobs)*

BELOW: Dr Bob Jacobs as a young lieutenant (left) and today (right). In 1964 he caught a 'flying saucer' craft on film firing beams of light to disable a dummy nuclear warhead on a speeding ICBM rocket fired from Vandenberg Air Force Base. When the US Air Force tried to deny the incident, Jacobs' commanding officer publicly backed his account. *(Courtesy Dr Bob Jacobs)*

Astronaut, Edgar Mitchell's official NASA photograph. Mitchell told a close friend of his, known here as 'The Spaceman', that he kept the secret of extra-terrestrial interest in the space program because to reveal it was 'treason'. *(NASA)*

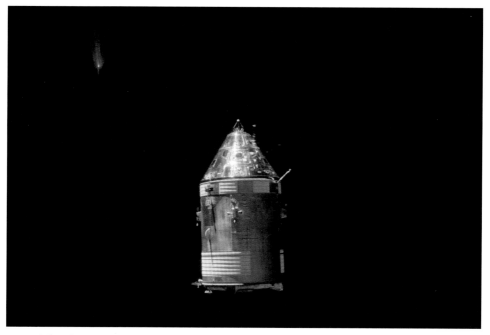

One of the objects (blue light, upper left) seen by Edgar Mitchell from Apollo 14's Lunar Module just before docking with the Command Module (centre). Mitchell always denied he saw a UFO but he told 'The Spaceman' he saw strange objects throughout his lunar mission in 1971. *(NASA)*

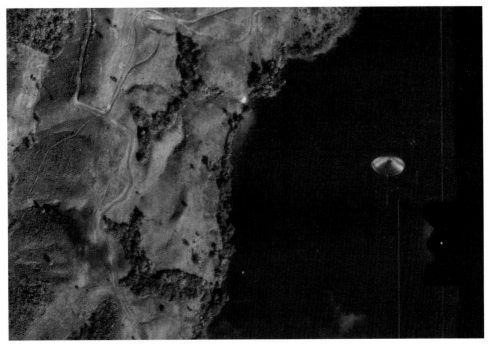

The Costa Rica UAP: in September 1971, a Costa Rican government aerial mapping team accidentally took this photograph of a metallic disc-shaped object, often hailed as the best UFO photograph ever. *(Costa Rican National Geographic Institute / Sergio Loaiza)*

US civil rights attorney Daniel Sheehan in 1977. While investigating what the US Government knew about UFOs for President Jimmy Carter, Dan was shocked to discover archival photographs of a 'flying saucer' craft being retrieved by US military. The images remain classified to this day. *(Courtesy of Dan Sheehan)*

Two of the air traffic controllers at Wellington Airport, New Zealand, control tower who witnessed the Kaikoura UFOs tracking a cargo aircraft in December 1978: Geoff Causer (front) and John Cordy (behind). Despite official assertions, Cordy says there was nothing wrong with the radar system that night and whatever it was, it was not fishing-boat lights reflecting off clouds, because he saw it on his radar. *(Courtesy of John Cordy)*

Twenty-year-old Melbourne-based pilot Frederick Valentich, who disappeared while piloting a tiny Cessna aircraft over Bass Strait in 1978. Shortly before he and his aircraft disappeared, Valentich was recorded telling Melbourne air traffic control that he was being followed by a huge illuminated shiny metal craft hovering above.

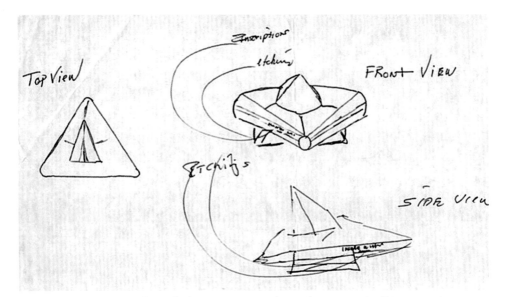

A sketch of the purported Rendlesham Forest UAP drawn by witness Staff Sergeant Jim Penniston. Mr Penniston and Airman John Burroughs claimed they saw the craft land in Rendlesham Forest near the RAF Woodridge base in Suffolk, England, on 26 December 1980.

Lieutenant Colonel Charles Halt, the deputy base commander at RAF Woodridge who led a patrol that witnessed what he describes as an 'intelligently-controlled' object moving through Rendlesham Forest.

Annie Farinaccio, who, in company with two Australian Federal Police officers, witnessed a UAP in 1991 near the then US-run Harold E. Holt Naval Communications Station in North West Cape, Australia. She saw a craft with lights underside, which did extreme manoeuvres and reached speeds far beyond acknowledged human technology. *(Author)*

The secretive defence base Harold E. Holt Naval Communications Station. In the event of war, this base was a prime Soviet nuclear target because it played a key role in sending out launch signals to US nuclear-missile-armed submarines. Was that why the base received some strange visitors? *(Alamy)*

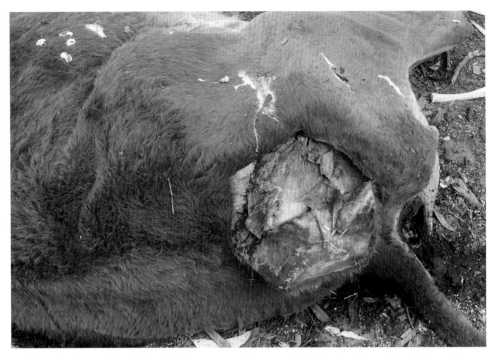

Mick and Judy Cook of Cloverly Station, north-west of Mackay in Queensland, Australia, have seen strange lights over their farm and have lost at least 15 head of cattle, discovered with missing organs and surgical cuts. This cow was discovered with a precise hexagonal cut into her body – and not a drop of blood spilt. *(Mick & Judy Cook)*

Area 51, also known as Homey Airport or Groom Lake, the super-secret US Air Force base within the Nevada Test and Training Range used to test experimental aircraft and weapons. Area 51 is frequently the focus of conspiracy theories about recovered ET craft and sightings of gravity-defying UAPs. *(DigitalGlobe / Getty Images)*

Robert Bigelow, space entrepreneur and paranormal/UFO investigator, with NASA Deputy Administrator Lori Garver. Bigelow founded the National Institute for Discovery Science and once owned Skinwalker Ranch, the site of multiple UAP sightings. *(NASA/Bill Ingalls via Getty Images)*

Punk rock star and UFO investigator Tom DeLonge, the man who founded To The Stars Academy and who secretly met with top officials in an apparent plan for UFO disclosure prior to the 2016 US presidential election. *(Joby Sessions/Getty Images)*

The story that forced the US Navy to admit that UAPs are real: retired US Navy chief petty officer and radar specialist Kevin Day, who, as a TOPGUN air intercept controller, monitored the strange Tic-Tac craft videoed and tracked by US Navy pilots in 2004. *(Author)*

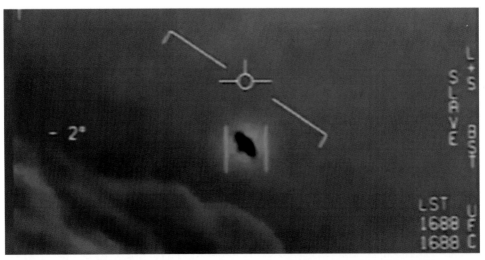

A still of the so-called 'Gimbal' UAP, from the official US Navy video of a 2014 or 2015 encounter. This video was taken by a navy fighter jet from the nuclear aircraft carrier USS *Theodore Roosevelt*, off the eastern seaboard, near the Florida coast. The Pentagon says the video is real and, officially, unexplained. *(US Department of Defense)*

Nat Kobitz, former Director of the US Navy's Science and Technology Development, who admitted to the author being briefed into secret programs allegedly involving the retrieval of and attempts to re-engineer alien spacecraft. He also examined a strange metal bulkhead from a craft of unknown origin. Kobitz was one of the most senior US Defense Department insiders ever to go public with claims of retrieved alien technology. *(Courtesy of the Kobitz family)*

Christopher Mellon, the former US Deputy Assistant Secretary of Defense for Intelligence, now prominent in pushing for UAP disclosure and transparency in the United States. *(Author)*

Former senior US Defense Department intelligence officer Luis Elizondo, who led the Pentagon's secret UFO investigation team, the Advanced Aerospace Threat Identification Program. Aptly, Elizondo lives near the Wyoming Devil's Tower Monument featured in the extra-terrestrial movie *Close Encounters of the Third Kind*. *(Author)*

Author and journalist Leslie Kean at home in New York, standing in front of her *New York Times* front-page scoop that revealed the existence of the Pentagon's secret UFO investigation program and detailed the leaked Tic-Tac video. *(Author)*

Chapter 15

Sharing the Guilty Secret

Sitting at his desk in Washington DC, this time as the campaign manager for Hillary Clinton's 2016 presidency bid, John Podesta had never heard of Victor Borisovich Netyksho, who headed unit 26165 of the Russian military intelligence agency, the GRU. But Netyksho certainly knew all about him. One unintended consequence of the crime Netyksho was about to commit against John Podesta was that it would corroborate Tom DeLonge's extraordinary claims that he met senior US government Defence Department officials, spies and military contractors whom, he alleges, admitted a secret government conspiracy to hide the truth about UAPs from you and me.

Boris Netyksho led a team of highly trained military hackers known as Fancy Bear,[1] who were doing politically motivated computer hacking for the Russian government in flagrant violation of international law – a kind of cyber-SMERSH. They hacked into the computer networks of the Democratic Congressional Campaign Committee and the Democratic National Committee. They were trying to dig up any embarrassing or damaging dirt on the Democratic presidential candidate Hillary Clinton. In front of glowing monitors, deep inside a secure GRU building somewhere in Moscow, Netyksho and Fancy Bear turned their efforts on Podesta.

Sometime in 2016, probably October, Podesta was working on his computer when he was prompted by his Gmail account to re-enter his password. Like most of us, he probably did not think twice about it; tapping in his password, he forgot about it. John Podesta had vastly more important things to worry about; he was a Washington DC Beltway insider on steroids and they were just weeks out from the finish line in Hillary Clinton's campaign to win the 2016 presidential election against Donald Trump. Just a couple of months earlier, on 28 July 2016, no one could quite believe what Republican presidential nominee Donald Trump said at a press conference in Florida. The candidate invited Russia to hack his rival Hillary Clinton's email account. 'Russia, if you're listening, I hope you're able to find the 30,000 emails that are missing,' he said. 'I think you will probably be rewarded mightily by our press.'[2]

It was a breathtakingly irresponsible comment because Trump knew that American intelligence believed Russian government sponsored hackers were responsible for earlier attacks on Democratic Party organisations. Trump later claimed he was being sarcastic but, within hours of his comments, the hackers began new penetration efforts against the Democrats; eventually their cyber-sniffing led them to John Podesta. You might be thinking that Netyksho's hacking was fairly harmless. Not a lot came out of the DNC leaks; one email revealed scuttlebutt that the White House rejected rockstar Ariana Grande from performing at a presidential gala because a video 'caught her licking other peoples' donuts while saying she hates America'.[3] Embarrassing for Ariana, but hardly Watergate. And a waste of good donuts.

The GRU is hardcore Dr Evil; it saw advantage for Russia in sabotaging the Clinton campaign. It was GRU hitmen who smeared novichok nerve agent poison on the doorknob of former

Russian military officer and double agent Sergei Skripal's home in Salisbury, England, in March 2018. In August 2019, it was a GRU agent who shot a Georgian citizen in a Berlin park. The bloody trail from the deaths of 298 innocent people on Malaysia Airlines flight MH17 over eastern Ukraine in July 2014 leads all the way back to the GRU's special forces Spetsnaz unit. There is a GRU unit known only by the number 29155 and its purpose, according to *The New York Times*, is to mount a 'coordinated and ongoing campaign to destabilize Europe' (and the US) executed by operatives 'skilled in subversion, sabotage and assassination'.[4] Presumably just a few doors down the corridor from the blood-spattered Unit 29155 hitmen, is Netyksho's Cyber Hacking Unit number 26165, whose job included cyber-subverting one of the world's oldest democracies.

Within minutes of Podesta clicking the fake Gmail link, which was actually a so-called cyber spear-phishing hack, his private communications were streaming back to Netyksho and his colleagues at GRU HQ in Moscow; in a few days, thousands of Podesta's emails were leaked on the *Wikileaks* website for all to read. Amidst them was a smoking gun that lent strong support to DeLonge's extraordinary claims: a string of exchanges between Podesta and DeLonge, revealing plans for a Google Hangout meeting between DeLonge, two US Air Force generals and Rob Weiss, the Lockheed Martin executive vice-president and general manager of its advanced development programs known as Skunk Works. Weiss was probably BossMan, the executive with whom DeLonge claims to have had his one-on-one chat discussing the potential disclosure of the US government's purported secret UAP program. Podesta was clearly DeLonge's anonymous 'top man' in government. While the planned Google Hangout meeting probably didn't happen, in the emails DeLonge briefed Podesta on some extraordinary meetings he had already had. 'I would like to bring two very "important" people out to meet you in DC,' he told Podesta. 'I think you will find them very interesting as they were principal leadership relating to our sensitive topic. Both were in charge of most fragile divisions, as it relates to Classified Science and DOD topics. Other words, these are A-level officials. Worth our time, and as well the investment to bring all the way out to you. I just need 2 hours from you. Just looking to have a casual and private conversation in person.'[5]

The endorsements on DeLonge's *SeKret Machines Book 1: Chasing Shadows* thriller reveal DeLonge's connections to a very senior former US Air Force officer. Until 2014, Major General Michael Carey was the special assistant to the commander of Air Force Space Command at Peterson Air Force Base in Colorado, the base for the super-secure NORAD Cheyenne Mountain facility. This is where the entire airspace of Canada and the US is monitored for anomalous aircraft or space objects; if any non-terrestrial object is entering Earth's atmosphere, NORAD should know all about it. Carey, who retired from the military in June 2014, wrote a glowing endorsement for DeLonge's 2016 thriller: '*SeKret Machines* scratches at the surface of "who do" we trust with our classified technology – certainly our adversaries are aware of our undertakings, as they are doing the same. But what of our citizens, our politicians, even our own military? ... Our military leaders have been saying space is a contested environment for years now, perhaps we should believe them!'[6] The general's blurb was a curiously positive endorsement for a book that includes fictional US military characters hiding the 'truth' about a secret government alien flying saucer program that (without giving away too much of DeLonge's storyline) has been subverted by traitors from within. Of course, the book is only fiction.

In another leaked Podesta email[7] dated 24 January 2016, a person calling himself 'Neil Mcc' responded to a Google Hangout invitation to check the time of another proposed meeting. The other meeting attendees were listed as DeLonge, Podesta, Skunk Works' boss Rob Weiss, an assistant to the Hillary Clinton campaign Milia Fisher, and retired Major General Michael Carey. It took another leaked email from the same day to piece together the identity of 'Neil Mcc'. In this email,[8] a Susan McCasland Wilkerson accepted the meeting invitation. She is an astrophysicist and former astronaut candidate with NASA, who also happens to be married to former Major General William Neil McCasland, the commander of the US Air Force's research laboratory at Wright-Patterson Air Force Base until July 2013. In the conspiracy-stricken world of ufology, few locations arouse more breathless speculation than the Wright-Patterson Air Force Base laboratory, which used to be known as the Foreign Technology Division. Numerous purported whistleblowers and insiders have claimed for years that this secure installation is a veritable underground carpark of recovered alien craft and technology, a claim adamantly denied by the US military. Today, the Foreign Technology Division has been rolled into the National Air and Space Intelligence Center (NASIC). Major General Neil McCasland was one very interesting guy to invite to the White House for a quiet chat about UAPs; mythology would suggest he knows a lot.

Another Podesta email suggested that the UAP meeting took place the following day, and that DeLonge came out of it disappointed that Neil McCasland had pulled his punches on the UAP issue. McCasland seemed to have told Podesta that he was a sceptic (presumably about aliens). 'He mentioned he's a sceptic, he's not,' a clearly frustrated DeLonge wrote after the 2016 meeting. 'I've been working with him for four months. I just got done giving him a four-hour presentation on the entire project a few weeks ago. Trust me, the advice is already been happening [sic] on how to do all this. He just has to say that out loud, but he is very, very aware – as he was in charge of all of the stuff. When Roswell crashed, they shipped it to the laboratory at Wright-Patterson Air Force Base. General McCasland was in charge of that exact laboratory up to a couple years ago. He not only knows what I'm trying to achieve, he helped assemble my advisory team. He's a very important man.'[9] This does appear to suggest that a crafty General McCasland made no admissions in his meeting with Podesta about a recovered alien spacecraft or the like. If DeLonge was telling the truth, however, it suggests that the general told DeLonge something very different in a private chat.

There was so much in these emails that is downright weird and extraordinary that it is possible to miss the one momentously significant fact that comes out of them: they revealed beyond any doubt whatsoever that punk rock star Tom DeLonge truly was in contact with one of America's most senior private aerospace chief executives, a campaign manager for Hillary Clinton, and two very senior recently retired air force generals – and UAPs were discussed. DeLonge was presumably not lying to Podesta about his sources. The real issue is the veracity of what they told DeLonge. Is there really a recovered 'lifeform' and an alien spacecraft in the possession of the United States? Could this possibly be true?

Because we can be sure that DeLonge was clearly telling the truth about the fact that he met with these military and defence insiders listed in Podesta's leaked emails, then it does add some small measure of credibility to his more off-the-wall claims that the official known only as The General and others were briefing him on extraordinary UAP technology held secretly by the US government. (I wrote to retired Major General Neil McCasland on the hunch he might be 'The General', inviting him to be interviewed for this book, but received no reply.) On balance, it does not seem unreasonable to assume that DeLonge was telling the truth when he said this meeting's purpose was to discuss disclosure of what the US government knows about UAPs; after all, what else could it be?

Tom DeLonge also divulged that when he flew to Colorado Springs to meet with serving officers from the US Air Force's Space Command, a high-ranking adviser implied there were multiple UAP crash retrievals beyond the 1940s. 'I said, "I'm gonna' be talking about some crashes, the crashes in the '40s". There was a pause, and he says, "Why just the '40s?" Gets you thinking a little bit,' DeLonge said.[10]

However, it needs to be emphasised that nothing in any of the leaked Podesta emails proves the truth of what was claimed in these briefings by these military insiders on alien visitations to this planet, or that Roswell and other purported crashes of extra-terrestrial craft happened or that the recovery of alien corpses happened. Maybe what DeLonge was told was part of some elaborate military disinformation program. It also does not prove that the US has secretly mastered anti-gravitic craft or that it is colluding in secret with other governments. But what it does prove is that Tom DeLonge definitely talked about UAPs with some very high-powered people in the US military and the defence industry. If DeLonge is lying about what he says they talked about, then why did these high-powered folks agree to meet him at all; what did they think they were there to discuss? Significantly, not one of them has publicly disputed the accuracy of what Tom DeLonge has claimed. All have stayed very quiet indeed. If you were a senior general in the US Air Force and a crazy rock star made bogus claims you had shared crazy stuff with him about UAPs, would you not want to at least correct the record? (I also wonder why on earth the mainstream US media is not chasing down these claims and asking these same questions, because there is no doubt these senior officials met with DeLonge. Surely the claims they purportedly made are a major story, worthy of further investigation?)

In one email DeLonge tells Podesta, 'The General (from Wright Patt R&D) and I talk every other day. He and I talked on the phone the other night and he is excited; he really thinks that the DOD is going to embrace my project because I am out to show all the positive things people have done on this topic. And I am eager to take direction from leadership to do a good and needed public service.'[11] What were they talking about if not about UAP disclosure? Neither General McCasland nor General Carey has explained what was going on. And why on earth would DeLonge offer to compromise by taking 'direction from leadership'?

There is another tantalising tidbit from the leaked emails. One intriguing line in the 24 September 2016 email[12] included recommendations from Neil McCasland for a White House memo, presumably to come from a future Hillary Clinton presidency, that would set out instructions for divulging 'information' in coordination with the Defence Department, the Director of National Intelligence and the National Oceanic and Atmospheric Administration. This sounds like General McCasland might have offered to set out a plan for UAP disclosure. What else could the dark secret be inside the US government that a very senior former general of the US Air Force felt needed carefully controlled disclosure from the highest levels of the US government, through the White House?

Maybe you are thinking it is possible that former Generals Michael Carey and Neil McCasland were, in sedate retirement, perhaps just shooting the breeze and chewing the fat over a few beers with their buddy Tom, that it was nothing official at all, nothing to do with the Department of Defence or the government. Just a couple of old Cold War warriors spinning yarns with a charismatic rock star who flattered them with his attention. Perhaps these former generals are actually hard-core punk rockers. Well, the problem with this interpretation is that DeLonge explained to Podesta in one email that he was also in touch with other current serving senior officers in the US Air Force Space Command; he said he planned to have dinner in September 2015 with 'current commanding officers at the Air Force Space Command in a couple [of] days in Colorado Springs to discuss how to move this project forward'.[13] DeLonge clearly never intended this admission to be public; he was sending Podesta this in confidence. So, whatever this planned disclosure was about, DeLonge's candid private admission showed his project enjoyed the involvement of very senior officers in the US Air Force Space Command. This is important. Seeing this independent corroboration gives Tom DeLonge's claims just that little bit more credibility in my mind; maybe this isn't crazy after all.

John Podesta has been very upfront publicly that he believes there is more to be told from within the US government about UAPs 'I think the American people can handle the truth about this,' he said while on the Hillary Clinton campaign. He also made it clear that he would be pushing for disclosure of the government's UAP files from the candidate everyone expected at the time to become President Hillary Clinton. 'I've talked to Hillary about that,' Podesta said in March 2016, from the campaign trail. 'It's a little bit of a cause of mine, which is, people really want to know what the government knows, and there are still classified files that could be declassified.'[14] As we have seen in previous chapters, Podesta is not easily dismissed as a tin-foil hat flying saucer looney. He is a senior and well-respected public servant who held top-secret/ SCI clearances in his past roles with both Presidents Obama and Clinton. He has enviable contacts throughout the national security establishment and he clearly believes someone in the government is hiding something about UAPs.

As the campaign rolled on, Hillary Clinton also made no secret of the fact that, if she became president, she would consider a taskforce to investigate the mysterious Area 51 military base in Nevada, long linked to UFO/UAP conspiracies. She also conceded it was possible our planet had been visited by aliens and she pledged she would make it a priority in her administration to get to the bottom of the UFO mystery.[15] So, in 2016, as the November Election date loomed, Hillary Clinton's presidential campaign potentially spelt trouble for anyone who might be, putatively, keeping The Big Secret about what the US government really knows about UAPs.

Here then is a completely fictional hypothetical scenario: Imagine you are a government insider who, for years, has been (criminally?) concealing evidence of advanced propulsion and free energy systems that the US has derived from recovered non-terrestrial (alien?) craft – all this paid for in secret by US taxpayers without their knowledge. It is a monstrous secret, a highly classified waived and unacknowledged Special Access Program shared only among a handful of corporate, defence, intelligence and political insiders, if at all. Since 1947, you and your predecessors have lied repeatedly to the public in press statements, in sworn evidence to Congress, and even to presidents and their advisers about what you really know. You have colluded with private contractors to hide this from Congressional oversight.

Billions of dollars diverted from taxpayer funded budgets to pay for insanely expensive research and technology programs, including hugely dangerous new space weapons, have been kept secret from all but a handful in the know. You and your fellow gatekeepers to The Big Secret have been reassuring yourselves for years that what you are doing is definitely in the best interests of the people. The excuse you use to convince each other that it all needs to be kept secret is that it is best the public does not know because they might get scared of the aliens you are planning to fight in a brand-new war that you are very excited about. You have even been able to announce a crewed offensive military Space Force without anyone asking why it is needed. The Space Force, the sixth and newest branch of the US military, was created in December 2019. Its Latin motto is unabashedly militaristic: *Si Vis Pacem, Para Bellum*, 'If you want peace, prepare for war'. Space Force's stated vision includes: 'A world-class team of space professionals developing combat-ready space forces and space warfighting capabilities'.[16]

Continuing this hypothetical and completely fictional scenario; you have convinced yourselves that admitting this incredible secret to suspicious senators or government oversight watchdogs (or, God forbid, the general public) is far too dangerous for 'national security'. Keep it under wraps, keep on spending the billions, keep them all in the dark. What they do not know does not hurt them. If they try to break into Area 51, rough them up a bit and give them a scare but reassure them it is all about national security and protecting new aerospace technology, even if we have not seen anything new come out of Groom Lake for 30 years. After all, it is all about protecting the Republic.

Imagine then that this demented evasion and disinformation strategy had been going fine for seven decades, until Hillary Clinton and her campaign manager John Podesta started making noises on the campaign trail about how they would demand the truth about UFOs/UAPs when and if they got into power. Initially you convince yourself that it is the kind of trendy thing politicians say just to woo the millennial vote, that they were not really serious. Then, throughout 2015 and 2016, the media becomes increasingly sure in its reporting that Hillary Clinton is a cert' for the presidency, that Donald Trump does not have a chance. As a gatekeeper, you are now getting very nervous that, come February 2017, post-inauguration, it might be you who is hauled in chains before a Congressional inquiry to explain why you hid The Big Secret. You start panicking that Hillary Clinton, and especially John Podesta, might not understand your protestations that it was all about protecting the Republic. Your sleep is interrupted by images of CIA interrogators (under Podesta's gleeful direction) slowly pulling out your toenails at Guantanamo to get the whole sorry story.

Then, imagine … along comes Tom DeLonge. He must seem like a gift. With a wink and a nod, he lets you know that he knows what you know. It is a huge relief to be able to share your guilty 70+ year secret with DeLonge. Even better, he is offering you a way to let the public know about it that makes the entire military-industrial complex cover-up sound like a bed of roses. Why, DeLonge even suggests he can make young millennials actually like you. He also reassures you that he understands all this national security stuff and that he will seek your permission and get your approval for what he is allowed to say about what you all knew about The Big Secret. You will get to control the disclosure narrative. Hell yeah, this is our sort of guy, you think.

So you start meeting DeLonge and his pals in the White House and the CIA. Podesta is a sure bet to be a senior official in the new President Hillary Clinton administration. You hedge your bets about how much you admit because this is The Big Secret after all; keep your cards close. You introduce DeLonge to all the guys in the gatekeeper gang and they cannot believe their luck either. Just to keep DeLonge onside, though, you talk about how much of a threat these darned aliens are and how important it is to spend so much taxpayer money in secret with little if any accountability or oversight. DeLonge says he completely understands; your relief is palpable. Come Hillary's inauguration day at the front of the Capitol Building in January 2017 you can be sure you and all the other gatekeepers of The Big Secret will be cast as the heroes who protected the Republic from the aliens, as Hillary finally announces to the world that we are not alone.

But … to everyone's shock and surprise, Hillary loses the election in November 2016. Incoming President Trump makes it clear he is sceptical about the aliens-are-visiting-Earth conspiracy theory. 'People are saying they're seeing UFOs. Do I believe it?' the president said. 'Not particularly.'[17]

Not long after, deep in an Area 51 cave under the plasma glow of a Fluxliner alien reproduction vehicle, the gatekeepers ease the cork out of a fine French champagne (paid for by those unwitting taxpayers). They slyly clink glasses, re-swearing their blood oath of absolute secrecy. They all agree that The Big Secret will be kept for at least another 70 years, that President Trump will be another pushover who can also be kept in the dark, like most presidents before him all the way back to Roswell 1947 and earlier. Think of the lunches and trips ahead with your chums in the fossil fuel industry and the aerospace conglomerates, who are benefiting from maintaining the status quo. Free energy would be downright inconvenient right now and who needs clean hypersonic and faster-than-light propulsion systems when you can flog kerosene burning combat jets at hundreds of millions of dollars a unit. Screw concerns about human-caused climate change. Pretty soon, you think, everything will go back to normal, just the way it has been for three-quarters of a century. But, in this completely fictional hypothetical scenario, the gatekeepers have forgotten about DeLonge. DeLonge is seriously pissed that The General is no longer taking his calls under President Trump. He starts talking to a few friends in the black world that he has made along the way. They actually care about UAP disclosure; they think the public has a right to know this stuff. They want humanity to go to the stars.

'To The Stars? … That would make a cool name,' DeLonge says to himself.

He pulls out a pen and paper and writes it down: 'Let's give it some gravitas … how about, To The Stars Academy of Arts & Sciences – TTSA … Hmmm,' he thinks, 'I can work with that.'

Chapter 16

To The Stars Academy of Arts & Sciences

On 11 October 2017, Tom DeLonge took to a Seattle stage to officially announce, as president and CEO, the formation of To The Stars Academy of Arts & Sciences (TTSA). It was a curious event; while essentially a pitch to make the public aware that there was now a new UAP research and disclosure group in town, the launch was online only and had no invited audience and no pesky press present. Media might well have asked some probing questions when they saw the backgrounds of some of TTSA's extraordinary roll call of confederates.

The undeniably impressive line-up of former spooks and defence insiders included Jim Semivan, one of the two co-founders of TTSA. Semivan was only recently retired from the Central Intelligence Agency's Directorate of Operations after 25 years as an operations officer working inside the US and internationally.

There was also the third co-founder of TTSA, Dr Hal Puthoff, a theoretical physicist who had led the previous controversial CIA and Defence Department research into 'psychic spies' or remote viewing. Another team member on stage, heading TTSA's aerospace division, was Steve Justice, who just a month earlier had finished as director of advanced systems at Lockheed Martin Skunk Works. The symbolism of this group of well-informed former insiders, all with top-secret compartmentalised security clearances, quitting the black world and joining a group to campaign for UAP research and plea for government transparency was profound.

TTSA's stated mission was 'to be a vehicle for change by inspiring a newfound appreciation and understanding for the profound, yet unresolved, mysteries of the universe that can have a positive impact on humanity'.[1] Everyone of course knew that was code for what TTSA was really all about: solving the mystery of UAPs.

Christopher Mellon was another of the people gathered on stage for the launch of the TTSA. Mellon was keenly aware of the UAP mystery from his past investigations as a Senate Intelligence Committee staffer and his senior Department of Defence role as the Deputy Assistant Secretary of Defence for Intelligence.

In his launch speech, Mellon pointed out that it was precisely 60 years ago to the month that, in the darkest days of the Cold War, the communist Soviet Union humiliated America by launching Sputnik in October 1957, the first human-made Earth satellite. That, while Sputnik was a shot across the bow for the US, it also prompted a massive government boost in spending on science and engineering to catch up with the Soviets, propelling the country into the space race. He argued Sputnik's significance to the UAP issue was that the US was once again in a race for technological innovation, but this time with an unknown challenger. He then segued to an account of what, at that time in 2017, was still the largely unknown story of the USS *Nimitz*'s F-16 encounters with the hypersonic Tic Tac UAP off the coast of San Diego. 'Bear in mind that naval aviators are the finest observers possible. All have top-secret clearances. All are drug tested, are ardent patriots, have excellent vision and understand aeronautics and aviation. Clearly this is not an experimental US aircraft but whose is it?' Mellon asked. 'How did it accomplish these feats? This story may sound like a sci-fi movie, but it is a true story and far from being the only one of its kind. ... Better yet the US government itself can verify the events involving the USS *Nimitz* on November 14th, 2004.'[2]

What was striking about the TTSA launch was the audacity displayed by each of these former US government employees and contractors, most from the secret world of defence and intelligence, directly challenging the government, the Congress and its oversight committees to investigate what everyone on stage clearly believed – that these unidentified aerial craft seen by military pilots are a real phenomenon and a direct threat to the technological superiority held by the United States since World War Two. Each member of TTSA's team sitting at that launch was keenly aware of something significant from their black world insights that motivated them to speak out. Here they were, goading the US government to do something about it, stretching the limits of their secrecy oaths and pushing for an investigation into the 'reality' of UAPs.

Two weeks after the TTSA launch, DeLonge did his extraordinary interview with Joe Rogan. DeLonge repeated claims long on the fringes of ufology conspiracy theories, suggesting that the US's recovery of a crashed alien spacecraft was the reason why, 90 days after the mythical 1947 Roswell crash, the US Air Force was created as a separate entity from the Army. He also claimed Roswell was why the US government enacted the 1947 *National Security Act*, to create the security apparatus, including the CIA, that had supposedly locked up the secret for nearly 75 years. It was implicit that DeLonge's insider sources had told him these incredible secrets, but was it true? Cold War historians would no doubt venture that America's 1947 national security laws had more to do with the US's realisation of the grim reality of confrontation with totalitarian communism during the Cold War but DeLonge told Joe Rogan, 'I absolutely think it had to do with aliens.'[3] As Annie Jacobsen also claimed, DeLonge averred he was told the Roswell crash was a Nazi-built Russian flying saucer, but neither he nor his insider sources have provided any evidence to substantiate such a sensational claim. If any of what DeLonge was saying was true, it would turn history on its head.

DeLonge also claimed the US already knew the secrets of free energy, so-called zero-point energy. 'One inch of air could power the US for hundreds of years,' he said. But when Joe Rogan pressed him on who exactly was telling him this, DeLonge went vague. 'You don't know what I know. I can't tell you some of the shit that I know,' he said. DeLonge implied that TTSA was being restrained from telling all by the government insiders feeding him information, but this raised a disturbing question. If TTSA had agreed to cooperate with the military in a government-controlled, drip-by-drip, soft disclosure, then DeLonge needed to explain why and justify that to his audience, many of whom were investing money in TTSA to see its promises fulfilled. They were assured their investment would 'allow gifted researchers the freedom to explore exotic science and technologies with the infrastructure and resources to rapidly transition innovative ideas into world-changing products and services',[4] whatever that meant. Needless to say, any breakthrough in anti-gravitics or free energy would bring unlimited riches to investors, but how realistic is TTSA's dramatic promise? And, is what DeLonge was purportedly told by insiders even remotely credible?

'Is there communication between the US government and aliens?' Joe pressed. DeLonge's answer did nothing to reassure listeners that he actually had any evidence. 'I personally don't know any of this stuff. I personally wouldn't doubt it, yeah. Different races are coming and they're trying to win—.'

Joe: 'More than one race?'

Tom: 'Oh yeah, I don't know how many. Some are very human. Some look like you and I.' He went on to claim that the mythical city of Atlantis was real and that there were links between the ancient Greeks and the writing supposedly seen on the Roswell craft. 'The sixth biggest Defence contractor in the world is SAIC. In the front of the building, you have Atlanteans on thrones. Eight-foot tall statues,' DeLonge told Rogan triumphantly, as if that proved anything. 'Do they have pickled alien bodies?' Joe asked. 'I believe they do,' DeLonge said. 'I can tell you other shit offline.'

I know Tom DeLonge is a rock star and rock stars are expected to say crazy things. But, at risk of making myself unpopular with ardent ufologists, it is important to put his claims on record because TTSA is not just a lobby group; it is a public company soliciting money from potential investors as a public benefit corporation pursuant to strict US government Securities and Exchange Commission laws and regulation. TTSA's 2019 *Offering Circular* says, 'The company's Aerospace Division is dedicated to finding revolutionary breakthroughs in propulsion, energy and communications.'[5] That is careful lawyer's language, making no huge promises. A prudent company president would never make unsubstantiated claims that might materially influence investors. But, in his interview with Rogan, DeLonge actually made an amazing claim – that TTSA expected to soon build a working anti-gravity craft. As recently as July 2020, DeLonge tweeted, 'Working on the first plans for @TTSAcademy's first anti-gravitic experiment. More to come.' This is literally the holy grail of modern aerospace, something we know numerous US corporations funded in the 1950s and 1960s, with no apparent result. If anti-gravity is real, then the world changes overnight. I wonder how Steve Justice, Chief Operating Officer of TTSA and former head of Advanced Systems at Lockheed Martin's Skunk Works felt when he heard DeLonge suggesting that TTSA had a good chance of being able to demonstrate a propulsion breakthrough within four years. But DeLonge went even further and promised a definite propulsion breakthrough within eight years.

'We think we have a 60 per cent chance within 36 months or so we will be able to demonstrate something pretty kickass. Within eight years we will be able to demonstrate something. One big name aerospace company is offering its material sciences division,' DeLonge claimed.[6] These were huge promises for a self-described public benefit company inviting the public to buy its shares. At time of writing, well over three years on from DeLonge's interview with Rogan, TTSA has less than a year to deliver on his predicted 60 per cent chance of a major breakthrough in anti-gravity technology. Should investors be asking for their money back?[7]

What Tom DeLonge achieved with TTSA's creation was initially impressive (albeit a pyrrhic victory for TTSA as history was to show). He persuaded a remarkable group of in-the-know people to come out from the shadows and join his public benefit corporation, notably raising public awareness of the UAP mystery.

One of the world's most powerful newspapers was also pre-briefed about a major scoop TTSA had up its sleeve. *The New York Times* revealed in December 2017, journalist Leslie Kean had secretly met with former Department of Defence counterintelligence officer Luis Elizondo one week before the TTSA launch, while he was still the director of the Advanced Aerospace Threat Identification Program, along with 'several present and former intelligence officers and a defence contractor'.[8] Luis Elizondo who was to join TTSA, revealed he had resigned from the Department of Defence just weeks before in protest at the excessive secrecy and internal opposition about the UAP issue inside the government. Elizondo had been working for the OUSDI, the Office of the Under-Secretary of Defence for Intelligence and Security. He had served in Afghanistan, the Middle East and Latin America, and was a trained senior Special Agent with top-secret compartmentalised clearances, who had led operations against some of America's toughest adversaries. The then US Deputy Secretary of Defence for Intelligence, James Clapper, a former director of the Defence Intelligence Agency, recognised Elizondo's skills and, in 2008, had personally hired him into the office that acts as the principal staff for the Department of Defence on sensitive intelligence-related matters, overseeing a cluster of three-letter DoD agencies, including the Defence Intelligence Agency and the National Security Agency.

Soon after joining OUSDI, Elizondo was tasked to join a special program described by a deliberately dull-sounding military acronym, AAWSAP, the Advanced Aerospace Weapon System Applications Program. Inside that program, he led the Advance Aerospace Threat Identification Program (AATIP), the secretive Pentagon unit set up at Senator Harry Reid's urging to study UAPs. As Elizondo's website acknowledges, his mission was 'to conduct scientific-based intelligence investigations of incursions by Unidentified Aerial Phenomena (UAPs) into controlled US airspace'.[9] While Senator Harry Reid's AAWSAP funding from Congress ran out in 2012, Elizondo maintains that the Pentagon secretly continued its investigations into UAPs.

In 2017, after nine years in AATIP and its Department of Defence replacement, Luis Elizondo left the Pentagon because his efforts to investigate UAPs were being obstructed from within. 'Why aren't we spending more time and effort on this issue?'[10] Elizondo complained in a letter to his former boss in Afghanistan, Jim Mattis, now Defence Secretary. 'Despite overwhelming evidence at both the classified and unclassified levels, certain individuals in the [Defence] Department remain staunchly opposed to further research on what could be a tactical threat to our pilots, sailors and soldiers, and perhaps even an existential threat to our national security.'[11]

Luis Elizondo presented as a duty-driven loyal former soldier spook from central casting. In the days after the *Times* story on the AATIP program broke, Luis Elizondo became the public face of TTSA, explaining why he had gone public about the secret work he did for the Defence Department investigating UAPs. 'We found a lot,' Elizondo told CNN. 'I think that what's important is that we have identified some very interesting anomalous type of aircraft, let's call them aircraft. Things that don't have any obvious flight surfaces, any obvious forms of propulsion, and manoeuvring in ways that include extreme manoeuvrability beyond, I would submit, the healthy G-forces of a human or anything biological, hypersonic velocities, low observability, positive lift. Again, seemingly defying the laws of aerodynamics.'[12]

One striking aspect of the TTSA launch was that, while everyone carefully said these unknown objects were not necessarily aliens, the possibility that these UAPs are an extra-terrestrial (or a non-human intra-terrestrial?) intelligence was the elephant in the room. When pushed by CNN's Erin Burnett on whether he thought the Tic Tac objects were aliens, Elizondo initially ducked the issue. 'What I wanted to do was to allow the data to speak for itself and then use that data to inform leadership, senior DoD leadership about the potential threat that these type of technologies pose to national security, especially over any types of controlled airspace that we might have. So, I'm not trying to be evasive in any way or vague with your answer, but I think there's a lot of possibilities,' he said, evasively. Burnett pressed the question, asking, 'Let me just ask you point-blank the question, do you believe that life from somewhere else while you ran this program, came here, visited, observed?'

Luis Elizondo answered, 'I will tell you unequivocally that through the observations, scientific methodologies that were applied to look at this phenomena, that these aircraft, we'll call them aircraft, are displaying characteristics that are not currently within the US inventory, nor in any foreign inventory that we are aware of.' That certainly sounded like Elizondo was talking about aliens, but Burnett did not let him get away without actually answering the extra-terrestrial question. She pushed, 'So I know you're using – you're being clear but, I mean, the answer's yes?' Then, in a response that will no doubt be remembered as a definitive (perhaps even, one day, an historic?) moment, the man who ran the Pentagon's secret investigations into the phenomenon finally said what he really thinks. 'Aaah, my personal – I can't speak on behalf of the government obviously, I'm not in the US government anymore,' Elizondo responded. 'My personal belief is that ah, there is very compelling evidence that we ah, *we may not be alone,* whatever that means.'

So, there we have it – it is about aliens … maybe. Elizondo's admission was a significant moment and there were no doubt audible intakes of breath in black world crevices of Washington DC when he said it. The big question on everyone's mind since is, what does Elizondo know from his time in the black world that convinced him so strongly that the US has 'very compelling evidence' that we may not be alone?

The CNN interview with Elizondo was a sensational story, perfectly timed for the 2017 Christmas holiday slow-down when families were sitting around their TVs. For a while there was a flurry of mainstream media interest around the world, but the news cycle moved on and, within a couple of weeks, UAP sceptic and astrophysicist Neil DeGrasse Tyson dismissively told CNN he was not convinced. 'Call me when you have a dinner invite from an alien,' he said. 'The evidence is so paltry for aliens to visit Earth, I have no further interest. The universe brims with mysteries. Just because you don't know what it is you're looking at doesn't mean it's intelligent aliens visiting from another planet.'[13] And Tyson was right.

Another sensational detail in the *Times* coverage was that Bigelow Aerospace (the enigmatic aerospace billionaire Robert Bigelow yet again) had 'modified buildings in Las Vegas for the storage of metal alloys and other materials that Mr Elizondo and program contractors claim were recovered from unidentified aerial phenomena'.[14] This was an astonishing claim: that there were samples, perhaps from a non-terrestrial craft, in human hands, stored away in a secure warehouse. It underlined that people inside TTSA actually believed the UAPs may well be intelligently constructed vehicles of some kind, yet not human-made ... alien. That was one hell of a claim. But *Times* reporter Ralph Blumenthal has since walked back from that claim in an interview, admitting they have now learned that 'no materials were provided'.[15] For TTSA to be associated with such claims was dangerous territory for a public company soliciting public investments. The TTSA *Offering Circular* wisely warned potential investors that 'Aerospace and scientific research and development can be risky, and there are no guarantees that any of the projects we undertake will lead to a commercially viable product'.[16] Careful lawyer's language again.

But, in his enthusiasm for his subject, DeLonge also made the claim in his October 2017 interview with Joe Rogan that one of these UAP samples he saw actually lost mass when it was radiated with terahertz frequencies. 'Something weird. It resonates some kind of harmonic and it gets lighter. And if you hit it with enough terahertz it'll float,' he claimed. 'So, we're going to be showing people this stuff. We're going to be bringing out hardware.'[17] What he was talking about is anti-gravity, which is still, according to disclosed mainstream science, only a theoretical possibility that aerospace scientists dream about. At the time of writing, however, nearly four years on from this interview, we are still waiting to see TTSA's anti-gravity metamaterials. Sooner or later, people will start asking DeLonge, where is the beef?

In another report on the Defence Department's UAP investigations, the *Politico* website journalist Bryan Bender was one of the first mainstream media journalists to start seriously addressing the growing concern inside the US military about sightings of anomalous craft around sensitive military facilities and exercises. He acknowledged that one possible theory to explain the unusual sightings of these unknown craft was 'that a foreign power – perhaps the Chinese or the Russians – had developed next-generation technologies that could threaten the United States'.[18] But he offered no evidence to support such speculation and he also coyly hinted at the extra-terrestrial hypothesis by citing Bob Bigelow's past outspokenness that he believes aliens frequently travel to Earth. Bender's story explained that some in government were 'uncomfortable with the aims of the program, unnerved by the implication that the incidents involved aircraft that were not made by humans'. For, in the face of overwhelming evidence that the UAPs were not Chinese or Russian craft, it is indeed a plausible possibility to at least consider that they were not human.

DeLonge's To The Stars organisation eventually posted three dramatic Defence Department videos of UAPs on its website. The first two were posted in mid-December 2017, timed for impact when *Politico*, *The Washington Post* and *The New York Times*[19] broke the story of the Defence Department's AATIP investigations into UAPs. One of those videos was the 76-second so-called FLIR1 video, depicting the Tic Tac, the egg- or oblong-shaped UAP filmed by the USS *Nimitz* pilot in 2004.[20] That FLIR1/Tic Tac film was posted on the TTSA site along with another undated 34-second video known as the 'Gimbal'.[21] The Gimbal video shows a UAP appearing to swivel on its axis in flight, manoeuvring in ways that defied known conventional aircraft capabilities. TTSA initially revealed very little about the Gimbal object other than that it was seen and videoed by US Navy fighter pilots at an unspecified location (it would later emerge that the Gimbal was almost certainly videoed sometime in late 2014 or early 2015 off the east coast of the US). The TTSA website said the Gimbal had 'low-observability' on both video and radar; it also had no distinguishable flight surfaces, no 'obvious propulsion system', 'never-before-seen flight capabilities' and, because of a strange shimmer on its surface, they speculated that it had a 'possible energy or resonance field of unknown nature'.

Three months later, in March 2018, TTSA posted another Defence Department video on its website, which it dubbed the Go-Fast video.[22] It also lacked any details on when or where it was shot, or who shot it, other than that it was captured by a US Navy FA-18 fighter using the jet's advanced targeting forward-looking infrared (ATFLIR) pod. On the 34-second video, the UAP appeared as a white oval shape moving at apparent high speed from top right to lower left of the screen flying very low over the water (although the claimed high speed is disputed by some). TTSA posted it online the same day that Christopher Mellon penned a fresh plea for the government to take the issue seriously. 'It is time to set aside taboos regarding "UFOs" and instead listen to our pilots and radar operators,'[23] he told *The Washington Post*'s readers. His story revealed that this latest newly declassified Go-Fast video was filmed off the east coast of the US sometime in late 2014 or early 2015.

TTSA's role in bringing these extraordinarily important videos to light should be acknowledged. They would elicit historic admissions by the US military. But, at the time of writing, TTSA's future role in UAP disclosure activism looks uncertain, for, in late 2020, TTSA imploded. Speculation had mounted for months that former Defence Department mandarin Christopher Mellon and key figures Luis Elizondo and Steve Justice were leaving TTSA. No detail was provided by TTSA on exactly why they were leaving, but it took Tom DeLonge several more months to formally admit to the Securities Exchange Commission not only their departure,[24] but also, a week later, Dr Hal Puthoff's resignation as a director. DeLonge announced he had 'recently taken steps to refocus [TTSA's] operations to scale back its initiatives in science and tech commercialization and to place a greater emphasis on the operations of its entertainment business. As a result, Dr. Harold E. Puthoff, one of TTSA's board members, has transitioned from his role as a director to serve on the company's scientific advisory board'.[25]

DeLonge put the best possible spin on the loss of his most illustrious talent but, any way you looked at it, it was a massive climb-down from TTSA's stated long-term objectives. People who had invested on the promise of a major breakthrough in anti-gravitic propulsion would be sorely disappointed. One thing for sure though – there was no putting the astonishing video evidence TTSA had flushed out of the black world back into the box.

Chapter 17

Verified Unidentified

In May 2019, a story broke in *The New York Times* that revealed even more astonishing UAP encounters with US military aircraft, this time over the Atlantic Ocean off the coast from Virginia Beach, just a short flight from Washington DC.[1] In late 2014, two pilots in Super Hornet F/A-18 fighter jets had been training for imminent combat operations in the Middle East, as part of a carrier strike group led by the nuclear-powered and nuclear-armed flagship aircraft carrier USS *Theodore Roosevelt*. The F/A-18 fighters were flying in tandem and, unlike those on the USS *Nimitz* ten years earlier, they had new advanced APG-79 electronic beam scanning radar systems. Carrier Strike Group Twelve, as it was known, also had a brand-new integrated data-link capability, giving commanders a comprehensive overview of the battlespace like never before. New E-2D Hawkeye airborne early-warning aircraft were also in the air.

For weeks, every pilot on almost every mission had been tracking strange objects in the sky. At first pilots assumed their new radars were faulty because they showed unknown objects apparently hovering for hours and then flying at instantaneous hypersonic speeds at altitudes ranging from 30,000 feet to sea level. But when their jets' infrared cameras started picking up the same objects, the pilots realised these were not false radar tracks at all. Something weird was indeed stalking the fleet up and down the coast, even if the pilots' eyes did not always see what their sensors were detecting. This was a grave issue for a military exercise in what was meant to be a closed training area; any potential adversary could learn how to anticipate and counter strategies if they saw enough.

On one occasion, the two fighters were flying in open skies barely 30 metres apart when, out of nowhere, a mind-bogglingly anomalous object hurtled through the narrow gap that separated them. What the pilots saw was a translucent sphere, like 'a giant soap bubble', that passed between the two jets. 'It was basically a cube inside a sphere with the points of the cube touching the outside of the sphere,' navy fighter pilot Lieutenant Ryan Graves said of the serious near-miss incident recounted to him by his anonymous pilot colleague who experienced it.[2] 'I almost hit one of those damn things,' Graves was told. Christopher Mellon gave more detail about the mysterious cube-inside-a-sphere object seen by the pilots in this incident: 'They're perhaps six to ten feet across. And they're transparent, like a soap bubble with a black cube inside. And the edges of the cube are touching the interior of the bubble …'.[3]

The *Times* story revealed that one of the Super Hornet pilots filed an official mishap report with the navy, only for it to be ignored. After the translucent soap bubble incident between the two F/A-18 jets, Lieutenant Graves' squadron filed a safety report to the navy, but they never heard back from anyone. In another sighting, fighter pilot, Lieutenant Danny Aucoin, personally encountered UAPs twice. 'The first time, after picking up the object on his radar, he set his plane to merge with it, flying 1000 feet below it. He said he should have been able to see it with his helmet camera, but could not, even though his radar told him it was there,' the

Times reported. 'A few days later, Lieutenant Aucoin said, a training missile on his jet locked on the object and his infrared camera picked it up as well. "I knew I had it, I knew it was not a false hit," he said. But still, "I could not pick it up visually".[4]

The stories from the east coast *Roosevelt* training exercises revealed how, as the training off the east coast rolled into 2015, pilots encountered these anomalous objects almost every time they flew. Defence reporter Tyler Rogoway also revealed that the sightings were not confined to Graves' squadron. The 'presence of the mysterious objects in the restricted training airspace off America's east coast was so pervasive that it was largely common knowledge among local flying units,' he wrote.[5] In fact, all of the Super Hornet squadrons equipped with the new APG-79 radars were detecting the objects on radar and ATFLIR and seeing them with their own eyes.

As well as the article in *The New York Times*,[6] the story was told in detail for a series TTSA made with the History Channel, called *Unidentified: Inside America's UFO Investigation*.[7] Graves told both the TV documentary and *The New York Times* that the publicly released Gimbal video was part of a much longer, higher-resolution video he viewed on board the *Roosevelt*. What he saw on the onboard video was a cluster of smaller craft flying in an inverted V-shape in front of the larger Gimbal object. The section of video publicly released by the Pentagon only showed the Gimbal by itself; the other objects were out of the picture. At one point, the Gimbal was stationary and then it apparently rotated through a 90-degree angle in the hover, a manoeuvre that is impossible for any known conventionally powered craft. 'It's just basic airplane physics,' Graves explained. The pilots rationalised that such a craft could not possibly be part of some covert US government project because the risk involved in deploying secret new technology against your own pilots without warning was immense and a flagrant breach of standard operating procedure. Just like the 2004 Tic Tac, the Gimbal had no visible flight surfaces, no visible propulsion, and no heat signature. It stayed stationary in one spot, even though there were 120 knots of wind against it, then it suddenly accelerated well above supersonic speeds. Even stranger, the cluster of objects it was part of stayed aloft for hours, far beyond the fuel duration of any known conventional craft. 'What's fascinating and interesting about these objects,' Graves said, 'is that they're up there when we take off, they're doing their thing for our hour-and-a-half, maybe two-hour flight, and then we land. And my buddy that takes off an hour later is seeing the same things.'[8]

Perhaps most disturbing of all was that when the USS *Theodore Roosevelt* left Florida in March of 2015 for the Persian Gulf to be part of the battle against ISIS in Iraq and Syria, these unknown craft apparently followed the carrier battle group to the other side of the world. Lieutenant Graves admitted the carrier had sightings while he was flying in the Middle East that year. 'I did occasionally see radar signatures that performed in ways that were consistent with our experiences back home, though at a significantly reduced rate,' he told *The War Zone*.[9]

You may be thinking, maybe it was a fault in the new radars installed on the navy F/A-18 Super Hornet fighters that they were showing false returns; perhaps they were not seeing anything real out there at all (which of course ignores the fact that multiple pilots say they also saw the objects with their own eyes). Navy Lieutenant Ryan Graves was asked about this and he countered that, on numerous occasions, his APG-79 radar tracked these objects kilometres away. When their jets' Advanced Targeting Forward Looking Infrared (ATFLIR) got close enough, it visually displayed the UAP, either electro-optically or in infra-red mode. 'We're getting them on radar and then picking them up on the FLIR,' he said. 'What appeared on the cockpit display was not the distinct outlines of an aircraft that one would normally see; typically, you can almost see the rivets.'[10] Whatever the objects were, they were seen on the ATFLIR or directly by both the pilot and his or her weapons system officer in the backseat, which all suggests these UAVs were real and not some illusion caused by the new radars. Sceptics feebly suggest that what the pilots saw was just a reflection off their cockpit or a strange cloud, but such explanations are incompatible with the overwhelming evidence. As former expert operators of the technology have explained, if it was simply a distant jet exhaust, the whole aircraft would have shown up clearly on the ATFLIR camera.

In the wake of the media coverage about the west and east coast sightings by the US Navy, pressure intensified in Congress for the military to explain what it knew. Republican Congressman Mark Walker of North Carolina, who sat on the Intelligence and Counterterrorism subcommittee of the House Homeland Security Committee, flatly accused the navy of withholding information about UAPs. He queried what resources the navy was dedicating to investigating the sightings and he asked if any physical evidence had been found to substantiate the claims, or whether foreign adversaries or private companies have developed this technology. 'Based on pilot accounts, encounters with these UAPs often involved complex flight patterns and advanced manoeuvring, which demand extreme advances in quantum mechanics, nuclear science, electromagnetics and thermodynamics. If the accounts are true, the unidentified crafts could pose a serious security risk to our military personnel and defence apparatus,' Walker wrote in a letter to the Secretary of the US Navy. 'They could also represent a tremendous opportunity for advancements in science and technology that can contribute to the public good.'[11]

He was told by Navy Undersecretary Thomas Modly that 'the Department of the Navy takes these reports very seriously and continues to log sightings and fully investigate the accounts'.[12] That was the kind of evasive answer spin doctors give when they really do not want to answer curly questions. So, Walker criticised the navy's apparently unwillingness to cooperate. 'While I am encouraged the Under Secretary of the Navy confirmed that UAP encounters are fully investigated, there is frustration with the lack of answers to specific questions about the threat that superior aircraft flying in United States airspace may pose,' he told *Politico*.[13]

The US Navy came out of the whole episode looking ridiculous. It took until September 2019 for the navy to formally acknowledge what everyone had long taken for granted – that it could not offer any satisfactory explanation for the phenomena its pilots are still witnessing to this day. 'The Navy considers the phenomena contained/depicted in those three videos [the Tic-Tac, The Go-Fast and the Gimbal UAPs] as unidentified,' a navy spokesman Joseph Gradisher told John Greenewald's *The Black Vault* website.[14] 'The Navy has not publicly released characterizations or descriptions, nor released any hypothesis or conclusions, in regard to the objects contained in the referenced videos.' That admission by the US Navy was historic. For the past 75 years, the US military has flatly denied, in public, that UAPs are an issue of national security concern, repeatedly playing down the notion they may be any threat and repeatedly suggesting (despite the protestations of many witnesses) prosaic explanations for the phenomena such as lenticular clouds, weather balloons or optical illusions. But this time, it was the navy's own sophisticated sensors and pilots that had caught the phenomenon on three apparently incontrovertible videos and the US Navy was forced to admit it had no idea what they were. The implication was that these craft were not American because even the US Navy acknowledged they were unknown. However, that does not exclude the possibility that the US Air Force was hiding such a technological breakthrough from the navy as well as from every oversight committee in the Congress. (In March 2021, *Politico*'s Bryan Bender wrote that the US Air Force and 'spy agencies' were 'blocking or simply ignoring the effort to catalogue what they have on "unidentified aerial phenomena"'.[15] His story was sourced to unnamed 'multiple current and former government officials'.) The *Roosevelt*'s Lieutenant Ryan Graves and other pilots were eventually summonsed to give confidential briefings to members of Congress. US Senators were also given a classified briefing by the Pentagon (including the Office of Naval Intelligence) about the UAV sightings; there were multiple requests from members of key Congressional oversight committees for more information throughout 2019. President Trump was also briefed.

If these craft are real, and numerous military pilots and sensor systems assert that they are, this is indisputably an issue of grave national security concern. These mysterious objects (craft?) display acceleration and manoeuvrability capabilities far beyond any acknowledged technology. They easily outmanoeuvre F/A-18s and the speeds and turns they achieve would humble even the latest F-22 or F-35 fighters.

To emphasise just how anomalous these unknown aerospace vehicles are, TTSA's Luis Elizondo coined a phrase, 'The Five Observables', the characteristics most commonly seen in UAPs.

- The first is that these UAVs are capable of 'positive lift or anti-gravity'. They display an apparent ability to fly without any apparent means of propulsion or lift.
- Secondly, they have 'instantaneous acceleration'. They reach a high rate of speed in a short amount of time. 'We are seeing objects that are doing 50, 100, 200 plus G-forces,' said Elizondo. 'Materials just aren't designed to withstand those forces.'[16]
- The third observable is 'hypersonic velocity'. These craft are travelling at speeds far beyond the speed performance limits of

any known aircraft. Elizondo said: 'As an object is travelling in three-dimensional space, the faster it goes, the more forces are placed upon it. And yet, here is an object that is doing well in advance of those speeds and I don't mean just three or four thousand miles an hour, potentially 8, 9, 10,000 miles per hour.'[17]

- The fourth observable, ironically, is 'low observability'. All of these craft can conceal themselves from any kind of radar or tracking. 'You're looking at an object that you should be able to detect very clearly and yet when you look at it with the naked eye it's opaque, kind of blurry, not well defined, I'm not really sure what I'm looking at. Other times it looks like it's jamming some of the best radar systems that we have in our inventory,' Elizondo explained.[18]

- Fifth and finally, the UAPs display 'trans-medium travel'. One of the most baffling attributes of these craft is that they seem to have the ability to seamlessly move through space, air and water with little if any apparent disruption to their motion. 'Everything we build is purpose specific for its environment. A plane looks like a plane, has wings, has engines, has a rudder, has a nose because it has to be aerodynamic. Yet here's an object that can operate just as easily in atmosphere, in space and potentially even underwater and yet it doesn't change its design characteristics. What type of technology could allow that? Any one of these, mind, would be an absolute game-changer for any foreign adversary to have. Just one of them. It would be a game changer and yet here we have things doing all five,' Elizondo emphasised.[19]

The first hint that the Pentagon was possibly changing its attitude to UAP sightings came in April 2019, when *Politico*'s Bryan Bender broke the story that the US Navy was drafting new guidelines for pilots and other personnel to report encounters. 'There have been a number of reports of unauthorised and/or unidentified aircraft entering various military-controlled ranges and designated air space in recent years,' a navy statement said. 'For safety and security concerns the navy and the [US Air Force] takes these reports very seriously and investigates each and every report.' The story also revealed that the navy had given briefings by senior naval intelligence officials as well as aviators to Congressional members and staff. 'To be clear, the navy isn't endorsing the idea that its sailors have encountered alien spacecraft,' Bender clarified. 'But it is acknowledging there have been enough strange sightings by credible and highly trained military personnel that they need to be recorded in the official record and studied – rather than dismissed as kooky phenomena from the realm of science-fiction.'[20]

On 27 April 2020, the US Defence Department officially released three of the previously published UFO videos taken by the US Navy pilots in 2004 and 2014–15. The Pentagon admitted, 'the aerial phenomena observed in the videos remain characterized as "unidentified"'.[21] This was the first time the Pentagon publicly confirmed the footage was authentic. Suddenly, after seven decades of denial, the US Defence Department was conceding that there is a superior unknown aerospace phenomena or technology being incontrovertibly recorded on video by its pilots that it could not identify.

There is absolutely no doubt that what the US Navy's pilots witnessed off the coast of Florida in 2014 and 2015 and off the west coast in 2004 was disturbingly weird and potentially dangerous. But perhaps the most bizarre observation to be drawn from this spate of sightings was the reaction that came from the senior brass of the US military, when its pilots complained about this apparent threat to air safety. The military command didn't react at all other than to give belated promises to investigate.

One of the most telling moments in the *Unidentified* History Channel documentary came when Lieutenant Ryan Graves described the reaction at sea of the Commander of the *Roosevelt* task force Rear Admiral Andrew L. Lewis, as he viewed a video of the UAPs recorded by the fighter jets: 'He looks at the video and goes "Hah!" and walks out,' Graves recalled.[22] That is not the sort of response you would expect from a responsible senior naval commander who was baffled by what he saw. It suggests that perhaps the commander already knew about these mysterious craft, that he was unsurprised. It could also explain why, soon after the USS *Nimitz* Tic Tac sightings, men clearly working for some arm of the US military or intelligence services arrived to collect the data drives. If the Tic Tac, the Gimbal and the Go-Fast UAPs were some super-secret government project testing a major technology breakthrough against US Navy pilots, then perhaps the boffins wanted to see as quickly as possible how their craft performed against the formidable might of two carrier battle groups. However, if the US military truly was test-flying some extraordinary new aerospace technology, it begs the question why no one told the pilots not to talk publicly about it? If this is a huge US technological breakthrough, it was compromised by an inept breach of security.

There is also indisputable evidence to show that the US government is definitely hiding something it does not want to tell you about these UAPs. In October 2019, researcher Christian Lambright made a *Freedom of Information Act* request to the US Navy's Office of Naval Intelligence (ONI), seeking records relating to the USS *Nimitz* Tic Tac UAP encounter. He cited the former fighter pilot who broke the original Tic Tac story, Paco Chierici, who wrote how he was allowed to view a classified ONI report before he wrote his article, a document that still has not been released by the navy. This confirmed ONI had conducted its own investigation and he asked for those records. The reply he received in December 2019 was intriguing; the navy admitted it does hold briefing slides that are classified top secret, stating, 'the release of these materials would cause exceptionally grave damage to the National Security of the United States'.[23] The Office of Naval Intelligence's refusal to release anything at all was revealing for what it suggests – that there is indeed something very sensitive being hidden from public scrutiny. A total ban on release like this is puzzling; it is understandable that the military might have to censor part of these documents in order to keep the full capabilities of its high-tech radar and ATFLIR systems secret, but what could possibly be so secret that the briefing slides could not be released in their entirety? The US government is indeed holding on to something about these UAPs it does not want you to know.

What is also baffling about this whole mystery is that Christopher Mellon, the former Department of Defence insider who should know if the US has anti-gravity craft capable of these extraordinary feats, categorically says these objects are not American technology: 'You know, as a former intelligence person, I'm a little frustrated that we spend $15 billion a year to try to avert strategic surprise and then we have vehicles with extraordinary capabilities, surveilling one of our aircraft carrier battle groups, and nobody's taking action to find out where these things are coming from and what they're doing there.'[24] Or, as TTSA's Steve Justice, former Lockheed Martin Skunk Works executive, said, 'My greatest fear is that an adversary did figure it out and we are just way, way, way behind.' These men would (or should) know. Their comments run counter to the cover-up theory; if these former black world insiders do not know about an anti-gravity craft built by the US government, then either it is being kept secret from them or it is not US technology at all. What is clear is that no one in the US military seems to care much about the possible threat posed by weird UAPs in their airspace. To many observers, that says volumes.

I find myself thinking back to Tom DeLonge's animated claims back in March 2016 to George Knapp, that he learned from his government insiders that the US had made a stunning secret technological breakthrough in anti-gravitic propulsion, and that the world was on the brink of learning about these extraordinary scientific achievements. 'Yes, we are building machinery that have anti-gravity. And yes, I was told that. It's a big deal,' DeLonge effused.[25] A conspiracy theory is swirling around that Tom DeLonge's TTSA, a supposedly public benefit corporation, was actually just a US government front, otherwise why would a bunch of spooks and scientists with top-secret clearances to protect hitch up with such an organisation. Tom DeLonge has acknowledged that his TTSA company provides the government with an opportunity for plausible deniability, to get what it knows out to the public without blowback. He told George Knapp, 'plausible deniability is something the government has always done and it's the way they operate, especially when they want to put out very serious information'.[26] But that does not prove he and his TTSA colleagues were government stooges. Maybe, though, there is something to the notion that DeLonge and his organisation are being used to get the story out, carefully.

Assume then that extra-terrestrial spacecraft have been recovered and re-engineered by the US (a huge assumption, I admit). This technology has been kept secret from the public and the Congress for 70+ years, and serious crimes have possibly been committed because officials presumably lied under oath to conceal what they knew. The conspiracy theory has it that one way of releasing this breakthrough to the public in a way that gets the keepers of The Big Secret off the hook for their crimes in hiding it is to use TTSA to dribble it out as their discovery. I surmise that, before TTSA's implosion, the plot required The General or his henchmen to quietly slip a blueprint for a flying saucer over a discrete café table in the back of Utah somewhere and, after a decent interval, up would bob TTSA's Steve Justice, Hal Puthoff and Tom DeLonge, slapping themselves on the back with the announcement that they have just discovered how to build a flying saucer with a warp drive. Just to add spice to the conspiracy theory, you will recall that back in March 2016, DeLonge made the curious promise that he could deliver a working craft within eight years, deadline 2024. How could such a promise have ever been possibly made if they truly were starting from scratch? Surely, the conspiracy goes, TTSA was getting a helping hand? Which brings us to something called the CRADA.

Chapter 18

Art's Parts

(Foreboding music rises as the camera closes in on the wreckage of a glowing flying saucer crashed in a lonely desert. We slowly track to a shocking close-up of a dead grey alien face in the smoking wreckage. Then we dissolve to a log fire in a family home and pan across to the pensive, weary face of an elderly gentleman in a wingback armchair, clearly weighed down with a great secret. Our narrator begins.)

'It is the captivating origin story linked to one of the most enduring myths of ufology …'

(Well actually, I suspect in all likelihood this particular story is a hoax, but it is important for you to hear it because people who should know better seem to believe it.)

The story has it that a short time before his death in 1974, an elderly grandfather gathered trusted members of his family together and confided he had been a member of a retrieval team sent to the crash site of the so-called Roswell flying saucer craft in 1947. At the empty desert location, his team found two dead alien occupants thrown from a largely intact metallic disc. Inside the craft, a lone ET survivor was found. The corpses of its dead alien comrades were sent to the Wright-Patterson Air Force Base in Ohio and the remaining craft debris was loaded onto three trucks.

The elderly narrator told his family the craft crashed because it collided with a meteor in orbit. In an act of selflessness, the aliens chose not to activate a powerplant that would have allowed them to escape to deep space because turning it on in the atmosphere would have obliterated New Mexico, Arizona, California and parts of Mexico. The occupants had instead ridden their stricken craft down, hoping for the best, choosing to sacrifice their lives for the sake of humanity. The grandfather revealed to his family how, for 26 weeks, he was part of a team that interrogated the lone surviving alien survivor of the Roswell crash. How, one day, the ET was placed onboard a US Air Force transport aircraft on a flight to Washington DC. But the plane and all aboard, including its alien occupant, disappeared during the flight in mysterious and disturbing circumstances. The fighter aircraft that scrambled to investigate a distress call from the transport plane suffered serious electrical malfunctions, hindering the air force efforts to find it. No trace of the US Air Force plane was ever found.

Roll forward 22 years to 1996. The army veteran grandfather had passed away but one of his grandsons was a serving US Army sergeant. The grandson felt conflicted over what to do with the earth-shattering evidence his grandfather had left him – a box containing a series of metallic samples recovered from the Roswell alien spacecraft, together with his grandfather's diary detailing his extraordinary role in one of the greatest moments in world history. In April 1996, the young sergeant finally overcame his reservations; he sat down and wrote to Art Bell, host of one of America's most popular radio shows, *Coast to Coast AM*, which covers fringe issues like UFOs and the paranormal. 'I agree with Neil Armstrong, a good friend of mine, who dared to say, at the White House no less, that there are things "out there", which boggle the mind and are far beyond our ability to comprehend,' the sergeant told Art Bell in a moving close to his first letter. His letter included a package of strange metallic samples.

Over the following weeks, the anonymous army sergeant, who only ever identified himself as 'A Friend', sent five letters with typed excerpts from his grandfather's diary.[1] Art Bell's self-described 'real x-files investigative reporter', Linda Moulton Howe, began investigating the claims and Art Bell started telling the dramatic story on his show as each letter arrived. At one stage, Howe even took a phone call from the anonymous letter writer, who explained he was currently serving in the US Army and was heading to the Middle East, 'and wanted me to know in case he didn't make it back alive'.[2]

As Linda Moulton Howe acknowledges on her *Earthfiles* website, the whole veteran grandfather story sounds like science fiction. There is more than a whiff of BS around the seductive narrative of the latest son in a family of American soldiers finally letting out Grandpa's incredible secret into the public arena before once again dutifully facing peril for his country. Selfless aliens sacrificing themselves for humanity also sounds, dare I say it, a wee bit of a tall tale. What also struck me is that the credibility of this story would be easy to damage by any thorough government investigator tracing the source of this ostensible mammoth leak to crossmatch the family connection between a 1947 Roswell retrieval member and a serving 1996 sergeant. It was probably a half-day's work for a competent investigator with access to computerised records, especially to find an army sergeant who admitted he knew America's most famous astronaut and who dropped enough hints about his army deployments as this one did. It left me wondering if whoever it was who wrote these letters was staying anonymous because they knew this story was complete bunkum. Yet, perhaps this was government disinformation, a cover story that allowed this physical evidence to be released in a sanitised way. It pays to be suspicious of sources who will not put their names to a story, especially if they refuse to identify themselves even off the record.

A fifth and final letter, sent in July 1996, revealed what the grandfather's diary recorded as the precise location of the crash site, 'near Roswell AAF within 30 mile radius of Base'.[3] The purported impact site was very close to where the first atomic bomb was tested in 1945. The most mythologised evidence from this story have long been the physical metallic samples sent with the letters. The grandfather's diary detailed what the military supposedly discovered about the first of these mysterious samples, that they were 'pure extract aluminium, as a conductor for the electromagnetic fields created in the propulsion systems'. Linda Moulton Howe says she sent the pieces to a scientist at a major midwestern US university for analysis, who confirmed they were 99 per cent aluminium. There is a photograph on Howe's website of the so-called 'UFO material' samples, which includes an image of fabricated sheets of louvred metal. This is where the cracks in the story widen. Mick West's *Metabunk* sceptics website points out that this louvred metal sample looks identical to louvred fin sheets used in car radiators since 1925,[4] a point that is yet to be addressed by anyone pushing the so-called 'Art's Parts' samples as authentic. It is one of several legitimate sceptical concerns about this whole story that just seem to be swept aside in the rush to believe. That is what Art Bell's listeners thought, too. When Art started telling the story, letter by letter, week by week, on his *Coast to Coast* show, his listeners responded sceptically; they did not buy it. 'I must say that I was somewhat surprised by the negative and close-minded responses directed your way, by some of your own listeners,' the clearly peeved anonymous sergeant wrote in a second letter to Art Bell.[5]

The third letter included six tiny pieces of metal, very different from the previous chunk of louvered metal. The writer claimed 'these scrapings came from the exterior underside of the Disc itself'.[6] Linda Moulton Howe's website has a picture of one of these pieces of metal, which is optimistically described as 'Micron-layered Bismuth and Magnesium Zinc from bottom of wedge-shaped UFO in late 1940s near White Sands Proving Ground, New Mexico'.[7] It is this curved lump of metal – the UFO 'Skin' – that has drawn an extraordinary amount of interest and speculation over the past quarter-century since it was sent to Art Bell. Incredible claims have been made over the years about these pieces of layered bismuth/ magnesium-zinc. Laboratory tests show the thin lines of bismuth range in width from one to four microns, less than the size of a human blood cell, which is about five microns in width. The magnesium-zinc is said to vary in width from 100 to 200 microns, which is about the diameter of a human hair. Howe says she was told by one exotic metals manufacturer in New Jersey that it simply was not possible to layer bismuth and magnesium in any known industrial process. 'It can't be done!' she was told. 'The layers won't bond with each other.'[8] An unnamed scientist is quoted by Howe as speculating that the 'waviness in the layers might be a fractal wave pattern calculated in the layered material's construction perhaps to better resonate with a specific frequency'. Soon the samples were being called metamaterials, promoting the notion that their structure somehow imbued them with extraordinary properties.

In his fourth letter, the purported sergeant again compromised his anonymity by admitting that, during a broadcast of one of Art Bell's recent radio shows, he was on a flight to Hungary for a 1996 military operation called Joint Endeavor. It would take a determined Defence Department leak investigator a few taps on a keyboard to find out how many sergeants were on a flight to Hungary on a certain date in May 1996 and who among them had a grandfather in the 1940s US Army. This bolstered the growing suspicion that this story was a tall tale. In a fifth and final letter, the sergeant claimed that 'in the late 70s' he had confided in a pilot friend about his grandfather's secret and they had talked about Roswell – and within hours, the friend, who was piloting a C-130 transport aircraft, was killed. 'You see, Mr Bell, my friend was carrying a Roswell sample. I have reasons to be fearful. C-130s don't normally get hit by lightning and explode,' the anonymous sergeant solemnly told Art.[9]

I have no doubt that most people reading this dubiously histrionic tale will have abandoned their suspension of disbelief and called it as utter BS, like I did, when they reached this professed crash account. One assertion in the letter that can be independently verified or refuted is the claim by the sergeant that his pilot friend's C-130 inexplicably crashed after it was hit by lightning. It is an extremely rare event for a lightning strike to down a huge and robust aircraft like a Hercules; modern aircraft are built to withstand lightning strikes. As best as I can tell, there is only one US military C-130 crash caused by lightning listed that might even remotely fit that claim. It happened in South Carolina on 30 November 1978,[10] four years after the grandfather supposedly imparted his solemn secret to his family. But, if this C-130 crash was the one he claims, then that was a full 18 years before the supposed US Army sergeant wrote his letter to Art Bell and Linda Moulton Howe. Based on the likely age range of a US Army sergeant, that means the letter's author was likely, at the oldest, a 12- to 14-year-old child when the US C-130 Hercules crashed due to lightning. It is clearly not plausible that a young teenage boy was exchanging confidences with a C-130 pilot about a super top-secret retrieved alien spacecraft hours before his plane crashed back in late 1978.

Aside from the spurious subject matter, there are also other reasons to be sceptical about this whole story. Debunkers claim that the Art's Parts bismuth-magnesium samples are not even unique or irreproducible at all, that the layered metal is simply slag from an industrial process called Betterton-Kroll, which removes bismuth from lead. So, the anonymous sergeant's story explaining the provenance of Art's Parts has major unresolved holes in it. It does not ring true at all.

If you are wondering why I have devoted so much energy into investigating the incredible and dubious claims being made about these mysterious pieces of bismuth-magnesium/zinc, it is because the US Army and TTSA are taking the Art's Parts purported UFO samples extremely seriously indeed, despite sound reasons to be sceptical. So seriously that, in October 2019, it was announced that To The Stars Academy of Arts & Sciences was partnering with the US Army to research alleged metamaterials that TTSA's sources claimed to have obtained from crashed craft.[11] Yes, this is for real. The US Army is collaborating in an investigation of purported alien spacecraft samples, including the dubious Art's Parts.

There was a disclosure notice by TTSA to the Securities Exchange Commission (SEC) revealing that in 2019 Tom DeLonge sold the same six 'Art's Parts' samples to his company for $35,000 and that Hal Puthoff would be analysing them for TTSA.[12] Researcher Keith Basterfield made the firm connection to the Linda Moulton Howe samples, noting that the SEC declaration stated that the purchased assets were '(i) One 1.75" x 1.25" x 0.25" piece of micron-layered Bismuth/Magnesium-Zinc metal; (ii) six pieces of Bismuth/Magnesium-Zinc metal; (iii) one piece of Aluminum that TTSA physicist Hal Puthoff already had in his possession that was on loan from Seller; and (iv) one round black and silver metal flake that physicist Puthoff already has in his possession currently on loan from Seller (collectively, the "Metal Pieces")'.[13] The filing also disclosed that Moulton Howe had previously held and studied these samples, 'reported to have come from an advanced aerospace vehicle of unknown origin'. The Art's Parts were sent to a US Army laboratory to test if they were from an alien spacecraft. It makes no sense to me that the US Army appears to have taken the Art's Parts' story seriously.

This agreement between TTSA and the US Army was secured under the terms of what is called a CRADA, a Cooperative Research and Development Agreement. A PR officer for the army declared that 'As materials research in general is of key interest to army research, the army is interested in any insights gained from investigating the properties of these materials, too … In this case, the army is providing the expertise and the facilities to analyse the materials, and TTSA is providing the materials themselves; both parties receive the result of the analysis. Just as there is no financial compensation to TTSA for the use of the materials, there is no financial compensation to the army for the use of the facilities.'[14] The army's official engagement with TTSA to aid in investigating these purported metamaterials gave the whole 'Art's Parts' metamaterials analysis project a huge credibility boost.

The CRADA stipulates army researchers will work with TTSA to develop advanced materials for the purposes of 'space-time metric engineering', 'active camouflage', 'quantum physics' and 'beamed energy propulsion'. It is only when you dig into what these terms actually mean that the supposed purpose of this cooperative agreement with the army becomes mind-boggling. 'Space-time metric engineering' is a term for a form of propulsion, the so-called Albucierre Drive, theorising a capacity to travel faster than light without actually doing so; in essence it is a real-life version of the *Star Trek*-style warp drive – as far as we know, still the stuff of science fiction. 'Beamed energy propulsion' is an idea already explored unsuccessfully by NASA – the possibility that spacecraft can be launched into space using a laser beam to leave the atmosphere. 'Active camouflage' is anyone's guess but, to continue the *Star Trek* theme, maybe it is a Klingon cloaking device. There are so many questions about why the army entered this CRADA with To The Stars Academy, not least why the army would see any advantage in working with TTSA to do research in areas that the US government has doubtless been funding for decades.

Before he left TTSA in 2021, the former Lockheed Martin Skunk Works engineer Steve Justice led TTSA's aerospace division but, even with his undoubted expertise, TTSA has never presented any evidence to date that it has the capacity to develop these theoretical technologies, nor whether anyone in the organisation has any experience that may help achieve a breakthrough. It declined to answer any questions about the CRADA when I sought comment, and declined any cooperation at all with this author. Steve Justice's decision to leave the company does not bode well for either the over-hyped metamaterials claims or Tom DeLonge's promised anti-gravitic propulsion system.

One clue as to why the army entered this relationship with TTSA came in a statement from an army scientist who works for its Combat Capabilities Development Command, Dr Joseph Cannon. 'Our partnership with TTSA serves as an exciting, non-traditional source for *novel materials* and transformational technologies to enhance our military ground system capabilities,' Dr Cannon claimed in a press statement.[15] The reference to TTSA being a source for 'novel materials' is the key point; it is presumably a reference to the purported mysterious metamaterials that TTSA has in its possession, which have supposedly been retrieved from suspected extra-terrestrial spacecraft.

An earlier 2018 disclosure TTSA made to the US Securities and Exchange Commission revealed that TTSA has already retained Hal Puthoff's EarthTech International Inc. to prepare plans on materials analysis and beamed energy propulsion launch systems[16] (which is probably why Dr Puthoff, although no longer on TTSA's board, remains on its Science Advisory Board). In a clear reference to the so-called 'metamaterials' that Tom DeLonge and others in TTSA have previously suggested came from extra-terrestrial craft, EarthTech's assigned role is 'to prepare a plan and advise on the collection and scientific evaluation of *material samples the company obtained through reliable reports of advanced aerospace vehicles of unknown origin*'. (My emphasis.) Another hint came in a tweeted TTSA announcement in 2019, when it posted an image of the strange bent lump of layered metal from the Art's Parts samples saying: '"The structure & composition of these materials are not from any known existing military or commercial application," said [then] COO Steve Justice. "We are focusing on verifiable facts and working to develop independent scientific proof of the materials' properties & attributes".'[17]

Just stop for a moment and think about the head-throbbing implications of this announcement. Tom DeLonge's TTSA, which has pushed the notion for years that the US military is concealing secrets about recovered alien spacecraft, agreed to share so-called UAP samples it had gathered from around the world with the very same US military that some of its members have accused of an egregious cover-up of recovered extra-terrestrial technology. Should they achieve a major breakthrough through testing these so-called metamaterial samples, the CRADA agreement allows for joint ownership of any invention that results. But, as we know, DeLonge has long claimed that the US government has already secretly developed anti-gravity technology, or that is what he was told by The General and his gatekeeper chums. What's in it for the US Army to collaborate in a venture like this, if Tom's extra-terrestrial-tech conspiracy theory is truly the case, if some arm of the military truly is hiding a recovered flying saucer in a cave somewhere? Moreover, why is the US Army allowing a taxpayer-funded laboratory to be used for the analysis of samples that, at the very least, seem to be of questionable provenance (especially the samples apparently identical to a car radiator fin that everyone seems to be politely overlooking)?

Some commentators with a dark conspiratorial bent suggest that the CRADA with the army is most plausibly a charade, a way for the US government to launder its secret anti-gravity discoveries made in the black world from back-engineering retrieved extra-terrestrial craft; that TTSA will supposedly 'discover' these breakthrough technologies in its collaboration with the army, which will then bring the discovery into the public arena without the need for any messy admissions about government cover-ups of alien tech for the past 75 years. Perhaps the implausibility of the US Army actually cooperating transparently with such research played a part in Steve Justice's departure?

Linda Moulton Howe has made stunning claims about the specific layered bismuth/magnesium Art's Parts samples over the years, including unproven suggestions that the material will levitate if it is hit with the right magnetic field, an anti-gravity effect. It is a whopper of a claim. Echoes here of Tom DeLonge's similarly dramatic assertion on Joe Rogan's radio show, mentioned earlier, that one of the metamaterials samples lost mass when it was radiated with terahertz frequencies: 'Something weird. It resonates some kind of harmonic and it gets lighter. And if you hit it with enough terahertz it'll float.' It is very important to note there that DeLonge did not say that the *hypothesis is* that it *may* lose mass or that it *may* get lighter; he stated it as a straight fact, implying this was verified. But nowhere has any evidence been publicly presented by anyone to substantiate such a claim.

Perhaps Dr Hal Puthoff, Steve Justice and Luis Elizondo, while at TTSA, knew something about some of the purported metamaterials samples they had recovered which they cannot reveal because of their national security oaths. They strongly hinted this was the case. There is no other reason to explain why they gave the Art's Parts samples such credibility. The sample is no longer just a scrap of metal; it is now invested with the status of a 'metamaterial', supposedly deliberately manufactured and purportedly capable of extraordinary properties if the right electromagnetic waveguide is put through it. When he was asked in May 2020 about the metamaterials, the former high-level Defence Department insider Christopher Mellon offered a curious answer. The conservative political commentator and conspiracy theorist TV host Glen Beck asked Mellon if he believed the United States had physical materials recovered from UAPs.[18] Mellon said some of the materials he was aware of had 'genuinely extraordinary properties', that some of the samples had different isotopic ratios from terrestrial metals. 'Some of these materials have different ratios than anything normally found on Earth, so it raises the question of whether someone was manipulating those in a lab somewhere on Earth at great expense, or whether these materials actually came from outside the solar system, formed in a different stellar explosion and different solar system,' Mellon said.

Based on what TTSA has so far revealed, there is simply not enough evidence yet to justify any conclusion that these samples are actually metamaterials or that they demonstrate extraordinary properties. We just have to take TTSA on its word. So, should we assume this whole claim about retrieved alien metamaterials is baloney? The US Army was clearly willing to give this claim credibility by allowing the use of its historical data, laboratories and scientists to do the tests; although, following DeLonge's announcement he is scaling back 'initiatives in science and tech commercialisation',[19] it seems inevitable that the whole CRADA with the US Army will fall in a heap. There has been no explanation to date from TTSA about what will happen to the much-hyped metamaterials, which presumably are sitting in a dark US Army laboratory or on a TTSA shelf gathering dust. I am still not sure what to conclude, but I suspect there is a lot we are not being told behind this deal between the army and TTSA. I strongly doubt the Art's Part sample truly came from a benevolent grandfather who surreptitiously peeled it off a flying saucer. To understand why everyone, including the US Army, was getting excited about these scraps of metal, it is important to understand what metamaterials are.

Chapter 19

The New Science of Metamaterials

Tom DeLonge's To The Stars Academy (TTSA) suggests that the Art's Parts samples are intelligently manufactured. One hypothesis is that their very structure may well work as a waveguide, so that when the right electromagnetic signal is put through the structure, the material might display miraculous properties such as anti-gravitic levitation. This might sound crazy, but this hypothesis is clearly being taken very seriously by some highly qualified and experienced scientists. Back in 1996 when these samples first surfaced, no one knew anything about the science of so-called metamaterials because it did not exist. Metamaterials are today not magical speculation, they are very real and, indeed, quite miraculous things are now being done with them by some very clever scientists.

Metamaterials are a major new field of science where the precisely conceived geometry of artificially constructed nanostructures can theoretically be used to manipulate forces like electromagnetic radiation, sound waves, and, it is speculated, perhaps even gravity. In essence, metamaterials get their properties not from their base materials but from their design.

Around the same time that Art Bell received the mysterious samples in the mid-1990s, a British theoretical physicist, Sir John Pendry, was beginning to conceive the idea of metamaterials. Pendry worked with Duke University in North Carolina, manufacturing metamaterials to create in reality the kind of magic of Harry Potter, such as a functioning invisibility cloak (albeit in its infancy, working at radar frequencies) that bends light waves. This is not the stuff of pulp fantasy or science fiction; this is a looming reality. The light Pendry has learned to manipulate with metamaterials is a form of electromagnetic radiation; light is essentially vibrations of electrical and magnetic fields. The theory goes that metamaterials can also potentially be used to alter magnetic properties, leading to further speculation that it might be possible to manipulate gravity with metamaterials. This is what is getting those in the know so excited – the notion that metamaterials may be one of the technological breakthroughs needed to achieve revolutionary propulsion systems such as anti-gravity.

That is why it is very important to test the claims being made about these so-called metamaterials, because a lot of TTSA's credibility is riding on them being something special, possibly not of this Earth, yet deliberately constructed. 'This one sample is engineered in layers thinner than microns through a process unknown on Earth, and for a purpose we can only guess,' journalist George Knapp excitedly told viewers in late 2018 over vision of what looked like the Art's Parts' bismuth/magnesium-zinc sample. His story quoted Dr Hal Puthoff saying, 'Nowhere could we find any evidence that anybody ever made one of these. When we talked to people in the materials field who should know, they said we don't know why anybody would want to make anything like this.'[1]

A letter from Dr Hal Puthoff (formerly with TTSA) to Linda Moulton Howe in 2012, revealed by journalist M.J. Banias on *Motherboard*, admitted that tests he did back then on the Art's Parts samples 'did not yield an interesting/anomalous outcome in the tests involving the application of various fields'.[2] But then Puthoff later told a Las Vegas conference in 2018 that the bismuth/magnesium samples 'turn out to be an excellent microscopic waveguide for very high frequency electromagnetic radiation terahertz frequencies'.[3] So, presumably something happened in the intervening six years for Dr Puthoff to find anomalies with the samples. Either Dr Puthoff is deluded, or he knows something about these samples that he is not yet revealing. In his 2012 letter, Dr Puthoff told Linda Moulton Howe that he did not have the equipment that would allow him to zap the Art's Parts' bismuth/magnesium sample with the required much higher frequency of 4.76–5.66 terahertz. That is presumably what the army was offering to TTSA under the CRADA. Assuming the conspiracy theorists are right, and the US military has already secretly mastered anti-gravity, then I am guessing the army scientists will make some attempt at slapping their heads in surprise and exclaiming, 'How about that?' when the test rig floats off the floor.

Of course, this also requires us all to uncynically accept that should the army, even in a best-case scenario, actually see an anti-gravity effect from TTSA's samples, it would not immediately tie TTSA up with national security proscriptions gagging them from revealing what they have discovered. If this is all true, and extreme scepticism is advised, are we really meant to believe that one of the greatest-ever scientific discoveries, potentially one of the most powerful weapons of all time, would actually be unselfishly shared with the world by the US military? As the Federation of American Scientists' *Project on Government Secrecy* explains, the *Invention Secrecy Act* of 1951 has long allowed the US government to impose secrecy orders on patent applications that contain sensitive information, which stops the inventor from either getting their patent registered or publicising their invention. In 2019, there were 5878 such secrecy orders in effect, most of them sponsored by the US military and many imposed on private inventors.⁴ For true believers in TTSA's laudable goal to bring this purported super-technology out into the open, there is good reason to be gravely suspicious about its CRADA with the US Army. I also think a lot of commentators are missing the most significant implication from the CRADA agreement – that the US Army was collaborating with TTSA to investigate something it had long maintained does not exist. Why is that so?

Credit is due to TTSA for avowing that it will do the solid science, but it is TTSA itself that raised expectations that these samples may be alien, especially with claims that extraordinary anomalous properties are already being detected. Just maybe it is possible that Tom DeLonge is about to be proved right with his claim that TTSA's metamaterials will float if they are hit with the right terahertz. Season one of TTSA's *Unidentified* documentary series on the History Channel has a sequence where Luis Elizondo tells the then Director of the company's aerospace division, Steve Justice, that they now have multiple metamaterials samples from numerous sources, including government sources. Again, it's a revealing admission. Why did the government retain samples from purported extra-terrestrial craft, and historical information about them, if, as it has said for years, this is all nonsense? And why on Earth would it allow them to be investigated by an outside UAP disclosure advocacy group like TTSA? As TTSA's aerospace expert, it fell to Steve Justice to deliver on the expectations raised by his colleagues. 'The expectations were huge. When the expectations are extremely high, performance has to follow. And so, performing is key to me now,' Steve Justice admitted.⁵ He was not kidding. No pressure. TTSA is very soon going to have to show some stunning results to support the claims it has made about these metamaterials because the fact that Steve Justice has walked away from the project suggests something came off the rails.

There were always grounds to be sceptical about TTSA, even before you consider this deal with the US Army. While rock star Tom DeLonge is CEO, the rest of the company was (and still is) largely made up of spooks, most of them with connections to the Central Intelligence Agency (CIA). Jim Semivan (who remains on TTSA's board and is still Vice President of Operations at time of writing) is a former senior operations officer and a former trainer for the CIA's Directorate of Clandestine Operations. Hal Puthoff worked for the NSA and CIA. Luis Elizondo was a former career counter-intelligence officer with the Defence Department, who worked most recently out of the office of the Director of National Intelligence. Chris Mellon was a former Deputy Assistant Secretary of Defence for Intelligence. TTSA advisory board member Chris Herndon is also ex-Defence Department. Norm Kahn, also on the advisory board, is a 33-year CIA veteran decorated with the spy agency's Intelligence Medal. The final advisory board member, Dr Paul Rapp, has a CIA Certificate of Commendation. These guys are all career military, defence and intelligence. This is a public benefit company top-heavy with black world spies, which claims it wants to develop supposed alien technology for profit with the US Army's help – and with a punk rocker as its front man. Seriously, what could possibly go wrong?

TTSA did nothing to reassure people of its credibility when it announced on Twitter in 2019 that it had acquired multiple pieces of metamaterials that 'are reported to have come from an advanced aerospace vehicle of unknown origin. We're enthusiastic about its potential use and how it can further our mission for discovery and innovation'.[6] It was pointed out that the photograph used by TTSA to support its dramatic Twitter claims about these purported metamaterials was, in fact, a downloadable commercial stock image of a natural layered stone called malachite;[7] and as I write this, the malachite stone image is still posted next to the TTSA tweet. At the very least, this was a misstep by a public company soliciting investors under strict Securities and Exchange Commission laws. TTSA has since used other images on Twitter of what look like Art Bell's bismuth/magnesium-zinc samples to promote its investigations into the so-called metamaterials. But, unless TTSA knows something that the rest of us do not know, it beggars belief that TTSA is giving credibility to the notion that the Art's Parts samples came from an extra-terrestrial craft. Why would a UAP disclosure activist organisation cooperate with the US military it has openly suggested is hiding these breakthrough technologies? I suspect the real agenda behind the deal with the military is that the CRADA will finally allow the military to share at least some of what it has known about metamaterials all along.

There is reason for caution for claims about samples purportedly retrieved from UAP craft; this is not the first time Hal Puthoff has publicly speculated that physical samples recovered from UFOs are of non-human origin. In a 1997 paper, Hal Puthoff commented about 'possible UFO artifact' samples recovered from a Brazilian UAP – the so-called Ubatuba object, which reportedly ejected pure magnesium metal fragments as it flew over Ubatuba in San Paulo province in Brazil in two separate incidents in 1954 and 1957. 'Laboratory analysis of the samples found the magnesium to be not only of exceptional purity, and anomalous in its trace composition of other elements, but 6.7% denser than ordinary pure magnesium, a figure well beyond the experimental error of the measurement,' Puthoff wrote in the same 1997 book review.[8] He reported claims that the only way to explain this observation was that the sample contains only the pure isotope Mg26 rather than naturally occurring terrestrial isotopes of magnesium. 'Since the only isotope separation on a significant scale in terrestrial manufacture is that of uranium, such a result must be considered at least anomalous, and possibly as evidence for extra-terrestrial manufacture,' Puthoff wrote in 1997. Once again, though, the problem with the Ubatuba samples is that they also came from an anonymous letter sent to a newspaper journalist. Moreover, more recent Stanford University analysis[9] and a 2020 analysis by Robert Powell of the Scientific Coalition for UAP Studies[10] has suggested there is no evidence at all that the Ubatuba specimens are of extra-terrestrial origin, nor that the magnesium is especially pure.

TTSA has also backtracked at times on some of its more dramatic early claims about these metamaterials. In October 2019, TTSA's then Director of Special Programs and former head of the Pentagon office that investigated UAVs, Luis Elizondo, was interviewed about these metamaterial samples by Tucker Carlson on the Fox News Channel.[11] The story introduction breathlessly asserted that TTSA might have actual physical proof of the existence of UAPs, but Lue Elizondo conspicuously cautioned about the provenance of at least some of the purported extra-terrestrial samples. 'Our company over the last year and a half has actually obtained quite a bit of material. And let me first preface, some of that material, its provenance is frankly hearsay,' Elizondo admitted. 'While other – the provenance of some of this material – is, has been substantiated.' He cautioned Carlson that it was only after all the tests had been done that TTSA would be able to reach a definitive conclusion. However, Elizondo went much further in a lecture he gave to the Scientific Coalition for UAP Studies in 2019. He showed his audience a composite picture of some of the retrieved metamaterials held by TTSA,[12] telling them, 'I won't point out which one's on that slide but there are some that are absolutely special and have been briefed to some very, very senior levels of this government. *And they do remarkable and extraordinary things.* [My emphasis.] And they're built in such a way that to this day, we still can't replicate them. To this day. So that should be very telling.'[13] If that is the case, TTSA has not yet publicised that research. The inconsistencies in how TTSA reports on the properties of these 'metamaterial' samples are troubling and it underlines the pressure that will be on TTSA to deliver, if it ever does.

Former Department of Defence intelligence insider Louis Elizondo has flagged that he is holding back on all he knows. In an interview with *Fox News'* Tucker Carlson in May 2019, Elizondo dismissed claims that the unidentified aerial phenomena objects do not exist, saying, 'It is an absolute fact that they are there. Now, what they are, where they are from, who is behind the wheel, we simply don't know.' He told Carlson it was unlikely they were foreign country adversaries flying craft in US airspace. Then, there was this revealing exchange:

'Let me ask you one last question,' Carlson asked. 'Do you believe, based on your decade of serving in the US government on this question, that the US government has in its possession any material from one of these aircrafts?'

'Oh … I do. Yes,' Elizondo responded.

'Do you think the US government has debris from a UFO in its possession right now?' asked Carlson, clearly surprised at Elizondo's candour.

'Unfortunately, Tucker, I really have to be careful of my NDA [non-disclosure agreement],' Elizondo answered, looking uncomfortable. 'I really can't go into a lot more detail than that—.'

'Okay,' Carlson said, moving to end the interview. But Luis Elizondo had not finished. He had something he clearly wanted to reveal. He talked over Carlson's wind-up to answer this momentously important question: does he think the US government has debris from a UFO in its possession?

'Aaah, simply put, yes.'[14]

This is one of the most significant statements ever made by a former or serving US government military official on the record about UAP. Not only did Elizondo imply that the UAPs are almost certainly extra-terrestrial or extradimensional, he stated categorically that he believed the US government has 'recovered UFO debris'. Elizondo's admission is at odds with the formal statement from the US government, the office of the president no less, flatly denying that the US has recovered extra-terrestrial technology. Elizondo says the United States government has recovered extra-terrestrial technology. Significantly, no one in the US government has since sought to rebut his claims or called him a liar. (The Pentagon did make a feeble attempt to suggest that Elizondo never ran the Pentagon's AATIP UFO research investigation, but the claim blew up in its face.) I also hear that Elizondo admitted to colleagues he copped a heavy reprimand from his former Department of Defence colleagues for his candour in that Tucker Carlson interview.

UAPs and hypersonic Tic Tacs are a fringe subject, but this was one hell of an admission from a former senior military intelligence official who had only recently worked out of the office of the Under Secretary for the US Defence Department with an extremely high security clearance. Elizondo said the US holds alien technology, period. That is big news. But there was no media, apart from researcher James Iandoli's Twitter feed, *Engaging The Phenomenon*. Iandoli asked former Bigelow National Institute of Discovery Science (NIDS) scientist Dr Eric Davis his views about Elizondo's claim of recovered extra-terrestrial debris. Davis sent this intriguingly mischievous reply: 'Luis Elizondo's very brief answer to Tucker Carlson's question about whether the US government is in possession of recovered, crashed *and landed* [my emphasis] UFO technology hardware is 1,000% accurate. My national security NDAs prevent me from adding any further comment on this.'[15]

This response went way further than Elizondo's limited admission about 'UFO debris'. Davis's statement boldly suggested that the US government *was* in possession of *recovered, crashed and landed* UFO technology hardware. This was an astonishing (and still wholly unproven) claim by an insider in a position to know (who, by the way, now works for the federally funded Aerospace Corporation on classified government projects). The deliberate choice of the word *landed* suggested he was talking about an intact craft and Dr Eric Davis no doubt knew his reply would cause a lot of mischief when he drafted it. James Iandoli told me that Davis made deliberate edits to his email response to emphasise the notion that the US government has something more than just samples or pieces. 'Dr Davis actually corrected the statement to portray what he felt was more accurate by including "landed" which was not in his initial statement,' Iandoli said.[16] I tried to get Davis to talk further on the record, but he responded that he has said all he wants to say publicly.

Davis recorded a cluster of extremely revealing interviews in late 2019 before he took up his new job at Aerospace Corporation, before he was bound again by the confidentiality constraints of the black world. All of them pushed Davis' line that he knew for a fact that the US was in possession of retrieved alien technology. He then surfaced in July 2020 in an interview with *The New York Times* (an interview apparently conducted before he joined Aerospace Corporation), where he admitted that the US held recovered physical UAP samples. He said examination of the materials had so far failed to determine their source and led him to conclude, 'We couldn't make it ourselves.' He also told the *Times* that he had given a classified briefing to a Defence Department agency three months earlier in March 2020 about retrievals from 'off-world vehicles not made on this earth'.[17]

Both Elizondo and Davis have asserted that the United States *is* in possession of technology from non-human craft, claiming their national security oath blocks them from saying anything more. What I find almost as amazing as their assertions is how little traction their claims gained in mainstream media. I suspect the default position for many media and scientists reading these claims of recovered UFO debris is to dismiss Davis and Elizondo as deluded fantasists and move on, because what they say is discomforting to their set world view. As author and journalist Leslie Kean told *Scientific American* magazine, 'I find it astonishing that there are still some scientists who adapt [*sic*] the position that it can't be, therefore it isn't. I don't have that choice, because I have witnessed many paranormal phenomena myself, and I know they exist. Those who don't want to believe these things will dismiss them no matter what they read, and they are unlikely to open themselves up to their own encounters with these phenomena.'[18]

Imagine for a moment if Dr Eric Davis sat down and wrote out what he knows, setting out chapter and verse of The Big Secret, the huge supposed government conspiracy to hide its knowledge of extra-terrestrial visitations to planet Earth, aliens, recovered flying saucers and re-engineered alien technology. Ideally, he would name names and set out the whole dastardly plot to conceal this incredible secret from the world. Crazy pipedream, eh? Well, that is exactly what many researchers believe has happened. They call it 'The Admiral Wilson Memo'.

Chapter 20

The Astronaut and 'the Spaceman'

I still remember the sense of wonder I felt as a child during the Apollo 11 mission in 1969, looking up at the Moon and thinking that, right at that very moment, there were actually human beings walking around on its surface, and we could watch them on our black-and-white TV. The whole astonishing expedition was of course prompted by terrifying Cold War brinksmanship with the Soviets, but the Moon landings were nonetheless hugely special. They underlined American exceptionalism and fired a sense that collective human endeavour could achieve anything it wanted to do, that anything was possible. *Ad Astra*, to the stars.

It is little wonder that the humans who pulled off this monumental achievement are remembered as heroes of aerospace history and, every year, folk travel to conferences across America to rub shoulders with the sadly ever-diminishing number of astronauts who made it happen. Australian architect and space exploration-buff James Rigney flew from his home in Melbourne, Australia, to attend a US space conference in 2013. Rigney had no way of knowing it, but his trip would put him at the centre of one of the most momentous UAP controversies of recent times. He was not a 'UFO obsessive'; what took him to America was his love for the adventure of space exploration. He deeply admired Edgar Mitchell and respected his intellectual curiosity. In Melbourne, Rigney served on the committee of his local space research association and had clashed with association members, who criticised Mitchell's post-NASA work investigating unidentified aerospace and paranormal phenomena. Rigney briefly met Mitchell in 2012 at the 40th anniversary celebrations of the final Apollo mission, Apollo 17. Over a few drinks at the 2013 Tucson Spacefest conference the following year, Rigney confessed his admiration for Mitchell to a fellow conference attendee, to whom we shall give the pseudonym 'The Spaceman'. What Rigney did not know was that The Spaceman, who wishes to remain anonymous, was a very close friend of the legendary Apollo 14 astronaut Edgar Mitchell. A year later, at another conference, The Spaceman made sure Rigney got the chance to have a long chat with his hero. 'What an honour to meet and spend time with this great man,' Rigney tells me. 'Dr Mitchell's work in both space exploration and the nature of human consciousness transcended conventional science as we know it. It was humbling to talk to a giant of science and exploration about how he felt our science and religious understanding had it all wrong.'

On 4 February 2016, Edgar Mitchell, the American hero who defied death by riding a giant highly explosive rocket 380,000 kilometres to the lunar surface, was felled by cancer, passing away peacefully at his Florida home, just one day before the 45th anniversary of his Moon landing. Before they die, elderly people often admit to traumatic or stressful events in their lives that they have never revealed before. Edgar Mitchell was one who did so. The Spaceman tells me the astronaut began confiding to him and other close friends about things he saw during his space odyssey that he had never talked about.

With an introduction from Rigney, I travelled to meet The Spaceman. His home is an extraordinary shrine to America's 1960s and 1970s Mercury, Gemini and Apollo spaceflight programs, an obsession that began when he was a young boy. He has a prodigious collection of space program memorabilia. Signed dedications and photographs from well-known astronauts and NASA officials cover his living room walls. At our first meeting, we watch much of Edgar Mitchell's Apollo 14 Moon landing and The Spaceman clearly knows the meaning of every phrase and instruction on that historic crackling audio. He has watched it hundreds of times and his lips move as Mitchell's voice calls the altitude as the lunar module comes in to land. The Spaceman has stacks of private correspondence with astronauts and NASA technicians, and those private conversations reveal an extraordinarily detailed knowledge of many of the untold stories behind that heroic enterprise. It is because he wants to protect his relationship with them that he insists on staying anonymous. 'These astronauts are my heroes,' he explains. 'Absolutely nothing has been done since that comes anywhere near what they achieved half a century ago. It's the greatest technological feat in human history, when the world held its breath and watched as man landed on the Moon. I was only a boy, but it changed my life. We need to remember these guys. They should be the story, not me.'

Throughout his life, Mitchell controversially expressed the view that there was strong evidence to show Earth was being visited by sentient life from either another dimension or somewhere else in the universe, and he spent a lot of time researching the phenomenon. That was why billionaire UAP investigator Robert Bigelow invited Mitchell to serve on the advisory board of his National Institute for Discovery Science research organisation. Mitchell's fascination was fired by locals he met near his hometown of Artesia, New Mexico, just down the road from the Roswell 1947 crash site. They told him, 'Roswell was real', that there truly had been a government cover-up. 'He was the local Roswell boy turned hero astronaut. Most of the people Edgar spoke to about Roswell never told anyone else what they saw. But they absolutely trusted him, and they told him what they knew, and they showed him what they had,' The Spaceman told me. Edgar Mitchell revealed to his friend that he was shown relics from the crash, including a sheet of memory metal that flattened back into its smooth-surfaced shape after it had been crushed. Mitchell later publicly accused the US government of a 'UFO cover-up'. The government's response to this living legend's accusations was always polite, but the US military has denied the cover-up accusation to this day.

Mitchell often talked about how the transcendent experience of seeing Earth from afar – the so-called Overview Effect – altered his life. 'From looking at Earth from space you come up with the question, who are we, how did we get here and where's all this going. And that's an ancient, ancient question that humans have asked for a long time. My experience was to realise that perhaps our science is wrong at answering these questions and perhaps our religious cosmologies are archaic and flawed. And given that now we are an extra-terrestrial civilisation ourselves, we need to re-ask these questions and do a lot more work to find the answers,' Mitchell declared.[1]

One thing that Mitchell always told the curious was that, in all his space travels, he 'never saw a UFO'. However, The Spaceman says that privately Edgar Mitchell confided he did see anomalous objects during his Apollo 14 mission that he could not explain. It was only in the last months of Mitchell's life that the astronaut finally took his friend into his confidence and told him that, incredibly, he believed – but could not prove scientifically – that every Apollo mission was closely watched by intelligently guided craft of unknown origin, and that he had seen these strange objects with his own eyes.

During the NASA mission, Mitchell confided to The Spaceman, he saw anomalous well-defined blue lights that appeared to have a structure behind them. A craft? One was captured in a photograph taken outside the lunar module on the Moon's surface, which shows Mitchell posing in the foreground and a blue light hovering in the distant blackness of space behind him. 'They'll say it's a lens artefact or a flare but it's not,' The Spaceman said the astronaut told him. 'He told me he saw it with his own eyes. He never said he thought it was aliens but like several other astronauts he was open to the possibility that it might have been.' Another even more intriguing cluster of blue lights reported by Mitchell to his friend appears on the high-resolution NASA lunar module film of the return journey from the Moon, as the Apollo 14 lunar module waited for the command module to rotate to allow docking. There to the left of the command module, clearly defined, is a trio of blue lights grouped in what looks like a dark triangular shape against the pitch black of outer space. It certainly looks like the outline of a triangle to me, as if there is a shape in a slightly lighter shade of charcoal, edged with the eerie blue lights, floating beside the command module. Or are my eyes playing tricks? It is impossible to be sure.

Anticipating claims the blue lights would be dismissed as some kind of lens flare or reflection, Mitchell told The Spaceman that the same supposed glitch appeared on two separate films from two separate cameras. The camera that took the shot of Mitchell on the lunar surface, with the mysterious blue light behind him, is still on the Moon; the camera that took the shot from the lunar module looking towards the command module, came back to Earth with Mitchell. Moreover, there were no blue lights that could have reflected from inside the lunar module; all the lights were white. Two separate cameras, but the same intriguing blue lights. We rewind the NASA vision two dozen or so times late into the night, straining to see form. If it was a craft, I ask myself, how could it possibly have escaped public attention for all these years? I find it hard to accept this could possibly be something real that has been overlooked. It seems absurd that this high-resolution digitised imagery of the NASA film has been available for decades and yet no one has ever queried the source of these strange blue lights.

Mitchell told The Spaceman there was nothing to be gained and a lot to lose by publicly revealing what he saw, and also, he could not be sure what the lights were. He could not prove they were alien, so he always maintained publicly he had never seen 'a UFO'. But he dismissed the possibility that what he saw were lens flares, reflections from inside the lunar module or camera glitches, because he saw the blue lights with his own eyes and went back later to check they were there on film. But he told no one, until that night with The Spaceman in the final months before he died. Mitchell also suggested NASA's astronauts were under an obligation of secrecy not to disclose anomalous sightings.

'I asked him why he always denied seeing UFOs and he would only say one word: Treason,' The Spaceman said. 'I took that to mean the astronauts were warned not to speak about UAP sightings and Ed certainly did not want to tell me any more about it.' I sat on the sofa, stunned by the implications of what The Spaceman was telling me, as he casually rattled off the other unusual sightings described to him privately by several other late astronauts he befriended, such as Al Worden, the command module pilot for Apollo 15, who died in March 2020. 'Al was in orbit for three days. Seventy-four times around the Moon. That's a long time looking at the moon. He just matter-of-fact told me, he saw lights, bright white lights, in craters on the Moon,' The Spaceman said. I have to be sceptical about such claims. Al Worden never asserted anything like that publicly, but he was open in his belief in extra-terrestrial life, even suggesting that humans were aliens from 'somewhere else'.[2]

The Spaceman was anxious I not ridicule Mitchell's extraordinary claims or legacy. I told him it was impossible to reach a definitive conclusion about the veracity of such astronaut sightings because I would have needed to hear it from Mitchell and Worden myself, and then test the evidence by putting it to NASA. 'They'll just say what they always say,' he laughed. 'Lens flares, camera glitches, reflections, tricks of light. That's why Ed never admitted what he saw. It was inviting attack. He stuck to what he felt he could prove.'

A few months later, I finally understood what he meant. After Edgar Mitchell died in February 2016, his nephew Mitch Harkins, who was living in Mitchell's home, took possession of several boxes of Mitchell's UAP and paranormal research files that he had retrieved from Mitchell's home study. Harkins was the son of Mitchell's late sister Sandra, and he had come to live with Mitchell after Sandra died. 'Ed took care of him,' The Spaceman told me. 'He was a redneck biker. He loved Ed.' Tragically, Mitch Harkins died in a motorcycle accident in mid-2018, but he had heeded his uncle Edgar's wishes to make sure his most sensitive files were preserved and passed on to the Spaceman. After months of negotiations, I was finally allowed by the Spaceman to see the original documents.

One of the first files I pulled out of Mitchell's archive was a November 1996 letter from a US Defence Department scientist (his name redacted) in the Weapons Sciences Directorate, referring to a 'metal artefact', which I speculated was from the mythical 'Art's Parts' purported extra-terrestrial samples. (The title given for the artefact was deleted on the document but when I typed in 'Art's Parts' in the same font, it fits.) It appeared to be written to a Los Angeles–based Hollywood TV show producer, perhaps one collaborating with Linda Moulton Howe or Art Bell, reporting on the results of scientific tests. The unnamed scientist asserted in his report, 'I must emphasise that, in my professional opinion, after thorough scientific testing, that the origin, manufacturing process, and function of the metal sample are unknown … Preliminary conclusions are, when the part is placed in a large electric field a lifting motion sideways to the electric field is observed. At this time, there are no known hypotheses that explain the observations.' It sounds like the artefact actually levitated when he zapped it. But, surely not. As far as we know to date, from the official accounts of the investigations into the so-called Art's Parts metamaterials, nothing anomalous was acknowledged to have ever happened. I could not resolve the provenance of the document because so much of it was redacted. I suspect the scientist's letter had been forwarded to Edgar Mitchell by Linda Howe or Art Bell to keep Mitchell briefed, but they had protected the name of the scientist by deleting a lot of the identifying information in the document. What it and other files reinforced for sure was that Ed Mitchell was a trusted confidant for many in the UFO community who were researching purported metamaterials and UFO crashes. There were numerous communications referring to famous events in ufology where the astronaut was let into ongoing investigations.

The paperwork also offered insights into the still-secret research undertaken by billionaire aerospace businessman Robert Bigelow and his National Institute of Discovery Science, while Ed Mitchell sat on the NIDS science advisory board. There were the aforementioned reports Dr Colm Kelleher wrote to NIDS about strange goings-on at Skinwalker Ranch and other parts of Utah and New Mexico. There was also a paper by Dr Eric Davis, where he wrote matter-of-factly about how UAPs used mimicry techniques to hide their form, 'entering the atmosphere with either the look or trajectory of a meteor or hidden within a meteor shower, behaving like dark meteors without the associated optical signature, hiding within an artificial or natural cloud, behaving as pseudo-stars sitting stationary over certain regions, or mimicking man-made aircrafts' aggregate features'.[3]

In his paper, Dr Davis referred to the infamous 1980 Cash-Landrum UFO case, covered earlier in this book, where the Landrum family reported a massive diamond-shaped UFO hovering over their car in the road near Dayton, Texas. As well as the trio reporting terrible burns from what experts declared was ionising radiation, one of the weirdest claims in the Cash-Landrum sighting was that they said they saw 23 helicopters, including massive CH-47 Chinooks, closely following the object. The US military denied any of its choppers were in the air nearby that night, and 23 of them in one place does sound implausible. Dr Davis's paper gave an explanation – that the helicopters were 'mimicry techniques employed for the manipulation of human consciousness to induce the various manifestations of "absurd" interactions or scenery associated with the UFO encounter. This in combination with the mimicry of man-made aircrafts' (helicopters) aggregate features were prominent in the Cash-Landrum UFO case'. There is no explanation for how Dr Davis reached this conclusion. No known science describes the capacity to manipulate human consciousness to induce hallucinations as described. Modern science would say it was science fiction.

However, an answer may lie in extraordinary PowerPoint slides we know now were prepared for a briefing of senior officials at the US Department of Defence, detailed online by *The Mind Sublime*. The individual behind that site told me he found the intriguing PowerPoint slides in early August 2018 while he was trawling through former US Deputy Assistant Secretary of Defence Christopher Mellon's personal website.[4] (This was shortly after *The New York Times* had revealed the existence of the previously secret Pentagon UAP investigation program.) *The Mind Sublime* researcher screenshotted his discovery to prove the slides came from Mellon's website, and, importantly, because the document was stated to be a PowerPoint for a briefing of the Deputy Secretary of the

Department of Defence. Perhaps it was these slides that prompted Senator Harry Reid to ask the Department of Defence for Special Access Program protection for the investigation – because what the slides said was momentous.

If the unredacted slides accurately reflect the Defence Department's knowledge of the UAP phenomenon, they are explosive. They reveal how the Pentagon's UAP investigation unit advised the Defence Department not only that the mysterious craft were a 'game changer' but that the US military was powerless against them.[5] One of the slides, headed 'AATIP Preliminary Assessments', shows that Elizondo's Advanced Aerospace Threat Identification Program privately advised the Defence Department that 'Preliminary evidence indicates that the United States is incapable of defending itself towards some of those technologies ... The nature of these technologies and the fact that the United States has no countermeasures is considered Highly Sensitive'.[6] The document, prepared for the Deputy Secretary of the Department of Defence, pushed for further investigation 'in order to determine the full scope of the threat and their capabilities to be either exploited or defeated'.

Another of the retrieved Advanced Aerospace Threat Identification Program slides found on Christopher Mellon's website was headed *DoD Threat Scenario*. It flatly asserted, 'The science exists for an enemy of the United States to manipulate both physical and cognitive environments in order to penetrate US facilities, influence decision makers and compromise national security.' If that was not enough to scare the willies out of you, the document further suggested that the phenomenon was capable of deploying 'Psychotronic weapons', which as best as I can understand means an ability to control the physical world with one's mind. The same document also suggested that whatever it is can also achieve 'Penetration of solid surfaces', which frankly sounds like magic. In a summary that would not be out of place in a science-fiction movie, the Department of Defence was also advised that whoever controlled the UAPs could achieve 'Instantaneous sensor disassembly ... Alteration/Manipulation of biological organisms' and that it could also effect 'Anomalies in the space/time construct' and 'Unique cognitive human interface experiences'. And, just to underline that the Defence experts thought it was real, the slide has a line stating, 'What was considered "phenomena" is now quantum physics'.

Many investigators have claimed the UAP phenomenon (assuming it is real) is benevolently intentioned towards humanity and that there is no reason to perceive the phenomenon as a potential threat. Dr Steven Greer has asserted, for example, that the whole alien threat narrative is a 'false threat narrative'.[7] Yet, if any of these claimed capabilities are real, then I can completely understand why they would give a superpower like the US the jitters. The described capacity to allegedly manipulate or alter biological organisms, for example, suggests an ability to influence human perception or decision-making; it would be the ultimate *Manchurian Candidate* scenario. It should be emphasised that there is not a shred of evidence on the public record to show that any of these capabilities have been proven, other than what has been revealed publicly and privately by the data from the Tic Tac, Gimbal and Go Fast encounters. Part of me just wants to shake my head and dismiss the claims made in this document out-of-hand as crazy nonsense, but we know these slides are real and we know that the highest levels of the Department of Defence were advised of these claims. The only issue is whether what the Deputy Secretary of Defence was told was true.

In June of 1997, just two months after Mitchell joined Steven Greer at his meeting with Admiral Tom Wilson at the Pentagon, Mitchell's files show he wrote to the powerful Republican Senator from South Carolina, Strom Thurmond – at the time the oldest and longest-serving member of the Senate. Mitchell's signed fax was sent in support of the contentious claims of Colonel Philip Corso in his then about-to-be-published book *The Day After Roswell*.[8] Corso asserted that there was indeed an alien spacecraft crash at Roswell in 1947 that was recovered by the US government. Senator Thurmond, who was the powerful chairman of the Senate Armed Services Committee, had unwittingly written the foreword for the book, praising his former staffer Colonel Corso as a man of integrity. Thurmond was embarrassed his support for Corso was being used to bolster claims of a US government UAP cover-up. 'I know of no such "cover-up" and do not believe one existed,' the Senator said in a statement.[9] Edgar Mitchell's fax privately assured the Senator that he was convinced the Corso story was true. In support of his case, he attached a letter to the Senator from Whitley Strieber, the author of *Communion*, a best-selling non-fiction account of Strieber's alleged contact with extra-terrestrials.

Strieber told the Senator in his letter that US Army Brigadier General Arthur Exon had told him personally in 1989 that there was a 'completely unequivocal cover-up' of a retrieved alien craft at Roswell and 'it went from [President Harry] Truman on down'.[10] Edgar Mitchell cited the Strieber letter in support of his case to the Senator that Colonel Corso's dramatic allegations be taken seriously. 'My initial scepticism of the Corso and Strieber type accounts has slowly turned to amazement as I dug through reams of documents and interviewed military colleagues,' Mitchell confided in his fax to Thurmond. 'The picture that emerges from the thousands of hours of interviews and data analysis is that there has been a systematic cover-up and denial by government of these matters of vital interest to all of us. Whatever rationale that existed fifty years ago for secrecy and denial has long since evaporated.'[11] Quite a claim from one of America's greatest heroes.

Chapter 21

Not Made by Human Hands

Nestled just along from the signed 1997 Thurmond fax in Edgar Mitchell's private archive is the document I have been looking for. It is best known as 'The Admiral Wilson Memo', but its real title is 'EWD Notes' – Dr Eric Davis' initials. It is this document – purporting to detail what Defence Intelligence Agency Admiral Tom Wilson admitted to Eric Davis in a private meeting in Las Vegas in 2002 – that many believers claim proves a supposed government UAP cover-up. The document was discovered by chance. In the US, Australian James Rigney befriended The Spaceman and learned he had the Edgar Mitchell files. In 2017, Rigney negotiated a viewing at The Spaceman's home. Rigney recalled, 'He came back with an armful of documents and dumped them on the table. I was going through them all, deciding very quickly what looks interesting because I only had about half an hour left before I had to go. I didn't have time to even read them there but weeks later he sent me copies of the ones I requested.' Among them was the 'EWD Notes'. 'I sat on it for months, knowing how important it was and not really knowing what to do with it,' he said.[1] Rigney sought out Canadian researcher Grant Cameron at a conference in November 2018 and showed him a copy of the document. The document finally appeared on the internet in June 2019. Researcher Richard Dolan has since dubbed it 'The UFO leak of the century'.[2] Debunkers assert the document has to be a fake.

For well over a year after the memo was first published on the internet, the former Defence Intelligence Agency official with whom Dr Eric Davis purportedly had this explosive conversation, Admiral Tom Wilson, made no comment. But, as rumours of an imminent *New York Times* story mounted in June 2020, Wilson finally issued a strong denial that any such meeting with Davis ever happened. I wish I could say Wilson's denial categorically resolved the issue once and for all, but I am not sure it did. The 'EWD Notes'/'Admiral Wilson Memo' deserve closer investigation.

The Spaceman, the keeper of Edgar Mitchell's archived files, told me he believes the controversial document was sent to Mitchell as early as late 2002 or in the first few months of 2003, probably by the recipient of the memorandum, Dr Hal Puthoff, who was Dr Eric Davis's boss at the time. If that timing is right, then it rules out the possibility the document was planted recently in Mitchell's archive. 'There is absolutely no doubt in my mind that the so-called Admiral Wilson document is real,' the Spaceman told me. 'There is a very clear historical line of paperwork all the way back to that 2002 meeting and there are earlier files than that that Ed Mitchell carefully put away.'

The reason the Admiral Wilson memorandum matters is because, on its face, it supports everything Dr Steven Greer, Edgar Mitchell, Commander Willard Miller, Stephen Lovekin and Shari Adamiak each said they were told by Admiral Wilson at their April 1997 Pentagon meeting, discussing the supposed UAP cover-up. If authentic, it means Wilson truly did tell them he investigated the codenames in a leaked document given to him by Greer, that he discovered a secret group working on recovered alien technology and that he was blocked from finding out any more about it. I have to admit, this all seems far too crazy and wild to be true. There are sound reasons to be intensely sceptical of claims in any document that an admiral who led the Defence Intelligence Agency just before he met Davis would be so candid with a stranger, even if Dr Davis was cleared to top-secret compartmentalised security levels and recommended by a close friend. One of the quotations attributed to Wilson in the memo has him saying to Dr Davis, 'If you blow my trust, I'll deny meeting you, deny everything said.'[3] Perhaps it is remotely possible that Admiral Tom Wilson was being a patriotic whistleblower, a courageous intelligence community insider who risked all at the end of his career to tell what he knew to someone he wanted to trust with his shocking secret. He was not prepared to go to the media, but he wanted someone with security clearances like Dr Eric Davis to know the truth.

I guess such a scenario might be possible, considering the laudable things I am told by his peers about Tom Wilson's honesty and high integrity. He sounds like the sort of principled guy who might reveal a sinister government cover-up. But we also need to weigh that with the fact that Admiral Wilson now categorically denies this conversation with Eric Davis ever happened. The only way to test this is to take a long hard look at the content of the purported 'EWD Notes'.

In his memo, Davis claims to have met the recently retired Director of the US Defence Intelligence Agency, Vice Admiral Thomas Wilson, on 16 October 2002, in a car parked in the carpark of a corporate office building in Las Vegas. Davis, who worked for Robert Bigelow's NIDS (National Institute of Discovery Science) was, more recently, chief scientist for Dr Hal Puthoff's Institute for Advanced Studies at Austin, Texas, and was briefly a member of Tom DeLonge's TTSA. He was then was hired in December 2019 by the federally funded Aerospace Corporation. He has repeatedly asserted knowledge of an ongoing cover-up inside the US government of recovered alien craft and attempts to engineer them. If his memorandum of this meeting is to be believed, he was meeting a top former Defence Intelligence Agency official who had investigated these astounding secrets five years earlier from the inside. You need to bear in mind, however, that Admiral Tom Wilson has told me this meeting never happened, that the memo is a lie.

The memo claims Admiral Tom Wilson made the astonishing admission that he discovered a shocking secret about a US government cover-up of recovered non-human craft. Wilson reportedly told Davis that he discovered the US government had long hidden a program secretly attempting to reverse-engineer recovered extra-terrestrial craft. This monstrous secret had been kept, and the alien craft hidden, ever since the Roswell crash in 1947. Since 1997, when an audit very nearly blew the whole operation's cover, the memo says the so-called 'Program' was hidden within the Office of the US Under Secretary of Defence for Acquisition and Technology. Wilson supposedly told Davis the people read into the Program – the 'Bigot list' – consisted of just 400–800 people, including Defence Department officials and an unnamed private corporation that was secretly storing the recovered alien craft. The Program apparently 'has recovered technological hardware not of this Earth and not made by human hands'.[4]

My instinct is to dismiss this all as completely nuts, the stuff of science fiction, and that is pretty much what retired Vice Admiral Tom Wilson told me in a June 2020 letter. 'The Dr Eric Davis memo contains somewhat detailed accounts of alleged efforts by me to get access to Special Access Programs ... and of meetings I supposedly had with various contractors or Special Access Program managers/overseers. I participated in no such meetings on these subjects. I never formally or informally requested any such access, was never denied such access and was never threatened to have my career "derailed" if I persisted,' he told me. Wilson denied visiting Vegas in 2002 and had no knowledge of ever meeting Dr Eric Davis. He said the only time he was ever in Las Vegas was for a Carrier Air Wing Three deployment to Nellis Air Force Base in 1979 or 1980. He says that in October 2002 he was on 'terminal leave' and retired from the navy for about three months, staying at an isolated camp in Maine before he started work for Alliant Technosystems in November.

As detailed earlier, we know for sure that Vice Admiral Tom Wilson met with UAP researchers in the Pentagon in 1997. Multiple first-hand witnesses from that 1997 meeting, including astronaut Edgar Mitchell, said that Wilson admitted he had discovered a secret US government UAP program. The 'EWD Notes' memorandum asserts Tom Wilson said the same thing to Eric Davis at this 2002 meeting. Frankly, at this point, it would also be a whole lot easier to write off the Admiral Wilson memorandum as a forgery and to ignore the uncomfortable (and implausible?) implications that flow from what it alleges. But if the document is fake, then why has its author Dr Eric Davis been welcomed into a highly classified government job inside Aerospace Corporation, a federally funded research and development centre that works on top-secret projects with the US military? Surely, if retired Admiral Tom Wilson, the former Director of the Defence Intelligence Agency, believed Dr Eric Davis was responsible for a bogus memo attributing a series of false claims to him, he would be demanding Davis be keel-hauled and stripped of his security clearances for such an outrageous breach of ethics and fraudulent misrepresentation?

The memorandum of their purported conversation, retrieved from Ed Mitchell's archives, runs to 15 pages. It reads as though the entire conversation was recorded but there is no acknowledgement of this in the memo. On the last page, Wilson reportedly asks

Davis, 'What will you do with this?' One possible interpretation of 'this' is that Wilson was referring to an audio recorder on the car seat between them. Davis responded by telling Wilson he would keep *it* for private and personal research. He assured Wilson he would keep his mouth shut.

The rumour is that Davis did keep an audio recording of the purported conversation. Dr Davis has come very close to admitting the memo is genuine, telling the *New York Post* journalist Steven Greenstreet[5] that the notes 'were leaked out of Ed Mitchell's estate and there's nothing I can say about it'. He said they were 'purportedly classified information. I'm not at liberty to confirm or verify any aspect of those notes and when you have security clearances that's something you don't want to violate'. His response effectively bolstered the document's credibility, admitting the notes did indeed come from the estate of Edgar Mitchell, thereby underlining their provenance as having been sent to Mitchell soon after they were apparently written by Davis in late 2002. Because Mitchell was on the NIDS science advisory board he was sent a copy by Dr Hal Puthoff

Davis's boss at the time, Dr Hal Puthoff, has also confirmed the authenticity of Davis's Admiral Wilson memo, even if he later claimed this was unintentional. Asked about the Admiral Wilson memo at an Arlington Institute address in February 2020, he responded, 'That is a question about the Wilson documents. They probably got leaked on the internet. *And Wilson was one of the joint chiefs of staff interviewed by my senior scientist colleague Eric Davis.* Since it discusses potentially ongoing programs, I have no comment.'[6] (My emphasis.) I have no doubt that Dr Hal Puthoff knew exactly what he was doing when he gave this answer because he explicitly claimed that Dr Eric Davis interviewed Admiral Wilson and referred to the notes as the 'Wilson documents'. Dr Puthoff did subsequently tell Keith Basterfield that he did not mean to confirm that the Wilson interview and notes were authentic, but his explanation does not address what he actually said.[7] His admission was very significant.

There is another issue arising from Admiral Wilson's June 2020 denial letter to me. In it, he said, 'The entire memo attributed to Dr Davis, including his characterization of my attitude, emotions and sentiments about other individuals is pure fiction. Many of the people (Oke Shannon, Mike Crawford, Linda, Rich, Doug) he characterises in the memo as people I interacted with are completely unknown to me, as are the conversations I purportedly had on Special Access Programs related to UFOs with senior officials in the Department of Defence. I did occasionally meet with some of these people, but not on anything remotely related to the content of the Davis memo.' Wilson is clearly suggesting that Oke Shannon in particular was 'completely unknown' to him. But journalist Billy Cox tracked down Oke Shannon, the navy-veteran scientist whom the memo asserts encouraged Admiral Tom Wilson to meet with Eric Davis in 2002. In his interview with Cox, Oke Shannon gave the impression that he actually knew Tom Wilson well. 'I don't know the provenance of that purported document – I don't know whether it's real or not real,' Oke Shannon told Billy Cox. 'Let's just leave it at the fact that I do know both of these gentlemen. Tom Wilson is an honourable man. And if this has embarrassed Tom Wilson, I am really sorry.'[8] Oke Shannon did not deny to Billy Cox that he had facilitated a meeting with Tom Wilson or that it happened. His response begged the question, what would Oke Shannon have to apologise for if he had not played a role in bringing the two men together? The easiest way for Oke Shannon to have killed the story was for him to deny he made any such introduction. He never did that at all; instead, he apologised for causing embarrassment.

The memorandum asserted that, after Admiral Wilson's 1997 'UFO briefing' with Greer and his colleagues, Wilson searched for the 'UFO files' in the Pentagon. The memo named a Department of Defence Major General Marshal Ward and William Perry, a former Secretary of Defence, as having told Wilson he should examine files in the Office of the Under Secretary of Defence for Acquisition and Technology. 'They told me of a special projects record group not belonging to usual SAP – a special subset of the unacknowledged/carve-outs/waived programs,' Wilson reportedly said in the memo. Davis then asked Wilson a series of questions, such as which Special Access Program compartment he found the Program hidden in and under which codename.

'Core Secret – won't say,' was Wilson's supposed reply. Davis then asked who was the Program's project contractor or the government agency that runs it.

'An aerospace technology contractor – one of the top ones in US,' was the purported reply.

'Who?' Davis pressed.

'Core secret – can't tell.'

The term 'core secret' was first acknowledged by defence writer Bill Sweetman in 2000. 'An unacknowledged SAP [Special Access Program] – a black program – is a program which is considered so sensitive that the fact of its existence is a "core secret", defined in USAF regulations as "any item, progress, strategy or element of information the compromise of which would result in unrecoverable failure",' Sweetman wrote. 'In other words, revealing the existence of a black program would undermine its military value.'[9]

If the memo tells the truth, Wilson did some extraordinary sleuthing inside the Pentagon, finding the Program hidden across different compartments with no obvious connection between them. Wilson told Davis in the memo that, by the end of May 1997, he had figured out who the Program's contractor and program manager were and that he even confirmed it with three people: Dr Paul Kaminski (Director of Special Programs in the office of the Under

Secretary of Defence for Acquisition, Technology and Logistics); Brigadier General Mike Kostelnik (Director of the Special Access Programs Coordination Office and executive secretary for the SAP Oversight Committee); and former Defence Secretary Bill Perry. The memo claims that at the end of May 1997, Wilson called the Program manager three times, one of them a conference call with the contractor's security director and corporate attorney. He reportedly demanded a formal briefing, 'Told them my not being briefed was an oversight they needed to correct – I demanded!'

Remember, in 1997 Vice Admiral Tom Wilson was the Deputy Director of the Defence Intelligence Agency and was responsible for briefing the generals who advised the president and Joint Chiefs of Staff. If anyone should be read into a secret program working with technology highly pertinent to national security, you would think Vice Admiral Tom Wilson was entitled to be briefed into The Big Secret. But that is not what we are told happened at all. The memo said that whoever it was he rang, demanding access, had the gall to hang up on him. Two days later, Wilson got a call-back and this time he was told they would not speak on the phone, but a face-to-face meeting was organised at the recalcitrant contractor's facility. Ten days later, in mid-June 1997, we read Admiral Tom Wilson was ushered into the private contractor's conference room within a secure vault. (This really does sound like something out of a James Bond movie; I half expected to read how the admiral arrived to find the evil villain Ernst Stavro Blofeld sitting there, stroking his white Persian cat.)

The corporate cover-up cabal waiting to meet Wilson comprised the unnamed contractor's program director, a security director and a corporate attorney, who the memo claimed had dubbed themselves 'the watch committee or gatekeepers'. Wilson reportedly described, 'Confusion on their part as to why I was looking for them and what I wanted from them or wanted to know about. Very testy tone from all of them ... They were agitated about my calling – surprised by call.' He asked about their crashed UFO program and MJ-12 (the supposed secret cabal of scientists, military and intelligence officials, and government formed in 1947 by President Truman to facilitate the recovery and investigation of alien spacecraft) and demanded a formal briefing as Deputy Director of the Defence Intelligence Agency and Assistant Joint Chief of Staff J-2.

The memo claimed 'the Program' was very nearly compromised some years back and, because of this, a formal agreement had been struck with the Pentagon Special Access Program Oversight Committee (SAPOC) to prevent this inadvertent security breach happening again. It was agreed that no US government personnel would be given access unless they met the criteria for access, which (incredibly) would be administered by a committee inside the private contractor company, 'irregardless [sic] of the tickets and position USG personnel possessed ... Literally their way or the highway'. If this is true, it was extraordinary, possibly illegal, and a complete abrogation of proper oversight procedures for a federally funded project. Wilson is quoted as saying he asked for the criteria allowing access and he was refused. 'Implication is now – to me – they operate without official oversight or any justification – politically dangerous place to be,' he says.

This is one hell of an allegation: that someone at the very apex of the Pentagon felt there was no proper oversight for possibly the most important potential national security issue of all time – recovered extra-terrestrial technology. Wilson reportedly admitted that he was angry that, even though his security classification 'tickets' were all confirmed, that was not enough to give him access to the Program. To compound the outrage, the memo asserts that no one in Congress, the White House or even any president is cleared to know The Big Secret, for they were not on the 'Bigot list' either. It implies that this mythical program is operating completely outside regular oversight procedures. If that is true, it suggests the Program is operating illegally.

What the memo recorded next raised major doubts in my mind about the credibility of the purported 'EWD Notes'. Although the memo said Wilson was told he was not on the Bigot list and could not be briefed on the Program, he was then told a major chunk of The (supposed) Big Secret regardless – that the contractor was working on a reverse-engineering program with recovered extra-terrestrial technology. There was this extraordinary allegation: 'program manager said they didn't know where it was from [they had some ideas on this] – it was technology that *was not of this Earth – not made by man – not by human hands*. Said were trying to understand and exploit technology; their program was going on for years and years with very slow progress,' Wilson reportedly revealed to Davis. The memo also claimed Wilson was told by the Under Secretary for Defence for Acquisition, Technology and Logistics, Dr Jacques Gansler, that 'UFOS are real, so-called "alien abductions" not real'. Dr Gansler was the third-ranking civilian at the Pentagon from November 1997 to January 2001, responsible for research and development and advanced technology. He died from melanoma cancer in 2018.

The memo asks us to accept that the unidentified contractor program manager suddenly backflipped on his refusal to reveal what he knew and admitted all. This surely raises a big red flag as it strains credibility that a private government contractor entrusted with protecting the biggest secret in US military and intelligence history, after telling Wilson he was blocked from knowing anything because he was not on the Bigot list, suddenly relented and told him a great deal about it being a supposed alien vehicle reproduction program – presumably the biggest secret in American military history. This might seem a curious reason for questioning the authenticity of the memo, but when I consulted three defence intelligence sources about it, this was the issue that raised the most doubt with people who knew how the United States government security compartmentalisation works. Why did they tell him anything at all if he was not on the Bigot list, I was told. Perhaps the gatekeepers felt that, by giving him some information and by playing down how much success they had had in reproducing the technology, they could limit the damage. But they did not have to tell him anything; they could have just shown him the door, or maybe the fiend Blofeld, the corporate gatekeeper masterminding the cover-up, could have just thrown the good admiral in the shark tank with a bit of blood and bone. End of problem.

As if the humiliation was not already enough, on his return to Washington, the memo claims Wilson complained to the Senior Review Group members overseeing the Special Access Program Oversight Committee inside the Pentagon, only to be threatened with his job if he caused trouble. He was shocked that they supported the contractor's denial of his access to the Program. 'They told me [TW] … that I was to immediately drop the matter and let it go – forget about it as I did not have purview over their project, it didn't fall within my oversight etc. I became very angry – started yelling when I should have kept my mouth shut,' the memo asserted Wilson as saying.

Wilson was supposedly told that, if he did not follow their suggestion, he would not be promoted to the Director of the Defence Intelligence Agency. He would also be sent into early retirement, and he would lose rank. 'Really incredibly angry – upset over this – livid!!!' Wilson reportedly told Davis. 'Why such a big deal over this considering the position of trust I have in the Pentagon – I do have relevant regulatory/statutory authority over their program – that's my position.' (Admiral Wilson, it should be emphasised, was very clear in his letter to me that he never requested nor was he denied such access to supposed UAP programs and neither was he threatened he would lose his career if he persisted.)

Numerous key officials are named in the Admiral Wilson memo, which suggests whoever wrote it had a complex understanding of who the Defence executives were at the time. However, none of those contacted support the memorandum's claims. We are left with the fact that, if the 'EWD Notes' memo is genuine, not one person who should know about the purported Admiral Wilson meeting is actually prepared to confirm its authenticity on the record. And the comments of Tom Wilson, his former Defence Department colleagues, and Commander Willard Miller pour cold water on its authenticity. It makes it impossible to resolve definitively whether the document is authentic. It should not be relied upon to support any allegation. It also strains my cynical journalist's brain to contemplate the possibility that such a preposterous secret could have been kept inside the notoriously leak-prone and gossipy bureaucracy frequenting the Potomac Washington swamp. But then, if it is a hoax, it is an extremely clever one.

On one side of the debate, there is a brilliant ufology researcher friend of mine I dub 'Cranium', who is absolutely convinced of a sinister cover-up conspiracy. Cranium sees huge significance in the fact that neither Hal Puthoff nor Eric Davis deny the memorandum's authenticity. 'These individuals have been given multiple opportunities to deny this document, and none of them have,' Cranium told me.[10] But without a senior Department of Defence official, Eric Davis, Admiral Wilson or Hal Puthoff, going on the record admitting to the veracity of the memorandum, its claims must be treated with extreme scepticism. It has to be treated as a hoax document until proved otherwise. For much of contemporary ufology, however, the memo will remain the ultimate smoking gun, whether the gatekeepers of The Big Secret admit it is true or not.

Cranium told me, 'It's really an atrocity that this vital information about not only our place in the universe, not only the fact that we're being visited by extra-terrestrials, but this godlike technology that could help our civilisation in so many ways, that could improve the human condition on this planet, has been sequestered by these private corporations for over seventy years.' He said all the evidence indicated that, in the 1950s, the US government was highly involved in gravity control research. Every aerospace company openly admitted it was investigating gravity control. 'And then all of a sudden, it went black. No one was talking about it. Everybody shut up. I believe that what happened was that they finally had success. Now, I believe they had success because they were able to have access to these crashed UFOs that gave them the information they needed to build their own,' Cranium said.

But, even if Cranium is right and assuming the 'EWD Notes' document, the 'Admiral Wilson Memo', is authentic, does accurately record what Eric Davis wrote, what I come back to is that it proves nothing. It is still only Dr Davis's claims. Needless to say, *if* anything Admiral Tom Wilson purportedly said is actually true, then the implications are mind-blowing. But Wilson has categorically denied the meeting with Dr Eric Davis ever happened. So, without further corroboration, end of conspiracy.

I figure the only way to resolve this mystery is to try to find someone, anyone, who is willing to talk and who knows what is going on. So I start writing letters. Many, many letters. I find the home addresses of senior military officers, spies, scientists, anyone who after months of research I guess might know something about 'The Program', if it actually exists. And I lick a lot of stamps. My thinking is that letters do not leave an electronic trail like emails and phone calls. I politely tell my correspondents how to contact me on secure communications apps or encrypted email, and reassure them of confidentiality. And then I wait. And hope.

Chapter 22

Gordon Novel: Fact or Fiction

'What are they gonna' do to me?' he said, in what turned out to be our last conversation, as we discussed his decision to tell me some of what he knew. The distinctive Brooklyn-accented voice of the man on the end of my phone in early 2020 was faltering and he occasionally took a pause to gather the energy to collect his thoughts and answer my questions, but the wait was no bother because I was thrilled by the privilege of speaking to the man who ran research for the world's greatest navy for nearly 30 years. Nat Kobitz, the former Director of Science and Technology Development for the US Navy, rang me one day out of the blue. He liked my letter.

I wrote to Kobitz chasing up a story told by a peculiar private investigator and CIA-linked spook named Gordon Novel. Mr Novel wrote a book,[1] two years before he died in 2012, in which he detailed the story of the so-called ARV (alien reproduction vehicle) Fluxliner. The Fluxliner story is one of the beguiling myths of modern UFO conspiracies. In his book, Novel describes how, in May 2001, a professional aerospace illustrator named Mark McCandlish testified to the Disclosure Project hearing at the National Press Club that the US government had successfully reverse-engineered a spacecraft retrieved from the 1947 Roswell crash site to build three so-called alien reproduction vehicles (ARVs). The only reason I am interested in Novel at all is because, in his book, he claimed to be in touch with a very senior US Navy scientist heading the navy's research and development, whom he pseudonymously dubbed Walter 'Wally' Katz. Novel's book claimed that Katz knew all about the secret work into these ARV Fluxliner craft and that, at a July 1993 Pentagon meeting between Gordon Novel and his son Sur and Katz, Katz let slip details to Novel of how they were back-engineered from recovered ET craft. It all sounded very improbable to me, but then I tracked down one of Gordon Novel's now elderly former-CIA contemporaries, who had helped me with another story about a dodgy CIA-front bank, the Nugan Hand Bank, that collapsed in scandal in Sydney in 1980 amid allegations of money laundering and drugs smuggling. He vouched for the access Novel had to some very high-powered people in the Congress, CIA and military top brass. 'Take it to the bank. Gord was very good at finding stuff out,' he told me gruffly. 'His biggest problem was not keeping his mouth shut.'

So, I took Gordon Novel's wild claims a little more seriously. The account he told of his supposed Pentagon meeting in his book put Mr 'Katz' smack in the middle of the official dark UAP cover-up conspiracy, asserting that 'Wally [Katz] admitted reluctantly that [the] ARV was, in fact, a reproduction of a universal UFO drive design ... he was willing to fund [Hal Puthoff's] zero point energy (ZPE) research and development program and secretly show us how to do it, but the antigravity system of ARV was going to have to remain a "Supreme Cosmic Secret" and the Number one national security issue.'[2]

Professional intelligence conmen like Gordon Novel generally know just enough to be dangerous and all of what he claimed to know should be taken with an equal dose of scepticism. His book has circulated for years among those who firmly believe the US government is hiding recovered alien technology. Novel was a seemingly implausible, but in fact real-life, character out of a spy thriller. When the CIA's Operation Mongoose covertly funded anti-Castro Cuban immigrants to plan an abortive invasion of Cuba in the Bay of Pigs debacle in 1961, Novel was among the plotters who stole weapons from a munitions bunker in Louisiana. He always touted his CIA links and there were allegations that secret written authority for his weapons heist came from the US Attorney General Robert Kennedy, who had a bit of a thing for covert actions. Novel also provided a way too gullible New Orleans District Attorney Jim Garrison with a CIA-Cuban-emigre link to the assassination of President John F. Kennedy by suggesting that, while working for the CIA, he knew both the alleged assassin Lee Harvey Oswald and Jack Ruby, Oswald's killer. Novel was indubitably a covert operator with strong CIA intelligence connections who, for decades, kept on bobbing up in the background of dramatic news events, including the JFK assassination, Watergate, Iran-Contra, Michael Jackson and the aftermath of the Waco siege. A whiff of Walter Mitty, I suspected.

Novel's book pumped up what he claimed to know of a purported secret government project re-engineering an anti-gravity propulsion drive from a crashed alien craft. Crucially, he dropped the names of two senior government officials to whom he gave the pseudonyms Wally Katz and Richard Cash, suggesting they were the two people he met who were most in the know. 'Barring someone like Wally Katz or Richard Cash, Esq, writing a tell-all book detailing *the program* and the route that the deep black money took to create, test and hide ARV etc., it is extremely doubtful that *the program* will ever be exposed,' Novel wrote.[3] 'Richard Cash' could only be Charles Richard 'Dick' D'Amato, former minority counsel for the Senate Appropriations Committee. It was a matter of public record that D'Amato did an investigation into 'UFOs'. I knew already he was not talking.

In a key chapter, Novel told a dramatic story of how, at a meeting in the Pentagon, the head of the US Navy's R&D, 'Wally Katz shook visibly (as my son, Lucky, will attest) when I presented him with an updated colorized version of McCandlish's ARV layout'.[4] Wacky as the claims in Novel's book appear to be, this was an allegation made by a purported insider that could actually be tested. It intrigued me that Novel also claimed he tape-recorded the conversations he had with all the insiders he met, including 'Katz', and that his son was a witness to this Pentagon exchange. If I can find Novel's son, I might be able to uncover the real identity of 'Wally Katz'. I anticipated I would soon find a sound reason to completely discount Novel's incredible assertions.

I eventually found Gordon Novel's son Sur, now living in Bangkok. Sur, a trained lawyer, was clearly conflicted by his late father. 'You know, he was always kind of paranoid, Dad. He exaggerated things and was always into the conspiracy theories,' Sur told me. 'He would find a conspiracy theory where conspiracies didn't exist because it was kind of like his calling card because he was involved in a lot of you know wild shit when he was younger, and you know with the JFK assassination. And then he was involved with these guys that were doing the Watergate shit and you know, up until Watergate, he was politically connected with the black ops and then those guys all kinda got wiped out because they were doing domestic operations in the US and that's not what the CIA is tasked to do.'[5] My head was spinning, pondering what black CIA covert operations a younger Sur must have naively witnessed; he casually name-dropped events and characters from Iran-Contra and Waco he saw with his dad. I asked Sur whether he ever accompanied his old man to a meeting in the Pentagon, and to my amazement he remembered it well. He confirmed the man they met was not a 'Wally Katz' but an official named Nat Kobitz, which is what I had assumed based on the book's description of his navy R&D role. (Katz-Kobitz.) Sur even remembered his father flourishing McCandlish's drawing of the ARV craft at Kobitz in his Pentagon office.

'The look on [Kobitz'] face was kind of like, what are you doing with this? It wasn't like, call the FBI and arrest this guy, national security or anything like that. It was just kind of like, you know it. You know,' Sur said. 'Basically, it's true you know, I did meet the guy. I don't know how Dad got a hold of him, but he had a lot of old CIA contacts and knew people, you know, from the black world.' I pushed Sur on Kobitz's exact reaction: 'What was the look on his face when he saw the image of the ARV Fluxliner?'

'Man, he was basically like, what are you doing with this, kind of type of deal … it didn't look like it was like, like a joke or anything like that,' he replied.

Sur is still convinced that his father was genuinely onto something in his belief that the US was secretly researching anti-gravity and that he was trying to work out how the technology actually worked. But, he declared, 'It looks like the United States' government already has their hands on it.' And what in part convinced Sur Novel of this was the reaction he claimed he saw from Nat Kobitz, the head of Navy Science and Technology Development, at that meeting in the Pentagon. The best way Sur could describe it to me was that Nat Kobitz seemed shocked by what the drawing showed. I have a sceptical hunch that Gordon Novel embellished what Kobitz said at this meeting to lure readers of his book into funding his 'anti-gravity propulsion' project.

I asked Sur if there is any truth to the claim that his father kept secretly recorded tapes of his conversations with insiders. He admitted that in his final years his father kept a storage unit with 'many tapes and documents in it'. My pulse quickened; I have a mental image of yours truly prying open a long-sealed dusty *Raiders of the Lost Ark* container full of the explosively incriminating taped confessions of pillars of the US military-industrial establishment. Sur dashed my hopes by telling me how his dad was 'down on his luck' shortly before he died, and after he passed, everything in the storage unit was, he assumed, tossed by the storage unit owner. 'They wiped out all the dirty, you know, CIA guys that were Dad's connections back then. And after that, he you know, he kind of got wiped out after that for a while. He had some legal troubles and things like that,' Sur explained forlornly. I can hear the relieved sighs across Washington DC right up to CIA HQ in Langley, Virginia, as the gatekeepers of The Big Secret read Sur's admission at this point.

I was about to miserably shelve my inquiries into Gordon Novel's claims when, over a quarter of a century on from that mythical Pentagon meeting, a kindly and clearly still sharp, albeit infirm, 92-year-old Nat Kobitz called me out of the blue from his home in Baltimore. He loved getting my letter from Australia and he spent the first 20 minutes explaining how Australia needed to get a certain type of Russian water bomber to fix the terrible bushfires then raging around Sydney. Tragically, Kobitz was fighting a terminal illness and, when his daughter Celia was out of earshot, he whispered that he knew he didn't have long. But he was in the warm embrace of his loving Jewish family and he told me he relished this opportunity to distract himself from the misery of his illness by talking about his remarkable career as a mega-boffin with the US Navy.

I listened enthralled for an hour as he told me the history of his US Navy R&D work. Kobitz was a navy defence aerospace legend, honoured for his distinguished service. He worked on the launch vehicle air frame for the Gemini space program, as well as numerous navy surface ship and submarine projects in a near 30-year career. In private consultancy, he worked on a special shroud for the lunar orbiter. Kobitz told me one self-effacing story about a navy unmanned aerial vehicle project he was involved in developing, called Sea Scout. He confided the hugely expensive prototype was lost when it flew too near the Texas wedding of President Bush's daughter and the president's security protection jammers knocked the drone out. 'We dug it four feet into Texas soil,' Kobitz told me with a chuckle. 'It cost a million bucks to build and we didn't have any more money. That was the end of the program.'

When I asked him if he ever worked on anti-gravity or field propulsion technology, he volunteered that he did and that the navy was researching it, but he would not tell me anything more, only that what he was working on was relatively unexciting. 'A propulsion system, very low energy ion propulsion,' he told me. 'The unit of force was MMF. Micro-micro farts.' In defiance of the claims in Novel's book, Kobitz confided that he did not think the United States had been able to crack the secret of anti-gravity despite years of secret research. 'I think eventually, before I retired, they would have sucked me into it,' he said with no hint of deceit.

We moved on to Kobitz's alleged Pentagon meeting with Gordon Novel and son in July 1993, one year before he left the navy, and I was very surprised when he confirmed the meeting. 'I remember Gordon very well,' he laughed. 'Unfortunately, a shoe salesman. Everything looked good on my feet.' It was clear Kobitz would not confirm much of what Gordon Novel claimed about their meeting and he told me that all he can remember about the ARV Fluxliner story was that 'it rings a bell'. Two days later, after I have sent him a detailed graphic of the purported ARV Fluxliner drawn by Mark McCandlish, he told me, 'Okay, I've seen that before. ... And my conclusion is that it's a hoax. I'm sorry,' he told me. I started to think this was another dud lead. However, as our conversation continued, it became clear that Kobitz had something to tell me, but he wanted me to ask the right question. So, I went for broke and showed my hand; I asked Nat Kobitz the billion-dollar question.

'Nat, were you ever read into any programs involving crashed UFOs or UAPs?' I pressed, repeating the question so he knew for sure what I was asking. There was a deep pause and then he said, 'Yes, I was. I was never read out of it. So, I really don't think it would help but I really can't speak about it.' The answer hung; he was expecting another question. I asked, 'Nat, are you aware of any recovered alien spacecraft inside the US government?' He responded cryptically, 'I only have hearsay information. I tried to be very careful not to fall into the category that a fellow did once when I was much younger. He was in his 90s and he said, "Kobitz, let me tell you, some of my greatest adventures never really happened".' Kobitz was intimating he was bound by a security oath not to talk about what he knew, and that he was not going to speculate about what he did not know directly.

So, I asked a different question, 'What have you *heard* about recovered alien tech?' Nat Kobitz answered without pausing, 'That we had recovered, several times, alien spacecraft. Or what was thought to be.' I recited the official US Air Force explanation for the 1947 Roswell crash to him – that the recovered Roswell debris was merely a high-altitude nuclear test surveillance balloon from a secret project codenamed Mogul. He laughed dismissively and replied, 'More than one person reported that it was not soft material. It was hard metal pieces and I've heard, but do not know of any actual space people.' He was clearly suggesting that colleagues had told him about extra-terrestrial wreckage. And had he just said 'space people'?

The former Director of US Navy Science and Technology Development had just told me he was read into a secret program involving crashed UFOs, alien spacecraft, possibly even aliens. I took a giddy pause to gather my thoughts. I recalled what Dr Eric Davis had claimed – that the US had so far failed to re-engineer the craft it has recovered – and then I asked, 'Are you able to confirm to me that the US has been trying to develop recovered alien technology?' Kobitz gave the question careful consideration. 'Yes, I can say that's so.'

In several long conversations over three weeks, Kobitz made it clear he would never breach the terms of his national security oath and reveal the full details of what he knew. But, as he wistfully acknowledged, his time was short, and I was asking him at just the right time because he was too sick for anyone to take any action against him for revealing just this much. He also told me of other UAP incidents he was caught up in, involving a navy pilot and a civilian pilot who both saw the same UAPs. 'One was a brilliant light which could not be accounted for at all. Because at one point it stood still, raced to another part of the sky and stood still again and then disappeared. The other was a solid vehicle that – the two differed on this shape – one thought it was triangular and the other thought it was elliptical,' he told me. He would not reveal any more, but it was clear to me that he knew a great deal more than he was willing to disclose.

Nat Kobitz left his Navy Director of Science and Technology role in 1994 and set up a private consultancy called NKA Science. NKA specialised in advanced manufacturing technology, especially what is called electron beam welding. This is a type of welding that uses a beam of high-speed electrons, focused using magnetic fields, to join materials. It gives a very precise and strong join with little discernible weld beading. Perhaps because of this expertise, Kobitz mentioned that, during his time at NKA, he was invited to visit Wright-Patterson Air Force Base in Dayton, Ohio, to examine some strange pieces of metal held under high security.

As quickly as he mentioned it, he changed the subject to talk about something else. On hearing the Wright-Patterson name, my ears pricked up. Wright-Patterson was the location of what used to be known as the Foreign Technology Division of the US Air Force. The UAP conspiracy theory has long alleged that Wright Field, now Wright-Patterson, was where the pieces of the supposed Roswell craft wreckage were taken in 1947 for further investigation.

Tom Carey and Don Schmitt's 2019 book *UFO Secrets – Inside Wright-Patterson* lists witnesses who claimed knowledge of the base's allegedly massive underground facilities, which housed the retrieved material, including strange, recovered memory metals that return to their original shape even when bent or twisted. Witnesses also claimed to have seen wreckage of a small circular craft at the base.[6] In 1994, Senator Barry Goldwater, the 1964 Republican candidate for the presidency of the United States, told an intriguing story to CNN's *Larry King Live* about his conversation with the Chief of Staff of the US Air Force, General Curtis LeMay. 'I think at Wright-Patterson, if you could get into certain places, you'd find out what the air force and the government does know about UFOs,' the Senator told King. 'Reportedly, a spaceship landed. It was all hushed up. I called Curtis LeMay and said, "General, I know we have a room at Wright-Patterson where you put all this secret stuff. Can I go in there?" I've never heard General LeMay get mad, but he got madder than hell at me and said, "Don't ever ask me that question again!"'[7] Goldwater was a very senior Senator; he served on the Armed Services Committee, the Aeronautical and Space Sciences Committee, and was a former chairman of the Senate Intelligence Committee. As a member of the so-called Gang of Eight in Congress, he was cleared to know America's most sensitive secrets. Goldwater was also a close friend of air force General William 'Butch' Blanchard who, as a colonel in 1947, was the commanding officer of the 509th Bomb Group at the Roswell

Army Air Field when the supposed Roswell UFO crash happened. Goldwater knew several people with direct knowledge of what actually happened at Roswell.

At the end of World War Two, the US did an enormous amount of work reverse-engineering recovered wartime Nazi technologies, including rocketry and aircraft, and, as the Cold War began, Wright-Patterson was the place where all foreign technology, including Russian and Chinese aerospace craft and space debris, was studied. The US Air Force Foreign Technology Division was formally created at the base in 1961. In 2003, it was absorbed into NASIC, the National Air and Space Intelligence Centre. This was why Nat Kobitz's admission that he was shown a strange metal at Wright-Patterson tweaked my interest. In his earlier conversation, he told me he wouldn't talk any further about the program working with recovered UAP technology, which he admitted he was read into during his time at the navy, but I figured that since this is clearly a separate issue, I could still ask him whether he actually saw any recovered alien technology at Wright-Patterson Air Force Base. So, what did he see, I asked?

'I saw a piece of piece of material that was reported to me as being a titanium alloy that was not known to the air force. I did not know what it was, I was not told what it was. It was a piece about three by maybe four feet. It showed no attachment except something welded to it. But it was not welded to it. It just was integral with, if you could think of it as a bulkhead, it was integral with the skin, if that helps,' Kobitz said. 'If you know something about electron beam, you know that it doesn't leave a little bead. They thought that this bulkhead was attached to the skin by electron beam, but it did not look like that to me. It looked like it was integral. It looked like the thing was cast. It was completely strange for me. When you see something cast in place, it is integral and shows no interruption. Even with electron beam, you'll sometimes see a small line. But this showed nothing, and this is what was strange about this to these manufacturing people.'

Kobitz's expert opinion was there was no known industrial process that could replicate the bond he saw on that curious fragment of metal at Wright-Patterson. He reserved judgement on whether the fragment was from some craft not of this world and he only chuckled when I flatly asked if he thought the metal was extra-terrestrial. There were so many more questions I still wanted to ask Nat Kobitz, but time, sadly, was catching up with him. Shortly after our last conversation, his daughter contacted me to say he had taken a turn for the worse. On 5 April 2020, his secrets passed with him. Nat Kobitz was a warm, generous and hugely intelligent patriot, who was fiercely proud of the work he did for the US Navy. I loved our chats.

In his final weeks, Kobitz introduced me to some friends of his. One of those he put me on to was a former boffin for the US Naval Weapons Centre in California at the massive China Lake base. Now retired, that person wants to stay anonymous – let's call him Sidewinder – but he was happy to tell me what he knew. After encouragement from Kobitz, Sidewinder told me a fascinating story about a person he came to know in the defence intelligence world who had agreed to meet Sidewinder and a group of other defence insiders at a suburban roadhouse one Sunday morning, to tell them what he knew about being invited into the US government's secret UAP program.

At this meeting, Sidewinder's defence intelligence friend described how he was invited to the campus of one of the many large aerospace firms located in Long Beach, Los Angeles, California. He was taken for a walk in the sprawling gardens and told by an executive, "'I want to offer you a job. This will be deep undercover. You'll have an office that you'll go to on a daily basis that will not be where you will be located. You'll have a person answer your phone and respond to questions and for all intents and purposes, you're an employee of this organisation. You have a job there. But in reality, you'll be working with us and others and as part of this job, you'll have access to the wreckage and the humanoids.'" Sidewinder told me, frustrated that he knows no more, 'That is the closest I've ever come to this thing being reality. That's the closest I've ever come.' His insider friend said the whole program was controlled by a relatively small group of people who were not all in the government, including people in the aerospace, intelligence and corporate financial communities as well as the Pentagon. 'And he said that if you're not in that circle, regardless of what organisation you're in, you won't know anything about it,' Sidewinder said. His friend declined to speak directly with me.

I talk over the following weeks with other anonymous insiders. To protect their identities, I cannot reveal much of the astonishing detail of what they told me but I am left in no doubt that they all assert that the US military, almost certainly the US Air Force, is in possession of retrieved non-terrestrial – alien – technology. Intriguingly, what I am told matches the claims made in the Admiral Wilson memo, that a private aerospace company now exercises control over this alien technology. (I was also told that the project was hidden inside the US Department of Energy for decades until it became a Federal agency in 1977, making it subject to Congressional oversight.) If such technology is being hidden away by the air force, it might explain why the US Navy recently admitted that it cannot prosaically explain the Tic-Tac, Gimbal or Go-Fast videos taken by its carrier battlegroup fighter pilots. Perhaps what is most effectively flushing out this incredible secret is good old-fashioned inter-service rivalry; that the navy is seriously pissed it is out of the loop.

Wild conspiratorial claims from believers in the ufology community are one thing. Hearing shockingly similar assertions from former senior government scientists the calibre of Nat Kobitz and his friend Sidewinder are another thing entirely. I am sure the debunkers will say that my quoted sources never saw any hard evidence of extra-terrestrial technology held by the US government, and they are absolutely right. In the end, what these men have said proves little. It was fascinating that Kobitz said he was read into a UFO-UAP 'program' involving crashed extra-terrestrial spacecraft, and that there was an active program underway attempting to back-engineer that technology. Even after talking to Kobitz and numerous other scientists and insiders, I struggle to accept the truth of what they told me. How could a government plausibly hide a secret as big as this? Surely this is science fiction? Or, is it?

Chapter 23

Dr Salvatore Pais's Puzzling Patents

Around 1.3 billion years ago, far across the universe, two black holes, the hugely powerful gravity fields left by collapsed stars, drew each other into a death spiral and eventually collided, releasing massive ripples in the fabric of space and time known as gravitational waves. In 1916, Albert Einstein predicted gravity waves must exist as part of his Theory of Relativity. Almost a century later, on 14 September 2015, those gravitational waves from that cosmic collision were detected for the first time ever by receivers in Louisiana and Washington, USA. Scientists announced the discovery in February 2016, and it is acknowledged as one of the most momentous scientific discoveries of the 21st century, winning the Nobel Prize in 2017. It's important to understand how little we actually know about gravity waves and how the science of even beginning to try to understand them is still taking baby steps. When Isaac Newton first observed gravity in 1687, he was at a complete loss to explain how gravity operated over the vast distances of space, later saying, 'I have not been able to discover the cause of those properties of gravity from phenomena, and I feign no hypotheses. (In the original Latin, this latter sentence read as *Hypotheses non fingo*)'.[1] Public science's understanding has not really advanced that much since.

Yet, within just eight weeks of the announcement of this momentous breakthrough, in April 2016, an unknown US Navy aerospace engineer named Dr Salvatore Pais filed a patent application for a revolutionary spacecraft driven by gravity waves that was straight out of *Star Trek*. As far as we know, nothing that Dr Pais said in his patent application had any basis in known and proven scientific technological breakthroughs and neither had it been subjected to independent peer review and scrutiny. Oddly, he still got his patent, largely because the navy vouched for his discovery. Intriguingly, the plans for his proposed craft resemble a triangular-shaped UAP. Dr Pais claimed to have discovered what he called an 'inertial mass reduction device', capable of generating the same kind of gravity waves whose existence had only just been confirmed weeks earlier. He asserted this incredible new propulsion system would allow his craft to travel at extremely high speeds in either water, air or outer space and, most incredibly of all, his navy boss alleged that the gravity wave propulsion system in Pais's invention would soon become a *reality*.

Dr Pais worked at the time for the US Navy's Naval Air Warfare Centre Aircraft Division, on the Patuxent River in Maryland. Over three years, he applied for a series of mind-bogglingly exotic patents for which the US Navy was the assignee. The first was a 'Room Temperature Superconductor';[2] the second, an 'Electro-magnetic Forcefield Generator';[3] and the third, a 'High Frequency Gravitational Wave Generator'.[4] The fourth patent, and by far the zaniest-sounding of all, was his so-called 'Craft Using an Inertial Mass Reduction Device',[5] which Pais's application described as being capable of extreme speeds and of operating in air, sea and the vacuum of outer space, courtesy of a supposed electromagnetic propulsion system that generates these high frequency gravitational waves.

The implications of Pais's patents are awesome: it means the US Navy officially claims to be developing an anti-gravity craft, a patent applied for in April 2016, 12 years after the USS *Nimitz* and its pilots tracked and videoed the Tic Tac UAP off the west coast. Is it just a coincidence that the craft is shaped exactly like the black triangles seen in the skies for decades? Or that the schematic diagram of the 'gravitational wave generator' looks just like … well … a Tic Tac?

As more than one sceptical scientist has pointed out to me, if UAPs and Dr Pais's gravity wave generator truly were pumping out gravity waves, then why do the super-sensitive Laser Interferometer Gravitational-Wave Observatory (LIGO) receivers in Louisiana and Washington not go off the scale every time Pais switches on his prototype generator, or as the supposed flying saucers zoom by America during their regular visits around Planet Earth? No one knows enough yet in the white world of science to be able to answer that question, but you would think that, if gravity waves were being emitted by such craft, they would be detected by some of the most sensitive sensors ever developed. Dr Pais's incredible patent also begs a more intriguing question: if the US Navy has cracked this technology, then where could he plausibly have got his ideas from? If what Nat Kobitz told me is correct – that a UAP reverse-engineering program was underway – is it totally outside the realm of probability that the US has been replicating an alien craft and is now about to make a light-speed leap in technological breakthroughs? (I can hardly believe I am writing this, as Kobitz's admission still astounds me.)

Pais's application for a spacecraft patent included a reference to a scientific paper he wrote in 2015, which suggested there was a theoretical possibility for 'superluminal craft propulsion in a Special

Relativity framework'. Superluminal is a cool word for faster than light – *Star Trek* warp speed stuff. Yet, one of the most inviolable postulates from Albert Einstein, the father of the relativity theory, holds that only massless particles can travel faster than the speed of light. No form of matter can ever travel faster than the speed of light. For this reason, it has always been thought that the speed of light is the cosmic speed limit. But Pais suggested that 'it is feasible to remove energy-mass from the system by enabling vacuum polarisation, as discussed by Harold [Dr Hal] Puthoff; in that diminution of inertial (and thus gravitational) mass can be achieved via manipulation of quantum field fluctuations in the vacuum'. This is all as clear as mud to me too, but I think what Pais is suggesting is that his electro-magnetic field generator can create a polarised energy field that creates a 'quantum vacuum' around the craft, which allows it to reduce mass. This enables it to repel any air or water molecules and supposedly also makes possible faster-than-light travel. It also means that any occupant does not feel aerodynamic or hydrodynamic forces, which would explain why they are not mashed into soup by the extreme g-forces any such craft would indubitably inflict.

Is it also just a coincidence that Dr Hal Puthoff, one of those who led the campaign through To The Stars Academy (TTSA) to get the US government to open up on what it knows about UAPs, is the boffin who the US Navy quotes in support of a faster-than-light spacecraft? At TTSA's October 2017 launch, Steve Justice, the then Skunk Works Lockheed Martin Program Director for Advanced Systems, stated that TTSA was working on a revolutionary Advanced Electromagnetic Vehicle that could 'dramatically reduce the current travel limits of distance and time. It mimics the capabilities observed in Unidentified Aerial Phenomenon by employing a drive system that alters the space-time metric'.[6] Maybe the navy was worried TTSA might get there first. Nothing like a bit of healthy competition to flush out a long-suppressed secret. Does Steve Justice's departure from TTSA mean that this revolutionary vehicle project was shut down?

The patent for the so-called hybrid craft was approved in 2018 and Pais presented a paper the following January, making challenging claims about his 'Room Temperature Superconducting System for Use on a Hybrid Aerospace Undersea Craft'.[7] A room temperature superconductor is one of the as-yet officially unachieved holy grails of modern physics. Superconductors are a material that show zero electrical resistance and the superconductors currently known to be in operation only work if the materials are super-cooled at huge expense to hundreds of degrees below zero. If Dr Pais truly has cracked room temperature superconductivity, then it is a stunning scientific achievement; the ability to flow a current over huge distances without losing any energy would revolutionise electricity grid transmission, for instance. An even more awesome implication is that a superconducting wire that never loses its charge could be used to store massive amounts of electrical energy. Conventional batteries slowly lose their power but, if Pais's room temperature superconductor truly does have zero electrical resistance, then it offers the potential for a machine capable of producing hugely powerful magnetic fields. This would revolutionise transport and space travel.

The timing of Dr Pais's patent applications, so soon after *The New York Times'* disclosures about the Tic Tac and other mysterious craft seen by the US Navy off the east and west coast, invited inevitable speculation that what the navy pilots saw were test flights of some still highly classified US craft. Pais's application does describe a strikingly similar craft to the mysterious Tic Tacs, a craft that 'can function as a submersible craft capable of extreme underwater speeds (lack of water-skin friction) and enhanced aerial/underwater stealth capabilities (non-linear scattering of

RF and sonar signals). This hybrid craft would move with great ease through air/space/water mediums by being enclosed in a vacuum/plasma bubble/sheath, due to the coupled effects of EM field-induced air/water particles repulsion and vacuum energy polarisation'.[8] (Remember that reference during the Tic Tac saga to an underwater object travelling at hundreds of knots?)

I talked to multiple military sources who dismissed the notion that the craft seen by the navy could possibly be of US origin or that this could explain the plethora of sightings of strange craft reported by reliable sources across the world. 'Why in hell would you test fly your most secret new technology in such an overt way that inevitably led to its existence being publicly compromised by the navy?' I was told by one retired very senior US Navy officer. 'To keep it in the black, you stay in the dark. That's why we have China Lake and Area 51.' Perhaps the best reason to doubt the test flight theory comes from Christopher Mellon, who speaks with authority because of the Defence Department clearances he has held. In an email sent to members of a private news group, Mellon responded to a posted video of a triangular craft recorded in 1997, addressing speculation it could be the mythical so-called TR3B, a rumoured super-hypersonic US stealthy anti-gravity craft,[9] which purportedly produces plasma to create a field of anti-gravity. Mellon says, 'My current and former colleagues at Lockheed Martin and the Skunk Works are very clear in private settings that if there is a TR3B it is not made by Lockheed. Perhaps my Skunk Works' friends are deceiving me, perhaps the SAP oversight process is broken; perhaps the USAF lied to the Office of the SecDef and the Chairman of the Senate Appropriations Committee; but that has been my experience with this issue. One would think there would have been an enormous spending line for something like that, but I at least never saw it, nor did I see evidence of such a craft during visits to Area 51 and adjacent ranges. Naturally, I could be wrong, but I remain sceptical for the simple reasons stated above. I am aware of one data point that suggests there could be a US connection, but it's a bit tangential, far from definitive and not in the public realm.'[10]

Physicists have expressed grave doubts about Dr Pais's claims to have achieved such a series of incredible technological breakthroughs. Frankly, if ever actually proven operable, any one of these patents would without question win him a swag of Nobel Prizes with a bow on it. It has been suggested that the navy filed these patents simply to stop the Chinese or Russians from claiming rights over any of these future technological breakthroughs, ensuring the United States would never have to pay royalties for their use. US patent law certainly has very liberal standards for what it allows to be patentable.

The drafters of US patent law[11] felt it was very important not to deny patents for revolutionary ideas that might seem impossible. Critics of the law have suggested this allows patents for inventions that are supposedly 'useful', but which have no scientific evidence to back their effectiveness, like patented cures for baldness.[12] Nothing in Pais's application proves he has actually mastered these technologies, as he asserts, which is why the approval of the patent for the hybrid craft in particular is so controversial, because when the US Patent Office knocked back Pais's application, the navy vouched for Pais's work in an appeal letter. Dr James Sheehy, the chief technology officer of the US Naval Aviation Enterprise, said, 'This will become a reality. China is already investing significantly in this area and I would prefer we hold the patent as opposed to paying forever more to use this revolutionary technology.'[13]

The navy went even further in backing two of Dr Pais's patents. Astoundingly, it formally stated that the room temperature superconductor and the high-energy electromagnetic field generator were both already *operable*. Patent Office documents show that the room temperature superconductor patent was rejected because it was determined by the examiner that the invention was 'inoperative and therefore lacks utility' because 'no assertions of room temperature superconductivity have currently been recognised or verified by the scientific community'. Pais's boss, Naval Aviation Enterprise Chief Technology Officer Dr James Sheehy, then wrote an extraordinary appeal letter, vouching that the room temperature superconductor 'is operable and enabled via the physics described in the patent application'.[14] The navy states, 'Dr Sheehy was the technical authority, and spokesperson for all basic, applied advanced research and transition for the Navy Air Systems Command of the Department of Navy for eleven years, and is the now the Chief Scientist for Naval Air Warfare Center Aircraft Division Human Systems and can be considered a subject matter expert ... Dr Sheehy states that the invention is operable and enabled.'[15] It is a crime to make false statements to the Patent Office and a false claim would also invalidate a patent, so by making a claim of *operability*, Sheehy truly was sticking his neck out.[16] He was verifying that the room temperature superconductor device actually works. However, it seems the Patent Office still did not buy the navy's evidence and, for now, the application has been abandoned. Which begs the question, why did the Patent Office give Dr Pais the patent for the hybrid craft if it did not accept the patent for one of the key technologies supposedly needed to power it?

Undeterred, Dr Pais and a navy attorney also made the same assertion of *operability* about his purported High Energy Electromagnetic Field Generator. In an interview with the examiner in July 2018, the attorney and Dr Pais 'presented information relating to the *operability* of the invention ... Mr Pais noted that the invention was a formative invention in its incipient stages'.[17] Dr Pais's application made some wild claims about his forcefield generator, including that it could 'generate an impenetrable defensive shield to sea and land as well as space-based military and civilian assets, protecting these assets from such threats as Anti-Ship Ballistic Missiles, Radar Evading Cruise Missiles, Top Attack for Main Battle Tanks (land and sea-based systems)'. He even claimed it could deflect an asteroid. The US Navy secured the patent for the supposedly operable forcefield generator. Go figure.

Then, just when you think it could not get any crazier, Dr Pais filed another patent application for yet another science-fiction sounding device, this time a Compact Fusion Reactor that is supposedly capable of generating power in the range of a gigawatt (1 billion watts) to a terawatt (1 trillion watts) output, with input power only in the kilowatt (1000 watts) to megawatt (1 million watts) range. This is a claim that seriously strains credibility for many because even the largest power station on the planet, the Three Gorges Dam in China, only generates 22,500 megawatts (2.25 billion watts). If Pais has mastered a car-sized compact fusion reactor that is capable of using magnetic fields to contain the huge temperatures and pressures necessary to sustain a fusion reaction, then that is a revolutionary achievement. Any existing fusion reactors are still very much in the experimental phase. Dr Pais's application for a 'Plasma Compression Fusion Device',[18] filed in March 2018 and published in September 2019, suggests it could be smaller than two metres in diameter. The obvious conclusion to be drawn is that this may be the potential power source for Dr Pais's proposed triangular hybrid spacecraft. As with every other of Pais's recent bizarre patents, the Compact Fusion Reactor application left most scientists baffled as to how he could possibly claim such a technological breakthrough. The fact that the navy did not apply for the patents to be kept secret under the US *Invention Secrecy Act*, as it could easily have done, suggests these applications are more about just sending a message to the United States' potential rivals, China and Russia. However, Dr Pais has given one interview, vigorously defending the science behind his discovery.

'The fact that my work on the design of a Compact Fusion Reactor was accepted for publication in such a prestigious journal[19]..., should speak volumes as to its importance and credibility – and should eliminate (or at least alleviate) all misconceptions you (or any other person) may have in regard to the veracity (or possibility) of my advanced physics concepts,' Dr Pais sniffily asserted.[20] Dr Pais went on to claim that his so-called 'Pais Effect' is a real phenomenon: 'the controlled motion of electrically charged matter (from solid to plasma states) subjected to accelerated vibration and/or accelerated spin, via rapid acceleration transients'. Pais said that 'my work shall be proven correct one fine day ...' but journalist Brett Tingley quoted one expert in rebuttal, suggesting the entire application was nonsense, accusing Dr Pais of using 'invented jargon, nonsensical statements, weak or absent evidence of an informed theoretical basis'.

Twenty years ago, aerospace journalist Nick Cook, then the aviation editor of *Jane's Defence Weekly*, the leading journal covering international defence issues, wrote a book detailing his ten-year investigation into the science of anti-gravity, *The Hunt for Zero Point*. Back then, Cook asked what had happened to anti-gravity research since a spate of articles appeared in the 1950s and early 1960s, suggesting an anti-gravity breakthrough was just around the corner. He chased down an elusive scientist named George S. Trimble, a former vice president with the Glenn L. Martin Company, which eventually merged to become part of the giant Lockheed Martin Corporation. In 1957, Trimble aggressively spruiked a golden age of anti-gravity, predicting it would sweep through the aerospace industry starting in the 1960s. 'So, what went wrong?' Nick Cook wrote. 'The evidence was suggesting that in the mid-50s there had been some kind of breakthrough in the anti-gravity field and for a small window in time people had talked about it freely and openly, believing they were witnessing the dawn of a new era, one that would benefit the whole of mankind.'[21] As it turned out, George Trimble mysteriously clammed up completely and Nick Cook suggested that US anti-gravity research might have had its origins in discoveries made by Nazi scientists during World War Two and that it had continued in secret since.

I befriended Cook early in my research and, as I descended into the rabbit hole that he had long ago traversed, every month or so he kindly mentored me from sliding into anti-gravity lunacy. Our Skype conversations generally happened as he was drinking his first coffee of the day in London, looking far too healthy, and I was starting my second glass of red wine in Sydney, steadying my nerves after a day trying to coax information out of media-shy American boffins. Never before had I found such a fruitful lode of initially promising leads that consistently faded away into nothing, with the trail disappearing all too often behind opaque US Defence Department black world projects. Something was clearly going on, but what? While Nick Cook found a lot of evidence two decades earlier that there was ongoing US research into anti-gravity and rumoured breakthroughs in exotically propelled new craft, his book left the issue an open question. I asked Cook what he thought now, 20 years on.

He said, 'The US Navy's talking about UFOs, officially admitting that it cannot explain the phenomenon, has validated my ability to talk about all this. And it's been quite liberating. Do I believe it is real? Yes, I do. Absolutely. Does that mean I think it's *all* real? Absolutely not. But there's a corollary to this and that is: what *do* I think is going on? The truth is, I still don't know. Do I think the US has cracked anti-gravity? I genuinely don't know. But that, to me, is almost incidental. If there is a kernel of reality in all this stuff, it is truly the most amazing story on the planet. And for me, at least, it's passed the sniff test. I've seen enough to know that that kernel of reality exists and that we are in for an amazing period in human existence.'[22]

I asked former US Navy R&D boss Nat Kobitz if he knew anything about Pais's patents and he made a few discrete inquiries. The answer came back that nobody Kobitz or his colleagues knew in the US Navy had any information on either Dr Pais or whether there were any working prototypes of any of his patents. 'If there is anything near a working AG (anti-gravity) craft, they've kept it very quiet,' I was told. Former Defence insider Christopher Mellon also tweeted online in July 2020 that 'I've looked into this and found disputes re whether the physics involved in Pais's patents is even viable. There's no indication of testing or prototypes. What our pilots are seeing is NOT secret US stuff. First thing navy and DoD did was check to make sure they weren't ours.'[23]

After months of digging, the only thing I find I know for certain is that while US anti-gravity research went dark in the 1960s, it never actually stopped. There is good reason to be sceptical that the US has cracked anti-gravity, but I am very sure that an intensive secret effort is clearly still underway. As for Dr Pais's curious patents, we will just have to wait and see if anything ever comes of them … but I have grave doubts.

Things are now happening very fast. In a dramatic reversal to decades of mockery of the UAP subject, in July 2020, one of the world's most esteemed scientific publications lent its weight to pushing for scientific investigation of UAPs. In *Scientific American*, scientists Ravi Kopparapu and Jacob Haqq-Misra opined that UAPs were a scientifically interesting problem and that 'we must simply let scientific curiosity be the spearhead of understanding such phenomena. We should be cautious of outright dismissal by assuming that every UAP phenomena must be explainable … Curiosity is the reason we became scientists'.[24] By any measure, this was a significant turning point in mainstream science's public view on UAPs.

There are rumours, too, of more revelations to come from *The New York Times*. Its reporter Ralph Blumenthal made a cryptic

comment to one reader in the online comments section of the *Times'*
24 July 2020 story, which featured allegations the US had retrieved
alien materials. A reader from San Francisco asked, 'Am I correct in
assuming ... The government, or people closely associated with it,
have successfully conspired for decades to suppress evidence of alien
visitation[?]'. Blumenthal responded that such an assumption might
not be far off.[25] It is very clear, from comments made by Blumenthal
and his *New York Times'* colleague Leslie Kean in an interview with
Project Unity[26] that both journalists believe there is substance to the
allegations that the US government has recovered alien spacecraft
or bits thereof – an incredible claim to be hearing from America's
newspaper of record. The paper that prints 'All the news that's fit to
print' has acknowledged UFO crash retrievals are possibly a thing.

Leslie Kean said, 'It's probably been the most difficult ... topic
to get out into *The Times* because for all the reasons you could
imagine, because of its controversy and because the information
about it is classified, and there's only so much that we can bring
forward and that makes it particularly difficult to report on that
topic, as well as it being so sensational.'[27] Blumenthal said in the
same interview, 'Crash retrievals is a classified subject.' If the *Times*
was suggesting that crash retrievals were actually a *classified subject*
inside the US government, then that was a dramatic admission.
Why would the US give crash retrievals a security classification at
all, unless crash recoveries were real?

In June 2020, President Donald Trump made an intriguing
comment about the mythical 1947 Roswell, New Mexico, UFO
crash in a cosy interview with his son Don junior. Don Jr. asked
his father, tongue in cheek, if he planned to release any more
information about the Roswell incident 'and let us know what's
really going on? Trump responded, 'I won't talk to you about what
I know about it, but it's very interesting.'[28] Why would the president
make such a comment if there was not more to reveal than the

very lame and prosaic US Air Force explanation for Roswell? The look in President Trump's eyes suggested he knew this question was coming and he was enjoying very much teasing his audience with his open-ended response.

In a turning point for disclosure, in late 2020, the US's powerful Senate Intelligence Committee also demanded US intelligence agencies and the Defence Department compile a report on all data collected on UAPs, including the navy pilot sightings. That report was due in June 2021 but was likely to be delayed. There is also the grave risk that whatever the public gets to see will be heavily redacted. However, as *Politico*'s Bryan Bender commented, 'UFOs are now on the agenda.'[29]

So, what do I know for sure, after two years down the rabbit hole? I have no doubt at all that the US government is hiding extraordinary secrets about The Phenomenon. The categorical statements made by defence and intelligence insiders Dr Eric Davis and Luis Elizondo (and the more qualified assertions by Christopher Mellon and former Senator Harry Reid) suggest that the United States has indeed recovered non-human intelligently manufactured technology, a conclusion that makes my head spin with its awesome implications, if true. Dr Davis leaves no room for doubt when he says whatever is propelling the Tic Tac, Go Fast and Gimbal UAPs is 'off-world vehicles not made on this earth'[30] and that is what he has told the Congress in private briefings. Irrefutably, there is technology operating in our oceans, atmosphere and orbit that is far beyond known human science. Intelligently controlled craft are flying around with impunity doing things way beyond human imagining, and they ain't ours.

It is hugely significant also that many of the claims made by punk rock star Tom DeLonge of TTSA were indisputably corroborated by the leaked Democratic National Committee emails. Meetings to discuss ways to disclose The Big Secret to the American public were being planned by a Hillary Clinton presidential campaign. Tom DeLonge truly was exchanging emails with very senior former US Air Force generals, with a top Lockheed Martin Skunk Works executive and with John Podesta, the confidant of Presidents Clinton and Obama. The only question is, was The General telling the truth about finding 'a lifeform' and recovered alien spacecraft? Or was the US military's play with Tom DeLonge and TTSA a clumsy attempt at deceiving new Cold War rivals about an apparent new American technological dominance? Are Dr Salvatore Pais's mind-blowing patents merely a pathetic bluff to scare off America's rivals?

Then I come to the esteemed navy scientist whose candour made me sit up and take the whole conspiracy seriously, the late Nat Kobitz, the former Director of Science and Technology Development for the US Navy. My fear is that malign black world types will run disinformation and charge that he was a confused elderly man suffering from a terminal illness, who told me what I wanted to hear. But to do so would betray the memory of an honourable American patriot, and defy the assertions of the associates he put me on to. I am in absolutely no doubt that Nat Kobitz told me the truth of what he knew and saw; that he was 'read into' a crash retrieval program and shown crafted bonded metal technology beyond anything he had ever seen before.

As incredible as it feels to write this, I strongly suspect from what my own sources tell me that technology not made by human hands has been recovered, not only by the US but by Russia and China. I venture the US has been wrestling for years with how to break this shocking news to the public, not least because it has flatly lied to its citizens for 75 years and criminally persecuted those who threatened The Big Secret. Too many insiders have dropped too many hints for me not to think that there is a reckoning coming.

I suspect the quest to unravel one of humanity's greatest mysteries will very soon have the beginnings of an answer.

ROSS COULTHART WELCOMES ANY FURTHER
INFORMATION:

Email: Muckraker@protonmail.com

Ross' personal website: www.RossCoulthart.com

Book website: www.InPlainSight-Book.com

For more on Ross' investigations: www.truestoryinvestigations.com

BIBLIOGRAPHY

Alexander, John, *UFOs – Myths, Conspiracies and Realities*, 2011,
   St Martin's Press

Asimov, Isaac, *The Roving Mind* (Revised Edition), 1997, Prometheus
   Books NY

Berlitz, Charles and Moore, William, *The Roswell Incident*, 1980, Granada

Bishop, Greg, *Project Beta, The Story of Paul Bennewitz, National
   Security, and The Creation of a Modern UFO Myth*, 2005, Simon &
   Schuster

Blum, Howard, *Out There*, 1990, Simon & Schuster

Bruni, Georgina, *You Can't Tell The People: The Definitive Account of the
   Rendlesham Forest UFO Mystery*, 2000, Sidgwick & Jackson

Cameron, Grant & Crain, T. Scott Jr, *UFOs, Area 51, and Government
   Informants*, 2013, Keyhole Publishing Co

Campbell Joseph, *Getting it Wrong: Ten of the Greatest Misreported
   Stories in American Journalism*, 2010, Berkeley, University of
   California Press

Carey, Thomas J. & Schmitt, Donald R., *Witness to Roswell*, 2009,
   Career Press/New Page Books

Carey, Thomas & Schmitt, Don, *UFO Secrets-Inside Wright-Patterson*,
   2019, New Page Books

Chalker, Bill, *The Oz Files*, 1996, Duffy & Snellgrove

Chichester, Francis, *The Lonely Sea and the Sky*, 1967, Pan

Condon, Edward U. & Gillmor, Daniel S. (editors), *Final Report of
   the Scientific Study of Unidentified Flying Objects*, 1969, Dutton/
   University of Colorado.

Cook, Nick, *The Hunt For Zero Point*, 2001, Penguin Random House UK / Arrow Books

Corso, Col. Philip with Birnes, William J., *The Day After Roswell*, 1997, Simon & Schuster Pocket Books

Davies, Paul, *Are We Alone?: Philosophical Implications of The Discovery of Extra-terrestrial Life*, 1996, Perseus

DeLonge, Tom with Levenda, Peter, *SeKret Machines: Man. Volume 2: Gods, Man, & War. An Official SeKret Machines investigation of the UFO Phenomenon*, 2019, To The Stars Inc

DeLonge, Tom & Hartley, A.J., *SeKret Machines Book 1: Chasing Shadows* 2016, To The Stars Academy

Dolan, Richard, *UFOs and the National Security State*, 2000, Hampton Roads Publishing Company

Dolan, Richard, *The Cover-up Exposed, 1973–1991 (UFOs and the National Security State Book 2)*, 2010, Keyhole Publishing

Friedman, Stanton co-authored with Berliner, Don, *Crash at Corona: The Definitive Story of The Roswell Incident*, 1992, Paragon House

Good, Timothy, *Need to Know: UFOs, the Military and Intelligence*, 2007, Pegasus Books

Good, Timothy, *Beyond Top Secret*, 1997, Pan

Greer, Steven, *Disclosure: Military & Government Witnesses Reveal the Greatest Secrets in Modern History*, 2001, Crossing Point Inc

Greer, Steven, *Hidden Truth: Forbidden Knowledge*, 2006, Crossing Point

Hastings, Robert, *UFOs & Nukes, Extraordinary Encounters at Nuclear Weapons Sites* 2017, 2nd Ed, Published by the Author

Hansen, Terry, *The Missing Times. News Media Complicity in the UFO Cover-up*, 2nd Ed. 2012

Hubbell, Webb, *Friends in High Places*, 1997, Beaufort Books.

Hynek, Dr J. Allen, *The Hynek UFO Report*, 1977, Sphere Books Ltd

Jacobsen, Annie, *Area 51: An Uncensored History of America's Top Military Base*, 2011, Orion Books/Hachette UK.

Kean, Leslie, *UFOs: Generals, Pilots, and Government Officials Go on the Record*, 2010, Three Rivers Press, NY

Kelleher, Colm A. Ph.D. & Knapp, George: *Hunt for The Skinwalker: Science Confronts the Unexplained at a Remote Ranch in Utah*, 2005, Paraview Pocket Books

Keller, T.L., *The Total Novice's Guide to UFOs: What you Need to Know*, 2010, 2FS Publishing

Keyhoe, Donald, *The Flying Saucers Are Real*, 1950, Fawcett Publications

Keyhoe, Donald, *Aliens From Space*, 1973, Signet Press

Keyhoe, Donald, *Flying Saucers: Top Secret*, 1960, G.P. Putnam's Sons, NY

Mezrich, Ben, *The 37th Parallel: The Secret Truth Behind America's UFO Highway*, 2017, Thorndike Press

Moseley, James W. & Pflock, Karl T., *Shockingly Close to the Truth: Confessions of a Grave-Robbing Ufologist* 2002, Amherst, NY

Numbers, Ronald L. & Kampourakis, Kostas, *Newton's Apple & Other Myths About Science* 2015, Harvard University Press

Ramsey, Scott & Suzanne & Dr Frank Thayer, *The Aztec UFO Incident. The case, evidence, and elaborate cover-up of one of the most perplexing crashes in history*, 2016, The Career Press Inc, NJ

Randle, Kevin D., *Project Moon Dust*, 1998, Avon Books, NY

Ruppelt, Edward, *The Report on Unidentified Flying Objects*, 1956, Ace

Scully, Frank: *Behind the Flying Saucers*, 1950, Henry Holt and Company

Vallée, Jacques, *Forbidden Science Vol Four: Journals 1990–1999 The Spring Hill Chronicles*, 2019, Lulu.com

ACKNOWLEDGEMENTS

I want to thank Bill Chalker, Keith Basterfield, Nick Cook, James Rigney and Paul Dean for their sage mentoring into the strange world of UAPs and for their generous research advice throughout; special thanks also to Keith for proof-reading my manuscript. There are so many people who have shown me kindness and extraordinary trust along the way, many of whom I cannot name because they are still bound by extremely tight security classifications that restrict what they are allowed to say about what America truly knows about The Phenomenon. I want to especially thank the family of the late eminent US Navy scientist Nat Kobitz, especially his daughter Celia Kibler. Special thanks also to the indefatigable Giuliano Marinkovic for his dogged and invaluable monitoring of UAP history. There will be so many honourable folk whom I may have inadvertently overlooked in these acknowledgements, but my deepest and warm appreciation goes to all of them, including: 'The Spaceman', Irene Previn, Jay Anderson, Jonathan Davies, James Fox, Shane Ryan, Robert Hastings, Dr Bob Jacobs, Dean Alioto, Jake Mann, Stephen Bassett, Sean Cahill, Billy Cox, Kevin Day, Luis Elizondo, Christopher Mellon, Leslie Kean, Grant Cameron, the late Mariana Flynn, Babcat, Megan Heazlewood, John Humphreys, David Marler, Franc Milburn, Joe Murgia, Damien Nott, Steve Oxley, Nick Pope, Scott & Suzanne Ramsey and Frank Thayer, Don Schmitt, Michael Schratt, Daniel and Paddy Sheehan, Brad Sparkes, the late Quentin Fogarty, Dennis Grant, James of *The Mind Sublime*, Dave Beaty, Deep Prasad, John

Petersen, Robert Powell, Annie Farinaccio, Nikolai Gordevich, Kate Faulmann, Adrian Arnold, Colin Kelly, Suesan Hill, Joy Clarke, Terry Peck, Andrew G., David Schindele, Bob Salas, P.J. Hughes, Gary Voorhis, George Knapp, Bob Greenyer, Niel X., John Cordy, Robert Fish and Admiral Tom Wilson.

From HarperCollins, I once again thank a stalwart team of highly skilled people who have enabled me to turn my love of investigation and storytelling into what I hope always to be insightful and informative books. I especially thank my publisher Jude McGee, editor Ed Wright and senior editor Lachlan McLaine, and the HarperCollins' CEOs during the writing of this book, James Kellow and Jim Dimetriou.

My warmest thanks go, as always, to my wife Kerrie Douglass and my daughters Lucy and Millie, who have had to tolerate my magnificent obsession and strange hours for two years.

ENDNOTES

1. Let's Hope They're Friendly

1. Air Marshall Sir George Jones, interview published in *Australian Flying Saucer Review*, No. 8, June 1965, p. 18. (UFOIC, Sydney edition).
2. Francis Chichester, *The Lonely Sea and the Sky*, Pan, 1967, p. 185.
3. RNZAF Press Release, 'RNZAF UFO Sighting Report', Jan 1979. Accessed online 17 Sep 2020: archive.org/details/NewZealandUFO/page/n75/mode/2up
4. 'Interim Report on UFO Sighting on the Canterbury Coast', Minister of Science NZ, Jan 1979. Accessed online 17 Sep 2020: archive.org/details/NewZealandUFO/page/n133/mode/2up, p. 134.
5. Asimov, *The Roving Mind*, Prometheus Books, NY (revised edition) 1997.
6. Ronald L. Numbers and Kostas Kampourakis (eds), *Newton's Apple and Other Myths About Science*, Harvard University Press, 2015.
7. Carl Sagan, 'Encyclopaedia Galactica' documentary episode, (December 14, 1980). *Cosmos: A Personal Voyage*. Episode 12. PBS.
8. Donald Prothero, 'UFOs & Aliens – What Science Says' (7 Feb 2020), TEDX. Accessed online 13 Feb 2020: www.youtube.com/watch?v=r8bgRABGLFg
9. Ibid, at 8 mins 9 secs.
10. Gallup Poll, accessed online 4 Feb 2020: news.gallup.com/poll/266441/americans-skeptical-ufos-say-government-knows.aspx
11. With acknowledgment to US journalist Billy Cox, reporter for the Florida-based *Sarasota Herald-Tribune* newspaper, who coined this phrase for his excellent (now defunct) blog, *Devoid*: devoid.blogs.heraldtribune.com/home/. *Devoid* was a great primer for anyone dipping their toe into the phenomenon, looking for serious mainstream journalistic coverage and analysis of UAPs until publisher Gannett recently (and perplexingly) axed Billy's blog.

2. Roswell: Implausible Denials

1. Associated Press report, 'Balls of Fire Stalk U.S. Fighters in Night Assaults Over Germany', *The New York Times*, 2 Jan 1945, pp. 1 and 4.
2. Adam Janos, 'Mysterious UFOs Seen by WWII Airmen Still Unexplained', History.com, 15 Jan 2020. Accessed online 9 Mar 2021: www.history.com/news/wwii-ufos-allied-airmen-orange-lights-foo-fighters
3. Joseph Campbell, *Getting It Wrong: Ten of the Greatest Misreported Stories in American Journalism*, University of California Press, Berkeley, 2010.
4. Timothy Good, *Need to Know: UFOs, the Military and Intelligence*, Pegasus Books, 2007, pp. 106–7 and 111. Document declassified in 1997, National Archives, Washington DC. USAFE Item 14, TT1524.
5. Researcher Keith Basterfield sourced these two *Adelaide Advertiser* reports for his summary of Australia's best UFO cases at: www.project1947.com/kbcat/kbmoreintoz.htm. The Port Augusta workmen sighting appears in the *Adelaide Advertiser*, 7 Feb 1947, p. 1. The Lock sighting was reported in the *Adelaide Advertiser*, 17 Feb 1947, p. 2. The Gogeldrie NSW sighting was reported in the *Murrumbidgee Irrigator* newspaper, 8 Jul 1947, p. 2.

6. Keith Basterfield, 'Four Months Before Kenneth Arnold', Keith Basterfield blog, 23 Jun 2017. Accessed online 22 Sep 2020: ufos-scientificresearch.blogspot. com/2017/06/four-months-before-kenneth-arnold.html?m=1

7. 'Supersonic Flying Saucers Sighted by Idaho Pilot', *Chicago Sun*, 26 Jun 1947, p. 2.

8. Richard Dolan, *UFOs and the National Security State*, Hampton Roads Publishing Company Inc, 2000, p. 19.

9. Ibid.

10. FBI Report from Project Blue Book files, in Dolan, *UFOs and the National Security State*, Ibid, p. 18.

11. Ibid, p. 22.

12. Thomas J. Carey and Donald R. Schmitt, *Witness to Roswell*, Career Press/New Page Books (Kindle Edition), 2009, Ch 21, para. 5.

13. 'RAAF Captures Flying Saucer on Ranch in Roswell Region', *Roswell Daily Record*, 8 Jul 1947, p. 1.

14. Stanton Friedman, co-authored with Don Berliner, *Crash at Corona: The Definitive Story of The Roswell Incident*, Paragon House, 1992.

15. Charles Berlitz and William Moore, *The Roswell Incident*, Granada, 1980.

16. 'Report of Air Force Research Regarding the Roswell Incident', 27 Jul 1994. Accessed online 22 Sep 2020: www.afhra.af.mil/Portals/16/documents/AFD-101201-038.pdf, P. 6.

17. Ibid, p. 9.

18. Thomas J. Carey and Donald R. Schmitt, *Witness to Roswell*, Ch. 11, para. 3.

19. US General Accounting Office, 'Results of a Search for Records Concerning the 1947 Crash Near Roswell, New Mexico', (1995) Publication # GAO/NSIAD-95-187.

20. Affidavit of Art McQuiddy/Roswell Morning Dispatch, Carey and Schmitt, *Witness to Roswell*, Ch. 21, para. 8.

21. Affidavit of First Lt Walter G. Haut, 26 Dec 2002, Carey and Schmitt, *Witness to Roswell*, Ch. 25.

22. Schmitt, interview with author, 20 Nov 2019.

23. Terry Hansen, *The Missing Times. News Media Complicity in the UFO Cover-up* (2nd edition) Xlibris, 2012, p. 178.

3. The Launch of Project Blue Book
1. Twining-Schulgen memo, 23 Sep 1947. Accessed online 24 Sep 2020: luforu.org/twining-schulgen-memo/

2. Edward Ruppelt, *The Report on Unidentified Flying Objects*, Ace, 1956, p. 35.

3. Dolan, *UFOs and the National Security State*, p. 64.

4. Ibid, p. 78.

5. Donald Keyhoe, *The Flying Saucers Are Real*, Fawcett Publications, 1950.

6. Ruppelt, The Report on Unidentified Flying Objects, p. 60.

7. FBI Website, 'UFOs and the Guy Hottel Memo', 25 March 2013. Accessed online: www.fbi.gov/news/stories/ufos-and-the-guy-hottel-memo

8. Dolan, *UFOs and The National Security State*, p. 82.

9. Dr J. Allen Hynek, *The Hynek UFO Report*, Sphere Books Ltd, 1977, pp. 63–4.

10. McMinville, Oregon sighting, 11 May 1950, *Condon Report*. Accessed online: www.project1947.com/shg/condon/case46.html

11. Frank Scully, *Behind the Flying Saucers*, Henry Holt and Company, 1950.

12. Wilbert Smith memo, 'Memorandum to the Controller of Telecommunications', 21 November 1950. Accessed online: www.docdroid.net/F3I5xly/smith-memo-pdf. Smith's papers are with the University of Ottawa: biblio.uottawa.ca/atom/index.php/research-on-wilbert-smith

13. Grant Cameron and T. Scott Crain Jr, *UFOs, Area 51, and Government Informants*, Keyhole Publishing Co (Kindle edition), 2013, Ch. 16.

14. Michel M. Deschamps Website, 'Robert Sarbacher Confirms UFO Crash Rumors', NOUFORS, Northern Ontario UFO Research & Study. Accessed online: www. noufors.com/Dr_Robert_Sarbacher.htm

15. 'Flying Saucers' [Report of OSI Study Group], 19 August 1952. CIA archives: www.cia.gov/library/readingroom/docs/CIA-RDP81R00560R000100020012-7. pdf, pp. 35–6.

16. Memo to Director CIA from Dep-Dir (Intelligence) Marshall Chadwell, 'Flying Saucers', 2 Oct 1952. CIA archives: www.cia.gov/library/readingroom/docs/ DOC_0000015339.pdf

17. Sara Schneidman & Pat Daniels, eds, *The UFO Phenomenon*, Barnes & Noble Books, NY, 1987, p. 110.

18. Hynek, *The Hynek UFO Report*, p. 13.

19. Ibid, p. 14.

20. Bill Schofield, 'Have You Heard' column, *Boston Traveler Magazine*, 5 May 1952, Editorial Page. As recovered from Project Blue Book archives by Dan Wilson for NICAP (National Investigations Committee on Aerial Phenomena) in 2006. Accessed online 22 Sep 2021: www.nicap.org/520314hawaii_dir.htm

21. Donald Keyhoe, *Aliens From Space*, Signet Press, 1973, pp. 65–6.

22. *Daily News*, 6 Jul 1952, as reported by Hynek, *The Hynek UFO Report*, p. 53.

23. Dolan, *UFOs and the National Security State*, p. 106.

24. Gerald K. Haines, 'CIA's Role in the Study of UFOs, 1947–90', Article from *CIA Studies in Intelligence*, p. 9. Declassified Jul 2002. Accessed online: www.cia.gov/ library/readingroom/docs/DOC_0000838058.pdf

25. Hynek, *The Hynek UFO Report*, p. 20.

26. 'Report of Meetings of Scientific Advisory Panel on Unidentified Flying Objects Convened by Office of Scientific Intelligence', CIA, 14–18 January, 1953. Accessed online 22 Sep 2021: documents.theblackvault.com/documents/ufos/ robertsonpanelreport.pdf

27. Dolan, *UFOs and the National Security State*, pp. 135–6.

4. A Worldwide Phenomenon

1. Timothy Good, *Beyond Top Secret*, Pan, 1996, pp. 227–9; Air Intelligence Information Report No. IR 193-55, 13 Oct 1955.

2. Good, *Beyond Top Secret*.

3. Gerald K. Haines, 'CIA's Role in the Study of UFOs, 1947–90', Article from *CIA Studies in Intelligence*, p. 9. Declassified Jul 2002. Accessed online: www.cia.gov/ library/readingroom/docs/DOC_0000838058.pdf Hynek, *The Hynek UFO Report*, p. 20. 'Report of Meetings of Scientific Advisory Panel on Unidentified Flying Objects Convened by Office of Scientific Intelligence', CIA, 14–18 January, 1953. Accessed online 22 Sep 2021: documents.theblackvault.com/documents/ufos/ robertsonpanelreport.pdf Gordon Thayer (U.S. National Oceanic & Atmospheric Administration), 'The Lakenheath England, Radar-Visual UFO Case, August 13–14 1956', CIA Library. Accessed online 28 Sep 2021: www.cia.gov/library/ readingroom/docs/CIA-RDP81R00560R000100010010-0.pdf

4. Gordon Thayer, Ibid.

5. US Air Attaché Afghanistan to COMATIC. WPAFB Ohio, (1956) Identifier: 1956-01-7340421 National Security Internet Archive.

6. Sydney Baker, 'Report on a Flying Object Sighting on 5th May 1954', in Dept of Supply, 'Reports on Unidentified Aircraft, Strange Occurrences etc Pt 1 1952–1968', National Archives of Australia, Series number D250, Control Symbol 56/483 Pt. 1, Barcode: 975473, p. 136. Accessed online: recordsearch.naa.gov.au/ SearchNRetrieve/Interface/ViewImage.aspx?B=975473

7. Dept of Supply, 'Reports on Unidentified Aircraft, Strange Occurrences etc Pt 1 1952–1968', p. 166–168, 'Flying Saucer Observed Over Woomera', 2 Oct 1952.

8. Ibid, p. 168.
9. Bill Chalker, 'The Secret Turner Report', 'UFOs Sub Rosa Down Under. The Australian Military & Government Role in the UFO Controversy' (1996). Accessed online 22 Sep 2021: www.project1947.com/forum/bcoz1.htm
10. Chalker, 'The Secret Turner Report'.
11. J. Hanlon, Report to the Range Commander, Maralinga, 'Unidentified Light – Wewak Area', 24 Jul 1960, Weapons Research Establishment Salisbury, SA, Dept of Supply and Royal Commission into British Nuclear Tests in Australia During the 1950s and 1960s, A6456, R029/284, Item number 417175 (Maralinga Project, Policy & Administration), p. 74 and 76. National Archives of Australia. Accessed online at: recordsearch.naa.gov.au/SearchNRetrieve/Interface/DetailsReports/ItemDetail.aspx?Barcode=417175&isAv=N
12. UPI wire story, 'Air Force Order on Saucers Cited. Pamphlet by the Inspector General Called Objects a "Serious Business"', *The New York Times*, 28 Feb 1960, p. 30.
13. NICAP, 'Statement on Unidentified Flying Objects by Admiral Delmer S. Fahrney USN (Ret) Chairman of the Board of Governors of NICAP', 16 Jan 1957. Accessed online: vault.fbi.gov/National%20Investigations%20Committee%20on%20Aerial%20Phenomena%20%28NICAP%29, p. 8.
14. Dolan, *UFOs and The National Security State*, p. 193,.
15. Major Donald Keyhoe, *Flying Saucers: Top Secret*, G.P. Putnam's Sons NY, 1960, pp. 266–7.
16. 'Air Force Order on "Saucers" Cited. Pamphlet by the Inspector General Called Objects a "Serious Business"', *The New York Times*, 28 Feb 1960, p. 30.
17. 'UFOs Serious Business', Inspector General Brief, USAF, No. 26, Vol XI, 24 December 1959.

5. Hard Evidence

1. Leslie Kean, 'The Retrieval of Objects of Unknown Origin. Project Moon Dust and Operation BlueFly', 2002. Accessed online: www.bibliotecapleyades.net/sociopolitica/esp_sociopol_mj12_3k.htm
2. Colonel Betz Memo, Dept of the Air Force, 'AFCIN Intelligence Team Personnel', 3 Nov 1961. Aka 'AFCIN-1E-0 Draft Policy', first released to Robert Todd, August 1979.
3. Howard Blum, *Out There*, Simon & Schuster, 1990, pp. 71–2.
4. Incoming Message, Dept of Air Force, (25 Apr 1961). Identifier: 1961-04-8677021 Pakistan Karachi. National Security Internet Archive.
5. Message from USDAO La Pas Bolivia to DIA, (17 Aug 1979), Defence Intelligence Agency FOIA documents.
6. CIA Information Report, 'Particulars of Bright Objects Seen Over South Ladakh, North East Nepal, North Sikkim and Western Bhutan' (11 Apr 1968). Released under FOIA 2001/04/02: CIA-RDP81R00560R000100070007-8
7. Kevin D. Randle, *Project Moon Dust*, Avon Books, NY, 1998, pp. 154–5.
8. Ibid, p. 154.
9. Dr Robert Jacobs, interview with author, 20 Apr 2020.
10. Hector Quintanilla, 'The Investigation of UFO's', Released 22 Sept 1993. Accessed online: www.cia.gov/resources/csi/studies-in-intelligence/archives/vol-10-no-4/the-investigation-of-ufos/
11. Dolan, *UFOs and The National Security State*, pp. 294–5.
12. Timothy Good, *Beyond Top Secret*, Sidgwick & Jackson, London, 1997, p. 162.
13. All Westall interviews with Joy Clarke and Colin Kelly were conducted by author onsite at Westall High School, 16 Nov 2019.
14. Terry Peck, interview with author, 14 Feb 2021.
15. Andrew Greenwood, interview with author, 16 Mar 2021.

16. Bill Chalker, 'Westall '66 – UFO or HIBAL? The answer is perhaps not "blowing in the wind"', 10 Aug 2014. Accessed online: TheOzfiles.blogspot.com.
17. Shane Ryan, interview with author, 22 Jul 2020.
18. *Tully Times*, 'I've Seen A Flying Saucer', Friday 28 Jan 1966, p. 1.
19. Edward U. Condon and Daniel S. Gillmor (eds), *Final Report of the Scientific Study of Unidentified Flying Objects*, Dutton/University of Colorado, 1969.
20. Dolan, *UFOs and The National Security State*, p. 308.
21. Condon and Gillmor, Final Report, 'Case 2: USAF/RAF Radar Sighting'.
22. Hynek, *The Hynek UFO Report*, p. 287.
23. US Air Force, 'UFOs and Project Blue Book. Fact Sheet', Public Affairs Division, Wright-Patterson AFB, Ohio, Jan 1985.
24. Good, Beyond Top Secret, Ibid, p. 537.

6. Cracking the Cover-up
1. O.H. Turner, 'Scientific and Intelligence Aspects of the UFO Problem', Minute Paper, Joint Intelligence Organisation, DoD Australia, 27 May 1971. Obtained by Australian researcher Keith Basterfield 2008 from National Archives Australia file 'Scientific Intelligence – General – Unidentified Flying Objects' Files series A13693, control symbol 3092/2/000, Barcode 300306606. A digital copy can be found online: recordsearch.naa.gov.au/SearchNRetrieve/Interface/ViewImage.aspx?B=30030606
2. Bill Chalker, interview with author, 3 Oct 2021.
3. '269: Memorandum for the Record. Washington, October 24/25, 1973, 10:30 p.m.–3:30 a.m'. CJCS [Chairman of the Joint Chiefs of Staff] Memo M–88–7. history.state.gov/historicaldocuments/frus1969-76v25/d269
4. These RAAF sightings reports were provided in 1974–56 to Moira McGhee of the UFO group UFOIC of Sydney and copies were subsequently provided to researcher Bill Chalker, who provided the author with copies. Chalker's account of this incident can be found in his book *The Oz Files*, Duffy & Snellgrove, 1996, pp. 154–9. A summary of this incident is available on researcher Keith Basterfield's blog: ufos-scientificresearch.blogspot.com/2013/12/north-west-cape-25-october-1973-initial.html
5. Bill Lynn communication with Keith Basterfield, accessed online: ufos-scientificresearch.blogspot.com/2014/07/william-gordon-lynn-25-october-1973.html
6. Kate Lynn communication with Keith Basterfield, accessed online: ufos-scientificresearch.blogspot.com/2014/07/william-gordon-lynn-25-october-1973.html
7. Affidavit of Eugene F. Yeates, *Citizens Against Unidentified Flying Objects Secrecy v National Security Agency*, Civil Action No 80-1562. Accessed online: www.nsa.gov/Portals/70/documents/news-features/declassified-documents/ufo/in_camera_affadavit_yeates.pdf
8. Grant Cameron, interview with author, 12 Feb 2020.
9. Dan Sheehan, interview with author, 17 Oct 2019 and 10 Jul 2020.
10. Daniel Sheehan, interview with author, 17 Oct 2019 and 10 Jul 2020.
11. Dolan, *The Cover-up Exposed, 1973-1991 (UFOs and the National Security State Book 2)*, Keyhole Publishing Co (Kindle edition), 2010, p. 136.
12. This story is well told by Richard. C. Henry in 'UFOs and NASA', *Journal of Scientific Exploration*, 1988, vol. 2, no. 2, pp. 93–142 (Permagon Press PLC).

7. Confusion or Cover-up?
1. John Cordy, interview with author, Wellington, New Zealand, 17 Sep 2020.
2. John Cordy, interview with author, 8 Jul 2020.

3.   Letter to Frank O'Flynn, NZ Minister of Defence, 25 Aug 1984. NZ Defence Force UFO Files 1984-89, p. 121. Accessed online 18 Sep 2020: ia600201. us.archive.org/11/items/NewZealandUFO/AIR-1630-2-Volume-1-1984-1989.pdf

4.   Quentin Fogarty, interview with author, 12 Feb 2016.

5.   Dennis Grant, interview with author, 18 Sep 2020.

6.   Timothy Good, *Beyond Top Secret*, pp. 56–77.

7.   Nick Pope, interview with author, Apr 2009. Sceptic Ian Ridpath has challenged Pope's claims about anomalous radiation at: www.ianridpath.com/ufo/rendlesham4.html

8.   Ian Ridpath, 'Rendlesham Forest UFO Case', (undated) www.ianridpath.com/ufo/rendlesham1a.html

9.   Col Charles Halt (retd), interview with author, Apr 2009.

10. Georgina Bruni, *You Can't Tell the People: The Definitive Account of the Rendlesham Forest UFO Mystery*, Sidgwick & Jackson, 2000.

11. Paul Steucke, Office of Public Affairs, Alaskan Region, Federal Aviation Administration, 'FAA Releases Documents on Reported UFO Sighting Last November', 5 March 1987, FAA/US Dept of Transport.

12. Philip Klass, 'FAA Data Sheds New Light on JAL Pilot's UFO Report', *The Skeptical Inquirer*, Summer 1987.

13. James W. Moseley and Karl T. Pflock, *Shockingly Close to the Truth: Confessions of a Grave-Robbing Ufologist*, Amherst, NY, 2002, pp 323–4.

14. Steven Greer, *Disclosure: Military & Government Witnesses Reveal the Greatest Secrets in Modern History*, Crossing Point Inc, 2001, pp. 79–93.

15. Interview with FAA Official John Callahan, 'FAA Official John Callahan   The Anchorage Incident', Sirius Disclosure. Accessed on YouTube 20 May 2020: www.youtube.com/watch?v=HUak1jfA2Hg (from 15:24).

16. Report of Squadron Leader Biddington, '[RAAF Headquarters Support Command, Victoria Barracks Victoria] UFO's [Unidentified Flying Object] reports [UAS - Unusual Aerial Sightings]' Series No: A9755 Control Symbol 5. Item ID: 3533434, p. 103.

17. John Alexander, *UFOs – Myths, Conspiracies and Realities*, St Martin's Press, NY, 2011, pp. 263–4.

18. UK Ministry of Defence, 'Unidentified Aerial Phenomena (UAP) in the UK Air Defence Region', Ch4 'UAP Work in Other Countries' (2000). Declassified 10 Nov 2012. The National Archives. Accessed online: webarchive. nationalarchives.gov.uk/20121110115327/www.mod.uk/DefenceInternet/FreedomOfInformation/PublicationScheme/SearchPublicationScheme/UnidentifiedAerialPhenomenauapInTheUkAirDefenceRegion.htm

8. The Black Triangles

1.   Retd Major Gen Wilfried de Brouwer, National Press Club Press UFO Conference for the Coalition for Freedom of Information, 12 November 2007, Washington DC.

2.   Leslie Kean, *UFOs. Generals, Pilots, and Government Officials Go on the Record*, Three Rivers Press, NY, 2010, p. 19.

3.   Brian Dunning, Skeptoid Podcast Episode 538 'The Belgian UFO Wave', 27 September 2016. Accessed online 28 Mar 2021: skeptoid.com/episodes/4538

4.   Sighting report: 11 Jun 1990 0208 hrs Exmouth, WA. Keith Basterfield, 'A Catalogue of the more interesting Australian UAP Reports 1793-2014', 15 Sep 2018. www.project1947.com. As provided to author.

5.   Timothy Good, Need To Know: UFOs, The Military & Intelligence, (2006) Sidgwick & Jackson, p. 382.

6.   Nick Pope, 'Britain's Real X-Files', 2 Feb 2005, Daily Mail, p. 13.8

7.   Author interview with Nick Pope, April 2009, Sunday Night, Seven Network Australia.

8. Martin Willis, *Podcast UFO*.
9. Bill Sweetman, 'Secret Warplanes of Area 51', *Popular Science*, 4 June 2006.
10. Leslie Kean, 'Is There a UFO Cover-up? A Government Insider Speaks Out', *Huffington Post*, 9 May 2016. Accessed online 11 December 2017: www.huffpost.com/entry/is-there-a-ufo-coverup-a-_b_9865184
11. Interview with author, 4 Apr 2020.
12. Harzan was the executive director of civilian UFO research organisation MUFON until his resignation in July 2020 after allegations he solicited sex from a 13-year-old girl.
13. T.L. Keller, *The Total Novice's Guide to UFOs: What You Need To Know*, 2FS Publishing LLC, 2010.
14. Richard Beckwith, interview with Jan Harzan of MUFON, 'Ben Rich: We Now Have the technology To Take ET Home', 29 August 2013. Accessed on YouTube 7 Jul 2020: www.youtube.com/watch?v=FB3ngWGwShs
15. John Andrews' signed transcription of his 10 July 1986 handwritten letter to Ben Rich, copy provided to the author by Jim Goodall.
16. Signed letter from Ben Rich to John Andrews, 21 July 1986, copy provided to the author by Jim Goodall.
17. Interview with Dave Fruehauf, 'The Storming of Area 51', 15 November 2019, *Ancient Aliens*, Season 14, Ep 20.
18. Jeremy Corbell, *Bob Lazar: Area 51 & Flying Saucers*, Netflix documentary, 2018, at 1:03:47.
19. Captain Bradley R. Townsend USAF, 'Space Based Satellite Tracking and Characterization Utilizing Non-Imaging Passive Sensors', March 2008, Thesis, Department of the Air Force, Air Force Institute of Technology, Wright-Patterson Air Force Base, Ohio.
20. Bob Fish email to Podesta, 'Leslie Kean book – DSP Program', 3 June 2015, *Wikileaks*, accessed online 22 Jul 2020: wikileaks.org/podesta-emails/emailid/54211
21. Bob Fish email to Podesta, 'Leslie Kean book comment', 3 May 2015, *Wikileaks*. Accessed online 22 Jul 2020: wikileaks.org/podesta-emails/emailid/47433
22. Bob Fish email to Podesta, 'Leslie Kean book – Blue Book', 3 June 2015, *Wikileaks*. Accessed online 22 Jul 2020: wikileaks.org/podesta-emails/emailid/31721
23. Bob Fish emails to author, February 2020.
24. Jacques Vallée, *Forbidden Science Vol Four: Journals 1990–1999 The Spring Hill Chronicles*, Lulu.com (Kindle edition), 2019, p 47. Account of meeting 21 June 1990.
25. Jacques Vallée, *Forbidden Science Vol Four*, pp. 92–3 (Kindle edition). Account of meeting 24 May 1991.
26. Statement of Dick D'Amato retrieved from his now-defunct website cricharddamato.com via Archive.org by researcher Giuliano Marinkovic of Omnitalk Radio. 26 May 2020. Also at: www.megalomediadesigns.com/dickdamato.html Accessed online 17 July 2020: www.theufochronicles.com/2020/05/senate-staffer-dick-damatos-ufo-statement.html?m=1

9. The Disclosure Project
1. Webb Hubbell, *Friends in High Places*, Beaufort Books (Kindle edition), 1997, p. 269.
2. For example: Joe Martin and William J. Birnes, 'Bill Clinton and UFOs: Did He Ever Find Out if the Truth Was Out There?', Salon.com, 29 January 2018.
3. Paul Davies, *Are We Alone?: Philosophical Implications of the Discovery of Extraterrestrial Life*, Perseus, 1996.
4. Dan Good, 'Bill Clinton Wouldn't Be Surprised if Aliens Exist', ABCNews.go.com, 3 April 2014.
5. Dr Greer's response: siriusdisclosure.com/dr-greers-response-to-former-cia-director-woolseys-denial-of-meeting/

6. Letter to Dr Steven Greer from James and Suzanne Woolsey and John and Diane Petersen, 16 September 1999. Accessed online 4 May 2020: siriusdisclosure.com/wp-content/uploads/2013/03/1999-Woolsey-Petersen-letter.pdf.
7. John L. Petersen, email to author, 15 May 2020.
8. Dr Steven Greer interview on Jimmy Church, 'Breaking: Dr Steven Greer speaks on the Davis/Wilson UFO Document Leak', 18 June 2019.
9. Steven M. Greer, *Hidden Truth: Forbidden Knowledge*, Crossing Point, 2006, pp. 149–51.
10. Leslie Kean, 'Third Cometa Article in VSD', UFO Updates. Accessed online: ufoupdateslist.com/2000/sep/m15-016.shtml. This is a draft article, a shorter version of which was subsequently published in French newsmagazine *VSD*, www.vsd.fr.
11. Tim McMillan and Tyler Rogoway, 'Special Access Programs and the Pentagon's Ecosystem of Secrecy', *The War Zone/The Drive*, 22 July 2019, Accessed online 5 May 2020: www.thedrive.com/the-war-zone/29092/special-access-programs-and-the-pentagons-ecosystem-of-secrecy
12. USAF NRO/Central Security Service, 'Memorandum for Record', 28 July 1991. Accessed on the SiriusDisclosure.com website 5 May 2020: siriusdisclosure.com/wp-content/uploads/2012/12/NRO-Doc.pdf
13. Steven Greer DVD, 'Dr Greer Presents Expose of the National Security State, Washington DC, November 21, 2015', DVD from Sirius-Disclosure.com.
14. Greer, *Hidden Truth: Forbidden Knowledge*, p. 151.
15. John Audette, interview with author, email 4 February 2020.
16. Dr Steven Greer and Ret. Commander Willard Miller, 'Insight into New Energy', 8 February 2013. Accessed on YouTube 11 May 2020: www.youtube.com/watch?v=XdoHAeaTc2A (at 29:42)
17. Steven Greer, interview with Art Bell, *Coast to Coast AM*, 8 May 1997: web.archive.org/web/19970605171829/www.artbell.com/topics.html
18. Steven M. Greer, *Hidden Truth: Forbidden Knowledge*, Crossing Point, 2006, p. 150.
19. Shari Adamiak/CSETI, Project Starlight, interview with Jeff Rense, 29 April 1997. www.renseradio.com. Accessed online 8 May 2020: archive.org/details/Sheri_Adamiak_-_CSETI_Project_Starlight (from 12:09)
20. Greer, *Hidden Truth: Forbidden Knowledge*, p. 152.
21. Greer, *Hidden Truth: Forbidden Knowledge*, p. xii.
22. Richard Dolan, *The Cover-Up Exposed, 1973-1991 (UFOs and the National Security State Book 2)*, Keyhole Publishing (Kindle edition), 2010, p. 539.
23. Signed letter from Vice Admiral Tom Wilson to the author, 'Coulthart response.pdf', received by email attachment, 30 June 2020.
24. Fife Symington interview CNN, 'Symington: I Saw a UFO in the Arizona Sky Event', CNN, 11 September 2007.
25. Podesta Press Conference, 22 Oct 2002. Excerpt from 'I Know What I Saw' documentary produced by James Fox. YouTube.com. Accessed online 16 Oct 2020: www.youtube.com/watch?v=smwQau3HtKM

10. Skinwalker Ranch

1. Zack Van Eyck, 'Frequent Fliers', *Deseret News*, 30 June 1996. Accessed online 2 Mar 2020 at: www.deseret.com/1996/6/30/19251541/frequent-fliers
2. Ibid.
3. Jessica Johnston, 'Cattle Mutilated in North Queensland', *North Queensland Register*, 7 Sep 2018: www.northqueenslandregister.com.au/story/5633519
4. Mick Cook, interview with author, 21 Mar 2021.
5. James R. Stewart, 'Cattle Mutilations – An Episode of Collective Delusion', *Sceptical Inquirer*, vol. 1, no. 2, Spring/Summer 1977, pp. 55–66.
6. Ben Mezrich, *The 37th Parallel: The Secret Truth Behind America's UFO Highway*, Thorndike Press, 2017.

7.   See Amy Bickel, 'Recent Cattle Mutilations Bring Memories of 1970s Attacks', *The Hutchinson News – Capital Press*, 15 January 2016; Jim Robbins, 'Unsolved Mystery Resurfaces in Montana: Who's Killing Cows?', *The New York Times*, 17 September 2001, Section B, p. 1.
8.   Ben Mezrich, 'Why I Believe in UFOs, and You Should Too', 19 December 2016, TEDxBeaconStreet. Accessed online 2 March 2020: www.youtube.com/watch?v=urKhVssiygA
9.   Erica Lukes, 'Dr Eric Davis, Skinwalker Ranch, NIDS and To The Stars Academy', 29 July 2018. UFO Classified, YouTube. Accessed online 19 December 2019: www.youtube.com/watch?v=nqBeuxB-9IM
10. Ibid.
11. Ibid.
12. Interview Dr Eric Davis with Alejandro Rojas, www.openminds.tv.
13. Ibid.
14. For example: Mick West, 'Black UFO at Skinwalker Ranch (a Fly)', 22 May 2020: www.metabunk.org
15. Dr Eric Davis Interview with Erica Lukes, *UFO Classified*, 28 July 2018.
16. Colm A. Kelleher Ph.D. and George Knapp, *Hunt for the Skinwalker: Science Confronts the Unexplained at a Remote Ranch in Utah*, Paraview Pocket Books, 2005.
17. Ibid, p. 147.
18. Ibid, p. 6.
19. Howard Blum, *Out There*.
20. John B. Alexander, *UFOs, Myths, Conspiracies and Realities*, St Martin's Griffin ed, p. 353.
21. Ibid, p. 354.
22. Ibid, p. 355.
23. Colm Kelleher, 'Summary Report of Utah Trip 7/30/1997-8/6/1997', NIDS. Document obtained by author from the estate of the late Edgar Mitchell.
24. Colm Kelleher, 'Report on Trip to New Mexico 9/15-9/19/1997', NIDS. Document obtained by author from the estate of the late Edgar Mitchell.
25. Ibid.
26. Ibid.
27. Ibid.
28. Ibid.
29. Greg Bishop, *Project Beta, The Story of Paul Bennewitz, National Security, and the Creation of a Modern UFO Myth*, Simon & Schuster, 2005.
30. Ibid.
31. Ibid.

11. Tic Tacs from Space

1.   Kevin Day, interview with author, 22 and 23 Mar 2021; Robert Powell, Scientific Coalition for Ufology, Interview with Kevin Day. Accessed online 8 February 2020: www.explorescu.org/post/nimitz_strike_group_2004
2.   Kevin Day, interview with author, 22 and 23 Mar 2021; Dave Beaty Interview with Kevin Day from documentary *The Nimitz Encounters*, first published 26 May 2019. Accessed online 4 Feb 2020: www.youtube.com/watch?v=PRgoisHRmUE
3.   Gary Voorhis, interview with author, 10 Mar 2021.
4.   Voorhis, interview with author, 10 Mar 2021; Tim McMillan, 'The Witnesses', *Popular Mechanics*, 12 November 2019. Accessed online 20 December 2019: www.popularmechanics.com/military/research/a29771548
5.   Joe Murgia/UFO Joe website, 'Notes and Quotes from the Military "Tic Tac" Witness Group Interview at UFO MegaCon', 27 March 2019. Accessed online 6 Feb 2020 at: www.ufojoe.net/?p=805

6. Interview with Kevin Day.
7. Robert Powell, Peter Reali, Tim Thompson, Morgan Beall, Doug Kimzey, Larry Cates and Richard Hoffman, 'A Forensic Analysis of Navy Carrier Strike Group Eleven's Encounter with an Anomalous Aerial Vehicle', SCU – Scientific Coalition for Ufology, (published online 25 April 2019). Accessed online April 2019: www.explorescu.org, p. 16.
8. Paco Chierici, 'There I Was: The X-Files Edition', *Fighter Sweep*, 14 March 2015. Accessed online 2 December 2019: sofrep.com/fightersweep/x-files-edition/
9. 'A Forensic Analysis of Navy Carrier Strike Group Eleven's Encounter with an Anomalous Aerial Vehicle', SCU – Scientific Coalition for Ufology, p. 8.
10. David Fravor, interview, *Fox News/Tucker Carlson Tonight*, 20 Dec 2017. YouTube, accessed online: www.youtube.com/watch?v=EDj9ZZQY2kA
11. 'A Forensic Analysis of Navy Carrier Strike Group Eleven's Encounter with an Anomalous Aerial Vehicle', p. 14
12. Ibid. p. 12.
13. Dave Beaty Interview with Kevin Day, p. 12.
14. Slaight Interview with ret'd USN Capt Tim Thompson, 'A Forensic Analysis of Navy Carrier Strike Group Eleven's Encounter with an Anomalous Aerial Vehicle', Ibid, p. 12.
15. Paco Chierici, 'There I Was: The X Files Edition'.
16. Tucker Carlson, interview with Fravor.
17. Robert Powell SCU interview with Kevin Day, from 6:15.
18. Frank Chung, 'What the Hell Is That? Navy Pilot Reveals Creepy Incident of Dark Mass Coming up from the Depths', *www.news.com.au*, 7 October 2019. Accessed online 8 February 2020: www.news.com.au/technology/science/space/what-the-hell-is-that-navy-pilot-reveals-creepy-incident-of-dark-mass-coming-up-from-the-depths/news-story/6a96202a189a58300b4c717e14b15422
19. Ibid.
20. Matthew Phelan, 'Navy Pilot Who Filmed the "Tic Tac" UFO Speaks: It Wasn't Behaving by the Normal Laws of Physics', *New York Magazine*, 19 December 2019. Accessed online 9 February 2020: nymag.com/intelligencer/2019/12/tic-tac-ufo-video-q-and-a-with-navy-pilot-chad-underwood.html
21. Beaty, 'The Nimitz Encounters'.
22. Author interview with Kevin Day.
23. Phelan, Ibid.
24. Eli Rosenberg, 'Former Navy Pilot Describes UFO Encounter Studied by Secret Pentagon Program', *Washington Post*, 19 December 2017.
25. Robert Powell SCU, interview with Kevin Day, from 8:50.
26. Hughes, interview, *UFO Joe*.
27. Tyler Rogoway, 'What the Hell Is Going on with UFOs and the Department of Defence?', *The Drive/The War Zone*, 26 April 2019. Accessed online 6 Feb 2020: www.thedrive.com/the-war-zone/27666/what-the-hell-is-going-on-with-ufos-and-department-of-Defence?

12. The Hunt for 'The Big Secret'

1. Robert Bigelow, interview with George Knapp, Part 2, 6 February 2021, *Mystery Wire/YouTube*. Accessed online: www.youtube.com/watch?v=9Sv66dG6Ldc
2. Eric Lach, 'Harry Reid Misses George W. Bush and Always Kind of Liked Bernie Sanders', *New Yorker*, 21 February 2020. Accessed online 27 February 2020: www.newyorker.com/news/the-new-yorker-interview/harry-reid-misses-george-w-bush-and-always-kind-of-liked-bernie-sanders
3. Ibid.
4. Senator Daniel Inouye, Closing Statement, US Senate Select Committee on Secret Military Assistance to Iran and the Nicaraguan Opposition, 3 August 1987.

Accessed 28 February 2020 online at C-Span (Inouye quote at 3:44:28-3:52:18): www.c-span.org/video/?9648-1/iran-contra-investigation-day-40

5. Eric Lach, 'Harry Reid Misses George Bush and Always Kind of Liked Bernie Sanders.

6. Lara Logan, 'Bigelow Aerospace Founder Says Commercial World Will Lead in Space', 28 May 2017, *60 Minutes*/CBS. Transcript accessed online 29 February 2020: www.cbsnews.com/news/bigelow-aerospace-founder-says-commercial-world-will-lead-in-space/

7. Tim McMillan, 'Inside the Pentagon's Secret UFO Program', *Popular Mechanics*, 14 February 2020. Accessed online 15 February 2020: www.popularmechanics.com/military/research/a30916275/government-secret-ufo-program-investigation/

8. McMillan, 'Inside the Pentagon's Secret UFO Program'.

9. George Knapp, Eric Davis interview *Coast to Coast AM*, 24 June 2018. Accessed online 21 March 2020: www.coasttocoastam.com/shows/2018/06/24

10. Robert Hastings, *UFOs & Nukes, Extraordinary Encounters at Nuclear Weapons Sites*, 2nd ed., 2017. Self-published manuscript.

11. Robert Hastings, interview with author, 7 April 2020.

12. Knapp, *Coast to Coast AM*, 24 June 2018.

13. Scott and Suzanne Ramsey and Dr Frank Thayer, *The Aztec UFO Incident. The case, Evidence, and Elaborate Cover-up of One of the Most Perplexing Crashes in History*, The Career Press Inc, NJ, 2016.

14. Art Bell Interview with Dr Colm Kelleher, 'Black Triangle Phenomenon', *Coast to Coast AM*, 24 April 2004. Accessed online 15 December 2019: www.coasttocoastam.com/show/2004-04-24-show/

15. Letter from Senator Harry Reid to William Lynn, Deputy Secretary of Defence, 24 June 2009. Letter first published by George Knapp of KLAS-TV. Accessed via the KLAS-TV website 2 August 2018: media.lasvegasnow.com/nxsglobal/lasvegasnow/document_dev/2018/07/25/Reid_letter_2009_1532565293943_49621615_ver1.0.pdf

16. McMillan, Ibid.

17. George Knapp, 'I-Team: Former Sen. Reid calls for Congressional Hearings into UFOs', *8NewsNow*, 31 January 2019. Accessed online 16 December 2019: www.8newsnow.com/news/local-news/i-team-former-sen-reid-calls-for-congressional-hearings-into-ufos/1743467461/

18. Gideon Lewis-Kraus, 'How The Pentagon Started Taking UFO's Seriously', *The New Yorker*, 10 May 2021, Accessed online 3 May 2021: www.newyorker.com/magazine/2021/05/10/how-the-pentagon-started-taking-ufos-seriously

19. Christopher Mellon interview with Joe Rogan, The *Joe Rogan Experience*, Ep1645, 5 May 2021. Accessed online 6 May 2021: open.spotify.com/show/4rOoJ6Egrf8K2IrywzwOMk

13. Would the President Know?

1. Melissa Bell, 'White House Denies Aliens Exist on Earth', *Washington Post*, 7 November 2011.

2. Steve Tetreault, 'Believers in Nevada Scoff as White House Denies UFOs Are Real', *Las Vegas Review-Journal*, 13 November 2011, p. 18A.

3. Annie Jacobsen, *Area 51: An Uncensored History of America's Top Military Base*, Orion Books/Hachette UK (Kindle edition), 2011, pp. 36–7.

4. Ibid, pp. 367–8.

5. Jimmy Kimmel, 'President Barack Obama Denies Knowledge of Aliens', *Jimmy Kimmel Live*, 13 March 2015. Accessed online 12 December 2019: www.youtube.com/watch?v=EYzRY2XpLBk

6. Michael Tedder, 'Blink-182's Tom DeLonge on UFOs, Government Coverups and Why Aliens Are Bigger Than Jesus', 17 February 2015, www.papermag.com.

Accessed online 9 March 2020: www.papermag.com/tom-delonge-ufos-interview-1427513207.html

7. Ibid.

8. Sam Law, 'Blink-182: The Inside Story of Enema of the State', Kerrang.com, 1 June 2019. Accessed online 9 March 2020: www.kerrang.com/features/blink-182-the-inside-story-of-enema-of-the-state/

9. Geoff Boucher, 'Hangin' Out with Rock's Rude Boys', *Los Angeles Times*, 11 May 2000. Accessed online 9 Mar 2020: www.latimes.com/archives/la-xpm-2000-may-11-ca-28718-story.html

10. Gavin Edwards, 'Punk Guitar + Fart Jokes = Blink-182', *Rolling Stone*, 20 January 2020. Accessed 9 Mar 2020: www.rollingstone.com/music/music-news/punk-guitar-fart-jokes-blink-182-63042/

11. Michael Tedder, *Papermag*.

12. Kelly Dickerson, 'Tom DeLonge Took a Break from Blink-182 to Focus on UFOs', 18 June 2016, www.mic.com. Accessed online 9 Mar 2020: www.mic.com/articles/140196/why-tom-de-longe-took-a-break-from-blink-182-to-expose-the-truth-about-aliens

13. Tyler Rogoway, 'Tom DeLonge's Origin Story for To The Stars Academy Describes a Government UFO Info Operation', *The War Zone*, 5 June 2019. Accessed online 8 Aug 2019: www.thedrive.com/the-war-zone/28377/tom-delonges-origin-story-for-to-the-stars-academy-describes-a-government-info-operation

14. Tom DeLonge, *SeKret Machines Book 1: Chasing Shadows*, p. XIII.

15. Ibid, p. XIV.

16. Ibid.

17. Ibid.

18. George Knapp, Interview with Tom DeLonge, *Coast to Coast AM*, 27 March 2016. Accessed online 5 Aug 2018: www.coasttocoastam.com/show/2016/03/27

19. Tom DeLonge with Peter Levenda, *SeKret Machines: Man. Volume 2: Gods, Man, & War. An Official SeKret Machines Investigation of the UFO Phenomenon*, To The Stars Inc, 2019, Prologue, p. XIII.

20. Joe Rogan, Interview with Tom DeLonge, 26 October 2017, *Joe Rogan Experience #1029*. Accessed online 2 February 2019: www.youtube.com/watch?v=5n_3mnJfHzY

14. We Can Handle the Truth

1. George Knapp, interview with Tom DeLonge, *Coast to Coast AM*, 27 March 2016. Accessed online 5 Aug 2018: www.coasttocoastam.com/show/2016/03/27

2. Tom DeLonge and A.J. Hartley, *SeKret Machines Book 1: Chasing Shadows*, To The Stars Academy, 2016, p. XV.

3. Knapp, *Coast to Coast AM*, hour 3 at approximately 07:05.

4. Ibid, hour 3 at approximately 24:37.

5. DeLonge, *SeKret Machines/Chasing Shadows*, p. XXX..

6. Joe Rogan, op. cit.

7. Ibid.

8. George Knapp, *Coast To Coast AM*, hour 3 at approximately 9:03.

9. Ibid.

10. Ibid.

11. Ibid.

12. Ibid.

13. Ibid.

15. Sharing the Guilty Secret

1. Netyksho was indicted by the US government in absentia on 13 July 2018. A full copy of the indictment is accessible at: www.justice.gov/file/1080281/download.

Analysis article by Zack Whittaker, 'Mueller Report sheds new light on how the Russians hacked the DNC and the Clinton campaign', 19 April 2018, Techcrunch. com. Accessed online 12 December 2019: techcrunch.com/2019/04/18/mueller-clinton-arizona-hack/

2. Ashley Parker and David E. Sanger, 'Donald Trump Calls on Russia to Find Hillary Clinton's Missing Emails', *New York Times*, 27 July 2016, p. A2.

3. Nigel M. Smith, 'Ariana Grande's Donut-licking Cost Her a Gig at White House, Wikileaks Reveals', *The Guardian*, 26 July 2016.

4. Michael Weiss, 'The Long, Dark History of Russia's Murder, Inc', *The New York Review of Books*, 18 December 2019.

5. Email from DeLonge to Podesta, 26 October 2015. Accessed online 2 February 2019: wikileaks.org/podesta-emails/emailid/2125

6. DeLonge, *Sekret Machines: Chasing Shadows*, back cover.

7. Email from Neil Mcc to Podesta et al, 24 January 2016. Accessed online. 2 December 2019: wikileaks.org/podesta-emails/emailid/5078

8. Email from Susan McCasland Wilkerson to Podesta, 24 January 2016. Accessed online 2 December 2019: wikileaks.org/podesta-emails/emailid/2635

9. DeLonge to Podesta email, 25 January 2016. Accessed online 3 December 2019: wikileaks.org/podesta-emails/emailid/3099

10. George Knapp, interview with Tom DeLonge, Coast to Coast AM, 27 March 2016. Accessed online 5 Aug 2018: www.coasttocoastam.com/show/2016/03/27

11. Tom DeLonge email to Podesta, 23 February 2016. Accessed online 2 December 2019: wikileaks.org/podesta-emails/emailid/19062

12. Tom DeLonge email to Podesta, 'Tom DeLonge Here', 24 September 2015, Wikileaks.org. Accessed online 2 December 2019: wikileaks.org/podesta-emails/emailid/33739

13. DeLonge email to Podesta, 24 September 2015. Accessed online 2 December 2019: wikileaks.org/podesta-emails/emailid/33739

14. George Knapp, 'I-Team: Clinton Aide Seeks UFO files'.

15. Ibid.

16. Space Force website. 'Star Delta Fact Sheet'. Accessed online 24 March 2021: www.spaceforce.mil/About-Us/STAR-DELTA/.

17. Devan Cole, 'Trump Calls Newly released UFO Footage a "Hell of a Video"', CNN, 30 April 2020. Accessed online 21 May 2020: edition.cnn.com/2020/04/30/politics/donald-trump-ufo-videos-response/index.html

16. To The Stars Academy of Arts & Sciences

1. Overview of TTSA mission, To The Stars Academy. Accessed online 8 March 2020: dpo.tothestarsacademy.com/

2. Transcript of Mellon speech by Alejandro Rojas/OpenMindsTV website, 'Transcript of TTSA Press Conference'. Posted 11 October 2017: www.openminds.tv/transcript-of-to-the-stars-academy-press-conference/41145

3. Joe Rogan, interview with Tom DeLonge, 26 October 2017, *Joe Rogan Experience* #1029.

4. News Release, 'To The Stars Academy of Arts & Sciences Launches Today', Cision PR Newswire, 11 October 2017. Accessed online 26 March 2021: www.prnewswire.com/news-releases/to-the-stars-academy-of-arts--science-launches-today-300534912.html

5. US Securities and Exchange Commission, 'Offering Circular dated July 12, 2019, To The Stars Academy of Arts & Sciences Inc'. Accessed online 30 March 2020: www.sec.gov/Archives/edgar/data/1710274/000114420419034515/tv525071_253g2.htm

6. Joe Rogan, Interview with Tom DeLonge, 26 Oct 2017, Joe Rogan Experience #1029, Ibid.

7. On 25 Jul 2020 Tom DeLonge tweeted 'Working on the first plans for @ TTSAcademy's first anti-gravitic experiment. More to come.'. Accessed online 28 Jul 2020 at: twitter.com/tomdelonge/status/1287067919243808769

8. Ralph Blumenthal, 'U.F.O.s, the Pentagon and The Times', *The New York Times*, 19 December 2017, p. A2.

9. Elizondo website, 'Lue at a Glance'. Accessed online 26 March 2021: luiselizondo-official.com/

10. Helene Cooper, Ralph Blumenthal and Leslie Kean, 'Real U.F.O.'s? Pentagon Unit Tried to Know', *The New York Times*, 17 December 2017, p. A1. Published online as 'Glowing Auras and "Black Money": The Pentagon's Mysterious U.F.O. Program': www.nytimes.com/2017/12/16/us/politics/pentagon-program-ufo-harry-reid.html

11. Joby Warrick, 'Head of Pentagon's Secret "UFO" Office Sought to Make Evidence Public', *The Washington Post*, 17 December 2017. Accessed online 26 March 2020: www.washingtonpost.com/world/national-security/head-of-pentagons-secret-ufo-office-sought-to-make-evidence-public/2017/12/16/90bcb7cc-e2b2-11e7-8679-a9728984779c_story.html

12. Erin Burnett, interview with Luis Elizondo, 'Ex-UFO Program Chief: We May Not Be Alone', CNN Outfront, 19 December 2017. Accessed online 12 December 2019: www.youtube.com/watch?v=-2b4qSoMnKE

13. Lindsey Ellefson, 'Neil deGrasse Tyson on UFOs: "Call Me When You Have a Dinner Invite from an Alien"', CNN, 21 December 2017. Accessed online 28 March 2020: edition.cnn.com/2017/12/20/us/neil-degrasse-tyson-ufos-new-day-cnntv/index.html

14. Helene Cooper, Ralph Blumenthal and Leslie Kean, 'Real U.F.O.'s? Pentagon Unit Tried to Know', *The New York Times*, 17 December 2017, p. A1. Published online as 'Glowing Auras and "Black Money": The Pentagon's Mysterious U.F.O. Program': www.nytimes.com/2017/12/16/us/politics/pentagon-program-ufo-harry-reid.html

15. Project Unity, interview with Ralph Blumenthal and Leslie Kean, *The New York Times*, 26 July 2020, Ibid. At 12:18. Accessed online: www.youtube.com/watch?v=KvOWnhNv-ys

16. US Securities and Exchange Commission, 'Offering Circular dated July 12, 2019, To The Stars Academy of Arts & Sciences Inc', p. 10.

17. Joe Rogan, interview with Tom DeLonge, 26 October 2017, *Joe Rogan Experience* #1029.

18. Bryan Bender, 'The Pentagon's Secret Search for UFOs', *Politico* Magazine, 16 December 2017. Accessed online 12 January 2018: www.politico.com/magazine/story/2017/12/16/pentagon-ufo-search-harry-reid-216111

19. Bryan Bender, 'The Pentagon's Secret Search for UFOs', Politico ; Eli Rosenberg, 'Former Navy Pilot Describes UFO Encounter Studied by Secret Pentagon Program', *Washington Post*, 19 December 2017; Helene Cooper, Leslie Kean and Ralph Blumenthal, '2 Navy Airmen and an Object That "Accelerated Like Nothing I've Ever Seen"', *The New York Times*, 16 December 2017, p. A27.

20. US Dept of Defence, '2004 USS *Nimitz* FLIR1 Video', 13 December 2017, TheVaulttothestarsacademy.com. Accessed online 29 May 2020: thevault.tothestarsacademy.com/2004-nimitz-flir1-video

21. US Dept of Defence, 'Gimbal: Authenticated UAP Video', 13 December 2017, TheVaulttothestarsacademy.com. Accessed online 29 March 2020: thevault.tothestarsacademy.com/gimbal

22. Department of Defence, '2015 Go Fast Footage', thevaulttothestarsacademy.com. 9 March 2018. Accessed online 29 March 2020: thevault.tothestarsacademy.com/2015-go-fast-footage

23. Christopher Mellon, 'The Military Keeps Encountering UFOs. Why Doesn't the Pentagon Care?', *The Washington Post*, 9 March 2018. Accessed online 20 March 2020: www.washingtonpost.com/outlook/the-military-keeps-encountering-

ufos-why-doesnt-the-pentagon-care/2018/03/09/242c125c-22ee-11e8-94da-
ebf9d112159c_story.html

24. Form 1U SEC filing by Tom DeLonge, 'Other Events', 17 February 2021. Accessed
online 26 March 2021: www.sec.gov/Archives/edgar/data/0001710274/000149315
221004131/form1-u.htm

25. Form 1U SEC filing by Tom DeLonge, 'Other Events', 24 March 2021. Accessed
online 26 March 2021: www.sec.gov/Archives/edgar/data/0001710274/000149315
221006682/form1-u.htm

17. Verified Unidentified

1. Helene Cooper, Ralph Blumenthal and Leslie Kean, '"Wow, What Is That?" Navy
Pilots Report Unexplained Flying Objects', *The New York Times*, 27 May 2019,
p. A14.

2. Ryan Graves, interview with Luis Elizondo and David Fravor, 'Unidentified:
Inside America's UFO Investigation' Ep 4, History Channel. First aired June 2019.
Accessed online 12 December 2019: www.history.com/shows/unidentified-inside-
americas-ufo-investigation

3. Christopher Mellon, interview with Harris Faulkner, 'Transcript – Mellon: Eight
Members of Congress Can Gain Access to The Most Sacred and Tightly Held
Special Access Programs (Crashed UFOs & Bodies?)', Fox News Channel – The Fox
News Breakdown, 5 June 2019.

4. Helene Cooper, Ralph Blumenthal and Leslie Kean, "Wow, What Is That?" Navy
Pilots Report Unexplained Flying Objects'.

5. Tyler Rogoway, 'Recent UFO Encounters with Navy Pilots Occurred Constantly
Across Multiple Squadrons', *The War Zone*, 20 June 2019. Accessed online 8 August
2019: www.thedrive.com/the-war-zone/28627/recent-ufo-encounters-with-navy-
pilots-occurred-constantly-across-multiple-squadrons

6. Helene Cooper, Ralph Blumenthal and Leslie Kean, "Wow, What Is That?" Navy
Pilots Report Unexplained Flying Objects', Ibid.

7. *Unidentified: Inside America's UFO Investigation* Season One, Ep 4, History
Channel.

8. Ryan Graves Interview with Luis Elizondo and David Fravor, 'Unidentified: Inside
America's UFO Investigation' Ep 4, History Channel.

9. Tyler Rogoway, 'Navy F/A-18 Pilot Shares New Details About UFO Encounters
During Middle East Deployment', *The War Zone*, 10 June 2019. Accessed online 18
December 2019: www.thedrive.com/the-war-zone/28453/navy-f-a-18-pilot-shares-
new-details-about-ufo-encounters-during-middle-east-deployment

10. Jan Tegler and Cat Hofacker, 'Mystery of the "Damn Things"', Aerospace America,
November 2019. Accessed online 12 January 2020: aerospaceamerica.aiaa.org/
features/mystery-of-the-damn-things/

11. Congressman Mark Walker, Letter to Hon Richard Spencer, Secretary of the US
Navy, 16 July 2019.

12. Bryan Bender, 'Navy Withholding Data on UFO Sightings, Congressman Says',
Politico, 6 September 2019. Accessed online 12 December 2019: www.politico.com/
story/2019/09/06/navy-withholding-ufo-sightings-1698396

13. Ibid.

14. John Greenewald Jr, 'U.S. Navy Releases Dates of Three Officially Acknowledged
Encounters with Phenomena', The Black Vault, 11 September 2019. Accessed
online 18 December 2019: www.theblackvault.com/documentarchive/u-s-navy-
releases-dates-of-three-officially-acknowledged-encounters-with-phenomena/

15. Bryan Bender, 'Military and Spy Agencies Accused of Stiff-arming Investigators on
UFO Sightings', 25 March 2021. Accessed online 26 March 2021: www.politico.
com/news/2021/03/25/ufo-sightings-report-478104

16. *Unidentified: Inside America's UFO Investigation* Ep 4, History Channel.
17. Ibid.
18. Ibid.
19. Ibid.
20. Bryan Bender, 'U.S. Navy Drafting New Guidelines for Reporting UFOs', *Politico*, 23 April 2019. Accessed online 12 December 2019: www.politico.com/story/2019/04/23/us-navy-guidelines-reporting-ufos-1375290
21. US DoD statement, 'Statement by the Department of Defence on the Release of Historical Navy Videos', 27 April 2020. Accessed online 24 May 2020: www.Defence.gov/Newsroom/Releases/Release/Article/2165713/statement-by-the-department-of-Defence-on-the-release-of-historical-navy-videos/
22. *Unidentified: Inside America's UFO Investigation*, Ep 4, History Channel.
23. Paul Dean, 'Office of Naval Intelligence (ONI) Admits to "Top Secret" Records and "Secret" Video from USS *Nimitz* "Tic Tac" UFO Incident', *UFOs – Documenting The Evidence Blog*, 8 January 2020. Accessed online 8 January 2020: ufos-documenting-the-evidence.blogspot.com/
24. *Unidentified: Inside America's UFO Investigation*, Ep 4, History Channel.
25. George Knapp, *Coast to Coast AM*, interview with Tom DeLonge, 27 March 2016.
26. Ibid.

18. Art's Parts

1. Linda Moulton Howe, '7-Part Mysterious Bismuth and Magnesium Zinc Metal From Bottom of Wedge-Shaped UFO', Earthfiles.com, 6 September 2019. Accessed online 12 January 2020: www.earthfiles.com/bismuth/
2. Ibid.
3. Ibid.
4. Mick West, 'Identified: Art Bell's "UFO" Aluminum Louvered Sheets – Heat Exchanger Fins', Metabunk.org, 30 July 2019. Accessed online 20 April 2020: www.metabunk.org/threads/identified-art-bells-ufo-aluminum-louvered-sheets-heat-exchanger-fins.11012/
5. 2nd letter of 22 Apr 1996, '7-Part Mysterious Bismuth and Magnesium Zinc Metal from Bottom of Wedge-Shaped UFO', Earthfiles.com, 6 September 2019. Accessed online 12 January 2020: www.earthfiles.com/bismuth/
6. 3rd letter of 27 May 1996, '7-Part Mysterious Bismuth and Magnesium Zinc Metal from Bottom of Wedge-Shaped UFO', Earthfiles.com, 6 September 2019. Accessed online 12 January 2020: www.earthfiles.com/bismuth/
7. Linda Moulton Howe, '7-Part Mysterious Bismuth and Magnesium Zinc Metal from Bottom of Wedge-Shaped UFO'.
8. Ibid.
9. Fifth letter of 5 July 1996, '7-Part Mysterious Bismuth and Magnesium Zinc Metal from Bottom of Wedge-Shaped UFO', Earthfiles.com, 6 September 2019. Accessed online 12 January 2020: www.earthfiles.com/bismuth/
10. C-130E 68-10936 crash, 30 November 1978, Charleston, Sth Carolina, 'Crash of a Lockheed C-130-E Hercules in Cottageville: 6 Killed', Bureau of Aircraft Accidents Archives, www.baaa-acro.com. Accessed online 17 April 2020: www.baaa-acro.com/crash/crash-lockheed-c-130e-hercules-cottageville-6-killed
11. TTSA, 'TTSA Announces CRADA with The U.S. Army Combat Capabilities Development Command to Advance Materiel and Technology Innovations', 17 October 2019. Accessed online 16 April 2020: www.prnewswire.com/news-releases/to-the-stars-academy-of-arts--science-announces-crada-with-the-us-army-combat-capabilities-development-command-to-advance-materiel-and-technology--innovations-300940211.html

12. SEC Form 1-SA TTSA, 27 September 2019. Accessed online 19 April 2020: www.sec.gov/Archives/edgar/data/1710274/000114420419046318/tv530141_1sa.htm
13. Keith Basterfield/Unidentified Aerial Phenomena – scientific research, 'TTSA's Metamaterials Acquisition – Some Details Revealed', 2 October 2019. Accessed online 20 April 2020: ufos-scientificresearch.blogspot.com/2019/10/ttsas-metamaterials-acquisition-some.html
14. John Greenewald/TheBlackVault.com, 'U.S. Army Releases Agreement with To The Stars Academy of Arts & Science', 18 October 2019. Accessed online 19 April 2020: www.theblackvault.com/documentarchive/u-s-army-releases-crada-with-to-the-stars-academy-of-arts-science/
15. TTSA Press Release, 'To The Stars Academy of Arts & Sciences Announces CRADA with The U.S. Army Combat Capabilities Development Command to Advance Materiel and Technology Innovations'.
16. TTSA Inc, 'U.S. Securities and Exchange Commission Form 1-SA Semi Annual Report Pursuant to Regulation A'. 25 September 2018. SEC.gov. Accessed online 12 March 2020: www.sec.gov/Archives/edgar/data/1710274/000114420418050766/tv503167_1sa.htm
17. @TTSAcademy tweet, Untitled, 26 July 2019. Twitter.com. Accessed online 12 December 2020: twitter.com/TTSAcademy/status/1154478173909766144
18. Joe Murgia transcript of Glenn Beck interview 8 May 2020 with Christopher Mellon and Lue Elizondo, 'Transcript: Mellon & Elizondo on Beck: F-18 Pilots Testified About Tic Tac UFO Before "Very Senior DoD Staff" In Secretary Mattis' Suite', 9 May 2020. UfoJoe.net. Accessed online 10 May 2020: www.ufojoe.net/mellon-elizondo
19. Form 1-U SEC Report, 24 March 2021.

19. The New Science of Metamaterials

1. George Knapp/INews-Channel 8 Las Vegas, 'I-Team: UFO Meta Materials', 31 October 2018. Accessed online 16 June 2019: www.youtube.com/watch?v=t-T4Aa4UPI8
2. M.J. Banias, 'UFO Researcher Explains Why She Sold "Exotic" Metal to Tom DeLonge', Vice.com, 15 November 2019. Accessed online 20 April 2020: www.vice.com/en_au/article/8xwp9z/ufo-researcher-explains-why-she-sold-exotic-metal-to-tom-delonge
3. Dr Hal Puthoff, 'Dr Hal Puthoff Address to the SSE/IRVA Conference, Las Vegas', 8 June 2018. Transcript accessed online 12 March 2019: paradigmresearchgroup.org/2018/06/12/dr-hal-puthoff-presentation-at-the-sse-irva-conference-las-vegas-nv-15-june-2018/
4. Federation of American Scientists, 'Project on Government Secrecy/Invention Secrecy Activity FY2019'. Accessed online 12 January 2020: fas.org/sgp/othergov/invention/
5. *Unidentified: Inside America's UFO Investigation*, History Channel.
6. TTSA Tweet, 26 July 2019. Accessed online 19 December 2019: twitter.com/TTSAcademy/status/1154436582021009408
7. Shutterstock stock photo, 'Malachite, Unique Background of Natural Stone'. Accessed online 19 December 2019: www.shutterstock.com/image-photo/malachite-unique-background-natural-stone-353092580
8. Hal Puthoff review of Paul Hill book, *Synopsis of Unconventional Flying Objects*, 7 March 1997. Accessed online 23 April 2020: www.ldolphin.org/hill.html
9. Peter Andrew Sturrock/Center for Space Science & Astrophysics, Stanford University, 'Composition Analysis of the Brazil Magnesium', *Journal of Scientific Exploration*, 2001, vol. 15, no. 1, 2001, pp. 69–95. Accessed online: citeseerx.ist.psu.edu/viewdoc/download?doi=10.1.1.557.5849&rep=rep1&type=pdf

10. Robert Powell YouTube presentation, 'Analysis of the "Ubatuba" Material by Robert Powell', 6 May 2020, Scientific Coalition for UAP Studies. Accessed online 26 July 2020: www.youtube.com/watch?v=NamnxaADugo

11. Tucker Carlson, Luis Elizondo interview, Fox News Channel, 4 October 2019. Accessed online 12 December 2019: youtu.be/Z7-DhPCG_II

12. Image from Luis Elizondo speech SCUAP Conference video 15 Mar 2019 'Luis Elizondo – UFOs ARE Real – SCAAP' @ 40', Slide entitled 'TTSA Material Collection And Analysis', YouTube. Accessed online 24 April 2020: www.youtube.com/watch?v=rhxmOAEFAh8

13. Luis Elizondo speech SCUAP Conference Video 15 March 2019, 'Luis Elizondo – UFOs ARE Real – SCAAP', 15 March 2019.

14. Tucker Carlson/Fox News/Tucker Carlson Tonight, 'Foreign Military Intelligence Official: "Low Probability" UFO Technology Is of This World', YouTube.com/ The DC Shorts, 31 May 2019. Accessed online 24 April 2019: www.youtube.com/watch?v=3Q5dbHj70i4

15. Eric Davis response to James Iandoli, *Engaging the Phenomenon*, 2 June 2019, Twitter.com. Accessed online 24 April 2020: twitter.com/EngagingThe/status/1135129992457838592

16. Iandoli, private email to author, 13 May 2020.

17. Ralph Blumenthal and Leslie Kean, 'U.F.O. Unit at Pentagon Will Publish Its Findings', *The New York Times*, 24 July 2020, p. A17.

18. John Horgan, 'Should Scientists Take UFOs and Ghosts More Seriously?', *Scientific American*, 18 May 2020. Accessed online 18 May 2020: blogs.scientificamerican.com/cross-check/should-scientists-take-ufos-and-ghosts-more-seriously/

20. The Astronaut and 'the Spaceman'

1. Alex Pasternack, 'The Moon-Walking, Alien-Hunting, Psychic Astronaut Who Got Sued by NASA', Motherboard/Vice.com, 14 May 2016. Accessed online 27 April 2020: www.vice.com/en_us/article/aek7ez/astronaut-edgar-mitchell-outer-space-inner-space-and-aliens

2. *Good Morning Britain* interview with Worden, 'Al Worden: The Man Who Flew Around the Moon 75 Times', 29 September 2017. Accessed online 18 May 2020: www.youtube.com/watch?v=yP05nhB2WLU

3. Dr Eric Davis, 'Semiotics, Incommensurability and the UFO Problem', Special for the NIDS Science Advisory Board, 7 April 1999. Edgar Mitchell Archive.

4. Christopher Mellon's website was www.globalsecurityissues.com. The researcher from *The Mind Sublime* wishes to remain anonymous but his website is: mindsublime.blogspot.com. His YouTube site is: www.youtube.com/channel/UCa54syVyf7iNrpVLlXeiAzw

5. *The Mind Sublime* blog, 'Advanced Aerospace Threat and Identification Program (AATIP)', 20 January 2020. Accessed online 21 January 2020: mindsublime.blogspot.com/2020/01/advanced-aerospace-threat-and.html

6. Ibid.

7. Dr Steven Greer email to subscribers of SiriusDisclosure.com, 'Dr Greer's comments re NYT article', 29 July 2020.

8. Col. Philip Corso with William J. Birnes, *The Day After Roswell*, Simon & Schuster Pocket Books, 1997.

9. Unbylined article, 'UFO Book Gives Thurmond Conspiracy-sized Headache', *Chicago Tribune*, 5 June 1997.

10. Letter from Whitley Strieber to Senator Strom Thurmond, 16 Jun 1997, Edgar Mitchell archive.

11. Fax from Edgar Mitchell to Senator Strom Thurmond, 'The Corso Matter', 17 June 1997.

21. Not Made by Human Hands
1.   James Rigney, interview with author, 22 July 2020.
2.   Richard Dolan, 'UFO Leak of the Century: Richard Dolan Analyzes the Admiral Wilson Leak', 9 June 2019. Accessed online 17 May 2020: richarddolanmembers.com/articles/article-ufo-leak-of-the-century-richard-dolan-analyzes-the-admiral-wilson-leak/
3.   Eric Davis Notes, 'EWD Notes – Eric Davis Meeting with Adm Wilson', 16 October 2002, p. 6. Edgar Mitchell Archive.
4.   Eric Davis Notes, 'EWD Notes – Eric Davis Meeting with Adm Wilson', p. 13.
5.   Steven Greenstreet, interview with Dr Eric Davis, 'Eric Davis on Working for Pentagon UFO Program', *The Basement Office/New York Post*, 27 May 2020, Accessed online 28 May 2020: www.youtube.com/watch?v=X3CcaP3yAkc
6.   Dr Hal Puthoff, Q&A session after speech 'DOD Unidentified Aerial Phenomena: The Back Story. The Forward Story', The Arlington Institute Berkley Springs VA, 8 February 2020. Private Audio of Puthoff courtesy of Giuliano Marinkovic.
7.   Hal Puthoff statement to Keith Basterfield, 'Unidentified Aerial Phenomena – Scientific Research', 9 February 2020/Update 20 February 2020. Accessed online 18 May 2020: ufos-scientificresearch.blogspot.com/2020/02/dr-hal-puthoffs-8-february-2020-talk.html
8.   Oke Shannon comments to Billy Cox, 'You Can't Always Get What You Want', 11 July 2019. Accessed 18 May 2020: devoid.blogs.heraldtribune.com/15854/you-cant-always-get-what-you-want/
9.   Bill Sweetman, 'In Search of the Pentagon's Billion Dollar Hidden Budgets. How the U.S. Keeps Its R&D Spending Under Wraps', 5 January 2000. Originally published in *Jane's Defence Weekly*. Available online: www.exopoliticssouthafrica.org/download/Sweetman_In_search_of_the_Pentagon_Dollars.pdf
10. 'Cranium', interview with author, July 2020.

22. Gordon Novel: Fact or Fiction
1.   Gordon Novel, *Supreme Cosmic Secret – How the U.S. Government Reverse-Engineered An Extra-terrestrial Spacecraft*, self-published manuscript, 2010.
2.   Gordon Novel, *Supreme Cosmic Secret*, p. 190.
3.   Ibid, p. 318.
4.   Ibid, p. 82.
5.   Sur Novel, interview with author, 16 January 2020.
6.   Thomas Carey and Don Schmitt, *UFO Secrets – Inside Wright-Patterson*, New Page Books, 2019, p. 22.
7.   Ibid, p. 61. Referring to *Larry King Live* show 1 October 1994.

23. Dr Salvatore Pais's Puzzling Patents
1.   Isaac Newton, *Philosophiae naturalis Principia Mathematica, General Scholium*, Third Edition, 1726, translated by I. Bernard Cohen and Anne Whitman, University of California Press, 1999, p.943. The *Hypotheses non fingo*' saying was first appended to his 1713 edition of the *Principia*.
2.   Inventor, Salvatore Pais, 'Piezoelectricity-induced Room Temperature Superconductor', Patent application filed 16 August 2017, Google Patents. Accessed online 15 July 2020: patents.google.com/patent/US20190058105A1
3.   Inventor, Salvatore Pais, 'Electromagnetic Field Generator and Method to Generate an Electromagnetic Field', Patent application filed 24 July 2015, Google Patents. Accessed online 15 July 2020: patents.google.com/patent/US10135366B2
4.   Inventor, Salvatore Pais, 'High Frequency Gravitational Wave Generator', Patent application filed 14 February 2017, Google Patents. Accessed online 15 July 2020: patents.google.com/patent/US10322827B2

5. Inventor, Salvatore Pais, 'Craft Using an Inertial Mass Reduction Device', Patent application filed 28 April 2016, Google Patents. Accessed online 15 July 2020: patents.google.com/patent/US10144532B2

6. Press Statement, 'To The Stars Academy of Arts & Sciences Launches Today', 11 October 2017. Accessed 16 July 2020: www.prnewswire.com/news-releases/to-the-stars-academy-of-arts--science-launches-today-300534912.html

7. Salvatore Cezar Pais, 'Room Temperature Superconducting System for Use on a Hybrid Aerospace-Undersea Craft', 6 January 2019, American Institute of Aeronautics and Astronautics 2019-0869. Conference Session: Robotic Precursor Missions and Technologies. Accessed online 16 July 2010: arc.aiaa.org/doi/abs/10.2514/6.2019-0869

8. Salvatore Cezar Pais, 'Room Temperature Superconducting System for Use on a Hybrid Aerospace-Undersea Craft'.

9. Military.com, 'TR-3B Anti Gravity Spacecrafts', 23 November 2013. Accessed online 20 July 2020: www.military.com/video/aircraft/military-aircraft/tr-3b-aurora-anti-gravity-spacecrafts/2860314511001

10. Email Chris Mellon, 'Re Video – Lockheed Antigravity Craft 1997 – Electrostatic – Electrogravitic propulsion', 11 February 2020. Obtained from confidential source.

11. S101 of 35 U.S. Code Title 35 – Patents, Part II Patentability of Inventions and Grant of Patents, Ch. 10. Patentability of Inventions, US Patent Act.

12. Daniel Rislove, 'A Case Study of Inoperable Inventions: Why Is the USPTO Patenting Pseudoscience?', (2006: 1275) Wisconsin Law Review.

13. Letter from James B. Sheehy, CTO, U.S. Navy NAE to Philip Bonzell, Primary Patent Examiner USTPO, 15 December 2017. This letter can be viewed through the USPTO online by searching for application number 15/141,270 and then clicking on the image file wrapper tab. It appears in the Appeal Brief documents filed 21 August 2018. Accessed online 16 July 2020: portal.uspto.gov/pair/PublicPair

14. Sheehy letter dated 27 November 2018 is within 'Affidavit-traversing rejectns or objectns rule 132' filed 23 Jan 2019. This letter can be viewed through the USPTO online by searching for application number 15/678,672 and then clicking on the image file wrapper tab. portal.uspto.gov/pair/PublicPair

15. 'Applicant Arguments/Remarks Made in an Amendment' document filed with USPTO by Navy 23 January 2019. Accessible on the USPTO online at portal.uspto.gov/pair/PublicPair by searching for application number 15/678,672 and then clicking on the image file wrapper tab. The Sheehy letter dated 27 November 2018 is also filed as 'Affidavit-traversing rejections or objections rule 132' filed 23 January 2019.

16. The criminal breach is under 18 U.S. Code S1001 'Statements of Entries Generally'. www.law.cornell.edu/uscode/text/18/1001. The invalidation of the patent if a fraudulent claim is made comes under: S. 2016 of the USPTO Manual of Patent Examining Procedures Chapter 2000, 'Fraud, Inequitable Conduct or Violation of Duty of Disclosure Affects all Claims'. 'A finding of "fraud", "inequitable conduct", or violation of duty of disclosure with respect to any claim in an application or patent, renders all the claims thereof unpatentable or invalid'.

17. US Patent Office Applicant-Initiated Interview Summary, Thomas Dougherty USPTO with Mark Glut, Attorney and Dr Salvatore Pais, Date of interview 10 July 2018. Accessed 16 December 2019: This document can be accessed via the USPTO online at: portal.uspto.gov/pair/PublicPair. Enter the patent application number 14/807,943 and then click on the image file wrapper tab, 19 July 2018.

18. Patent application: 15/928,703, filed 22 Mar 2018. This document entitled 'Specification' can be accessed via the USPTO online at: portal.uspto.gov/pair/PublicPair. Enter the patent application number 15/928,703 and then click on the image file wrapper tab.

19. *Institute of Electronic and Electronics Engineers, Transactions on Plasma Science.*
20. Brett Tingley, 'The Secretive Inventor of the Navy's Bizarre "UFO Patents" Finally Talks', *The War Zone*, 22 January 2020. Accessed online 18 July 2020: www. thedrive.com/the-war-zone/31798/the-secretive-inventor-of-the-navys-bizarre-ufo-patents-finally-talks
21. Nick Cook, *The Hunt for Zero Point*, Penguin Random House UK/Arrow Books, 2001, pp. 15–16.
22. Nick Cook, interview with author, 22 July 2020.
23. Tweet @ChristopherKMe4, Christopher Mellon Twitter account, 21 July 2020. Accessed online 22 July 2020: twitter.com/ChristopherKMe4/status/1285691560991088640
24. Kopparapu and Haqq-Misra, '"Unidentified Aerial Phenomena", Better Known as UFOs, Deserve Scientific Investigation', *Scientific American*, 27 July 2020. Accessed online 28 July 2020: www.scientificamerican.com/article/unidentified-aerial-phenomena-better-known-as-ufos-deserve-scientific-investigation/
25. To access this comment and response, go to the end of the online story and click on the Comments tab, Ralph Blumenthal and Leslie Kean, 'No Longer in Shadows, Pentagon's U.F.O. Unit Will Make Some Findings'.
26. Project Unity/Jay Anderson interview with Ralph Blumenthal and Leslie Kean, 'First Interview on Their NYT Article', YouTube/Project Unity, 26 July 2020. Accessed online 28 July: www.youtube.com/watch?v=KvOWnhNv-ys
27. Ibid.
28. Aamer Madhani/AP, 'Trump Says He's Heard "Interesting" Things about Roswell', MilitaryTimes.com, 19 June 2020. Accessed online 20 June 2020: www.militarytimes.com/news/pentagon-congress/2020/06/19/trump-says-hes-heard-interesting-things-about-roswell/
29. Bryan Bender, 'Senators Want the Public to See the Government's UFO Reports', *Politico*.com, 23 June 2020.
30. Blumenthal and Kean 'No Longer in Shadows, Pentagon's U.F.O. Unit Will Make Some Findings Public'.

ACRONYMS

AATIP Advanced Aerospace Threat Identification Program (US Department of Defense)

AAWSAP Advanced Aerospace Weapons Systems Applications Program (US Department of Defense)

AISS Air Intelligence Service Squadron (US Air Force)

ATFLIR Advanced Targeting Forward Looking Infrared (airborne weapon targeting and vision system)

BAASS Bigelow Aerospace Advanced Space Studies

CIA Central Intelligence Agency

CRADA Cooperative Research and Development Agreement (US Army)

CSETI Center for the Study of Extra-terrestrial Intelligence

CSI Committee for Skeptical Inquiry

CSICOP Committee for the Scientific Investigation of Claims of the Paranormal

DAFI Directorate of Air Force Intelligence (Australia)

DIA US Defence Intelligence Agency

DSP Defence Support Program (US satellite system)

DSTI Directorate of Scientific and Technical Intelligence (Australia)

ET extra terrestrial

FBI Federal Bureau of Investigation

GRU Glavnoje Razvedyvatel'noje Upravlenije (Russian military intelligence agency)

NASA National Aeronautics and Space Administration

NICAP National Investigations Committee on Aerial Phenomena

NIDS National Institute for Discovery Science

NORAD North American Aerospace Defence Command

NRO National Reconnaissance Office (US)

NSA National Security Agency (US)

ONI Office of Naval Intelligence (US)

OSI Office of Special Investigations (US Air Force)

OUSDI Office of the Under-Secretary of Defence for Intelligence and
     Security

RAAF Royal Australian Air Force *also* Roswell Army Air Field

SAP Special Access Program (US security access protocol)

SCI Sensitive Compartmented Information

SETI Search for Extra-Terrestrial Intelligence

TTSA To The Stars Academy of Arts & Sciences

UAP Unidentified Aerial Phenomenon

UFO Unidentified Flying Object

USAF United States Air Force

USAP Unacknowledged Special Access Program

WUSAP Unacknowledged Special Access Program

INDEX